מסורה

The ArtScroll Series®

Rabbi Nosson Scherman / Rabbi Meir Zlotowitz

General Editors

A TOUCH
OF WISDOM

Published by

Mesorah Publications, ltd

in conjunction with

ACHIASAF PUBLICATIONS

A TOUCH OF WIT

A sparkling treasury of Jewish anecdotes, ideas and advice

by Shmuel Himelstein

FIRST EDITION
First Impression . . . May, 1991

Published and Distributed by
MESORAH PUBLICATIONS, Ltd.
Brooklyn, New York 11232

Distributed in Israel by
MESORAH MAFITZIM / J. GROSSMAN
Rechov Harav Uziel 117
Jerusalem, Israel

Distributed in Australia & New Zealand by
GOLD'S BOOK & GIFT CO.
36 William Street
Balaclava 3183, Vic., Australia

Distributed in Europe by
J. LEHMANN HEBREW BOOKSELLERS
20 Cambridge Terrace
Gateshead, Tyne and Wear
England NE8 1RP

Distributed in South Africa by
KOLLEL BOOKSHOP
22 Muller Street
Yeoville 2198, South Africa

Typography by Compuscribe at ArtScroll Studios, Ltd.

Printed in the United States of America by Noble Book Press
Bound by Sefercraft, Quality Bookbinders, Ltd. Brooklyn, N.Y.

In loving memory of my father

ר׳ **אברהם מרדכי** ב״ר **ראובן יהודה הכהן** ע״ה

A master storyteller

ও Contents

◆§ Holy Days

Introduction

Judaism is something alive. It is lived every moment, not a religion which is stored in a closet to be taken out when needed. This book is a record of Judaism as it has been *lived* through the ages — in the form of anecdotes, stories and aphorisms, each of which serves to throw light on a section of the whole.

The entries were drawn from a vast pool, and the choice was deliberate. Each story serves a purpose: to give a Torah viewpoint on a particular topic, as illustrated by an individual's conduct; to show a proper trait worth emulating; to indicate the greatness of a specific individual; to teach how great sages regarded those outside the fold, and so on. At the same time, though, every effort was made to choose stories and anecdotes which would prove interesting or even entertaining.

Most of these stories have been handed down orally — some of them for many generations before finally being recorded. It is not surprising, then, that there were instances where the same story was attributed to different individuals, or where thee are different versions of the same story. While I hope that the attributions are correct, I cannot be sure. It is the message, though, which is of cardinal importance, and it is this that has been my main concern.

We are told by our Sages that "even the everyday talk of Torah Sages needs to be studied." It is my hope that these stories will, while proving entertaining, nevertheless serve as food for thought, and even study.

Shmuel Himelstein

Between Man and God

Emunah – Faith

◆§ The Right Purchase After All

R' Leib Mirkes, father of the author of *Shulchan Shlomo*, was a very saintly person. He lived in Mir and had a fabric store. His wife would mind the store, while he would sit and learn.

Once, his wife said to him, "All the merchants are traveling to the Leipzig fair. Please go there too, and buy fabric for the coming year."

R' Leib agreed to go, and prepared himself for the trip. His wife wrote a list of what fabrics and quantities to buy, as well as the price which he should pay. She even sewed the money he would need into his coat, and he traveled to Leipzig.

When he arrived in Leipzig, he found out that the fair was to last for a month. He said to himself: "What's the rush? I will have to remain here until the end of the fair so that I can return with the other merchants. I will buy my fabrics on the last day of the fair, just before I am ready to return home. Meanwhile, I will sit and learn." R' Leib's faith in Hashem was so great that he was certain that he was required only to show an effort; if he was worthy, Hashem would provide his livelihood. If not, he could work day and night for all thirty days and he still would fail.

He spent the entire month in a *beis midrash* learning. On the last day of the fair he went to the market to buy fabric, but, by then, all the merchants had sold out their stock. Finally, he found a single merchant with fabric, but it was a very costly red fabric used by the nobility. A large store might sell ten yards of it in a year. R' Leib used all the money he had, and bought two bolts.

When he arrived home, he dropped off his purchase and immediately set out for the *beis midrash* to learn. His wife opened the packages and was horrified. How long would it take to sell two bolts of this cloth? And what could she do without either cloth or money? She ran to the *beis midrash* in tears.

"What have you done?" she cried. "In twenty years we won't sell the fabric that you bought. How will we earn a living?"

"Woman, why are you weeping?" said R' Leib, trying to calm her. "Don't you believe that a person's income is decreed on *Rosh Hashanah*? What difference does it make which fabric I buy?"

A few days later a servant came from the lord of the region. He had instructions to buy a few hundred yards of this particular cloth because his majesty wished to use it for livery for all his servants. R' Leib's wife sold all the fabric, and with the proceeds they had enough to keep them comfortable through the year.

◆§ It Depends Upon Whom You Rely

R' Mordechai of Lechovich was extremely poor, despite his best efforts. Even bread was often missing from his table, and the entire family knew what it was to go hungry. He tried to encourage his wife and children to have faith, but he was not always successful.

Once, one of his relatives came to visit. R' Mordechai's wife complained to the relative about their terrible situation. In her distress, she burst into tears.

The relative went into R' Mordechai's room and found him pacing back and forth, joyfully humming a melody.

"I don't understand," said the relative. "Your wife and children are all crying, but you are singing."

"They are crying," said R' Mordechai, "for good reason. They look up to *me* to sustain them. But my eyes are lifted up to Hashem for our sustenance, and that is why I sing."

∽ *"They're Looking!"*

R' Zundel of Salant was once being driven in a horse-drawn cart. When they came to a field full of hay, the driver stopped and said to R' Zundel, "Please keep watch for me while I get some hay for my horse."

R' Zundel remained silent.

The driver got off the cart. As he picked up a load of hay, R' Zundel called out, "They're watching! They're watching!"

The driver dropped the hay and ran back to the cart. He jumped onto the seat, and in no time at all he had the horse galloping away at full speed. As he drove away he turned. He didn't see a soul about.

"You lied to me," he said reprovingly.

"Heaven forbid," said R' Zundel. "I told you the truth. They were watching."

"Who?" asked the driver. "I didn't see a soul."

"Up there," said R' Zundel, pointing to the heavens.

∽ *Exceeding His Authority*

When R' Chaim Leib of Stavisk became very ill, the townsfolk brought a famous doctor from Warsaw to check the patient. The doctor came in, examined him and told the family that there was no hope. When the family members heard this, they all began to cry. But they cried softly, so that R' Chaim Leib should not hear.

R' Chaim Leib sensed that they had been crying and told them, "I don't understand why you are crying. Are you concerned about what the doctor told you? He is not the one who determines such matters. Our Sages tell us that the verse, 'He shall surely cause him to be healed,' teaches us that doctors have the right to heal a person. But this verse only tells us that a doctor has the right to *heal* a person. He does not, though, have the right to determine who will die."

◆§ Worrying Quickly

Before R' Elye Baruch Kamai came to Mir, he was the rabbi of a small village. His salary was very meager, and his family was constantly in terrible want. His wife was always worried. Their needs were great, their children growing up, and soon there would be weddings — and all this on R' Elye Baruch's tiny salary. R' Elye Baruch, on the other hand, was joyful by nature. Even in the worst of times he did not worry.

Once his wife said to him, "Elye Baruch, don't you worry about your home and children? My life is nothing but constant anxiety because of all of our needs, yet you don't seem to be at all upset."

"You know that I have a reputation for being a quick thinker," said R' Elye Baruch. "What is the difference between a person who thinks quickly and one who doesn't? One who does not think quickly spends a week pondering the same material that the quick thinker grasps in an hour or even an instant. What worries you for an entire week worries me for only an instant."

◆§ Only a Moment

When R' Moshe Leib of Sasov was in distress, he would say, "What has passed has passed. As for the future, I expect Hashem's salvation to come at any instant. Thus, my troubles will only last for a moment. Is there any person who can't bear troubles for an instant?"

‌ You Have to Have Faith

R' Menachem Mendel of Rimanov would give his married son money each week to pay for the week's expenses. The amount given was always three rubles less than the son needed. Once his son asked him, "Father, as you are willing to support me, couldn't you give me three more rubles each week?"

"No," answered his father. "If I give you enough to cover all your expenses, I will, Heaven forbid, take away your need to have faith in Hashem."

‌ Different Generations

R' Eizel Charif said: "See the difference between the earlier generations and the later generations. The generation of the desert discarded their gold and silver in order to make themselves a god, while the later generations discard their G-d in order to make themselves gold and silver."

‌ Do Not Give up Hope

R' Yisrael of Ruzhin would say: "If a man gives up hope of recovering what he has lost, and another subsequently finds the object, it belongs to the finder.

"That rule was meant as a penalty to the one who gives up hope. This teaches us that a Jew may never give up hope."

‌ Only the Forty-Ninth Rung

R' Chaim of Brisk would say: "We are told that Moshe reached the forty-ninth rung of understanding. Why did he not reach the last, the fiftieth rung?

"So that he would still be able to fulfill the *mitzvah* of having faith in Hashem."

⊷§ *Worrying About the Future*

The young daughter of R' Eliezer Shulewitz, *rosh yeshivah* of the yeshivah, came and asked her father, "Father, I had five nuts. I gave two of them to my friend for her birthday. On her next birthday, I will give her two more. However, what will I do the third year, when I only have a single nut left?"

R' Eliezer said, "My daughter, you are worried about missing a single nut three years in the future. But you must realize that the one who gave you the five nuts today can give you many more tomorrow and afterwards. It is unfortunate that many adults also spend their time worrying about tomorrow but don't realize that the One who has sustained us until now can sustain us tomorrow and afterwards as well."

Torah Study

⚜ Page Two

R' Levi Yitzchak of Berdichev was once asked: "Why do all the *masechtos* (tractates) in *Shas* (the Talmud) begin with Page ב, the second letter of the Hebrew alphabet, which is used for the numeral 2, rather than on Page א , which stands for the numeral 1?"

R' Levi Yitzchak answered, "So that a person should realize that no matter how much he has studied, he has still not started to study the first page of even one work."

⚜ True Dedication

R' Chaim of Volozhin was once in Vilna for *Shabbos*. Before he had time to unpack and prepare for the holy day, an urgent message came from the family of the Vilna Gaon that he was needed immediately.

R' Chaim dropped everything and rushed to the Gaon's home. He was told that the sage had been in his study for three days and three nights. During all that time, he had not seen a soul or touched any food.

R' Chaim entered the Gaon's study and was shocked at what he saw. The Gaon, his face flushed, his head wrapped in a towel, sat struggling with a difficult text. When he saw R' Chaim, the Gaon was overjoyed and said, "I am baffled by this very difficult passage in the *Yerushalmi*, and am unable to go on. Can you possibly explain it?"

R' Chaim went over the passage and finally said, "Rebbe, in my humble opinion the meaning of the passage is as follows. . ." and he explained it at length.

The Gaon's face lit up, he removed the towel from his head, and asked that a meal be prepared for him.

◆§ A Quick Response

R' Chaim of Volozhin would say: "I, too, can answer questions the way R' Akiva Eiger does, but I am unable to begin with the words, 'Your letter reached me today.' "

◆§ A Path to Torah

Once R' Chaim bought a pair of heavy boots, the type used by peasants. Whoever entered his room and saw the boots wondered why R' Chaim would need them, but no one was willing to ask him about them.

Once, in mid-winter, after a snowy night, R' Chaim was seen at daybreak walking in these boots from the market to the yeshivah and back. "Rebbe," they asked him, "why are you walking in this deep snow?"

"I am breaking a path for the students of the yeshivah," he answered.

❧ No One Ever Again Arose in Israel Like Moshe

The *Chasam Sofer* would say: "It is not surprising that Moshe attained what he did. Had I had a teacher such as his teacher (Hashem), I, too, would be equal to Moshe. Now if you wish to know why I didn't have the same teacher, the answer is that I am not Moshe."

❧ Smoking Away Torah

When R' Shalom of Belz was a young man, he smoked a pipe.

One day, he saw another young man preparing to smoke his pipe. First he cleaned the pipe thoroughly, then he filled it with tobacco, and finally he lit it. In the time it took the young man to get his pipe ready, R' Shalom learned an entire page of *gemara*.

Immediately thereafter, R' Shalom put away his pipe, and never smoked one again. "If this thing can cause a person to waste the time of an entire page of Torah learning," he thought, "I want to have nothing to do with it."

❧ A Shade of Difference

R' Yosef Ber, the *Beis Halevi*, would say: "What is the difference between me and my son, R' Chaim? If someone asks me a question in *gemara*, that person and I are both happy. If someone asks my son a question, neither of them is happy. I study the question carefully and finally find an answer. We are both happy: he because he asked a good question, and I because I gave a good answer. If someone asks my son a question, he immediately shows that there is no question in the first place. Thus both he and the questioner feel frustrated."

◄§ Only a Little

A young chasid once came to R' Yitzchak Meir of Gur, author of the *Chidushei HaRim*.

"Do you know the Torah?" R' Yitzchak Meir asked him.

The young man was in a quandary. If he answered that he did know, his knowledge paled into insignificance before the Gerer's. On the other hand, if he answered that he didn't know, he would be lying. Finally, he said to the Rebbe, "I know a little."

"And who," R' Yitzchak Meir asked him, "knows more than a little?"

◄§ Learning or Teaching

A young *chasid* once came to R' Menachem Mendel of Kotzk, and the rebbe asked him: "What knowledge do you have of the Torah?"

"Rebbe," he replied boastfully, "I have learned all of *Shas*."

"Really?" said the Kotzker. "Then could you tell me what all of *Shas* taught you?"

◄§ A True Teacher

Once the Sanzer came to his home town. He immediately went to greet his first teacher, who had taught him the *aleph-beis* (alphabet). In the same town lived the rebbe who had taught him *Mishnah* and *gemara*, but the Sanzer made no effort to visit the man. The latter was hurt, and asked him, "Rebbe, why did you not come to visit me? After all, I taught you more than your first teacher."

"You taught me *gemara*," said the Rebbe, "but as I became older and understood more, I realized that the true interpretation of the *gemara* is much deeper than what you taught me. On the other hand, no one argues that an *alef* is an *alef* and a *beis* is a *beis*. I am sure that whatever my first teacher taught me is the truth."

☙ Moving on

A rabbi wrote to R' Yitzchak Elchanan Spektor and complained: "I have a tremendous problem with a certain *sugya* (topic) in *gemara*. I have struggled with it and cannot solve it. As a result, I am simply unable to continue further."

R' Yitzchak Elchanan sent him a short reply: "Look up *Menachos*, page so and so, the *Tosafos* that begins with words such and such."

The rabbi took out his *gemara* and checked the reference, but found that it was on a completely different topic.

Again he wrote to R' Yitzchak Elchanan: "I have checked the source you gave me and found nothing to help me with my problem. The *Tosafos* you indicated discusses an entirely different topic, asks a question, and does not answer it. I wonder if you possibly gave me the wrong reference."

R' Yitzchak Elchanan replied: "That was exactly what I meant. Even the *Ba'alei Tosafos* sometimes ask a question for which they have no answer. Yet as you can see, there is another passage of *Tosafos* immediately after this. They didn't stop their learning just because they were left with an unanswered question."

☙ The Force of Torah

R' Chaim Leib, the *rosh yeshivah* of Mir, was once at a festive gathering with his yeshivah students. As they discussed various matters, he said to them: "Do you know, my children, that the *masmid* in our yeshivah who learns day and night prevents Rothschild in Vienna from converting?"

The yeshivah students all looked up in amazement, and one of them finally blurted out: "Rebbe, what has one got to do with the other?"

"The *masmid* in the yeshivah learns twenty hours a day," said R' Chaim Leib. "The average yeshivah students learn only fourteen hours a day. The former yeshivah students, who work for a living, learn three hours a day. The merchants of Minsk learn an hour a day. The merchants of Warsaw pray three times a day. The merchants in Moscow keep *Shabbos* according to the *halachah*. The merchants of London eat kosher food. Finally at the lowest rung is Rothschild in Vienna, who has not converted. If the *masmid* in the yeshivah learns less than twenty hours a day, the others will learn less than before; the former yeshivah students will stop learning Torah regularly; the Minsk merchants will stop learning an hour each day; the Warsaw merchants will no longer pray; the Moscow merchants will not keep *Shabbos*; the London merchants will eat unkosher food; and Rothschild will convert."

◆§ A Fast Sleeper

R' Heshel of Chelm slept very little each night.

"Rebbe," his friends asked him, "how are you able to get along with so little sleep?"

"It's the easiest thing in the world," R' Heshel replied. "There are some who eat quickly; others write quickly. I sleep quickly."

◆§ The True Tally

R' Shlomo of Karlin preferred to learn a small amount Torah in depth, rather than learning a great deal superficially. He would say: "Hashem doesn't count the pages one learns, but the hours."

◆§ Truly Engrossed in Torah Study

R' Meshulam Igra, the Rabbi of Pressburg, was always involved in learning. Not for an instant did he stop. Even when he walked about, his mind was constantly evolving *chidushim* — new interpretations.

Once, he was deeply absorbed in a certain topic as he walked through the market square, and a speeding horse and cart ran him over. Those present ran to extricate him from underneath the wheels of the cart. As they finally managed to pull him out, they heard him say to himself, "The *Rambam* is nevertheless correct."

◆§ The Master Thief

R' Menachem Mendel of Kotzk and R' Yitzchak Meir of Gur were once "talking in learning." Finally, they discussed a very difficult passage of *Tosafos*. R' Menachem Mendel read over the *Tosafos* and said, "According to the comment by the thief of Vilna, in his *Hagahos HaGra*, there is no problem with this *Tosafos*."

Everyone present looked up in shock. How could the Kotzker refer to the Vilna Gaon as a thief?

"Let me explain myself," said the Kotzker. "We know that when Moshe went up to Heaven to receive the Torah, he was told all its secrets, including any thought of any person in the future. Now there were a few souls present at Sinai that stole up behind Moshe and listened to all the secrets as they were being told to Moshe. Among them was the Vilna Gaon. In his *Hagahos HaGra* he answers the most difficult of questions with a single word. That is why I say that the Gaon was a master thief!"

◆§ The Pain of Learning

The Kotzker would say: "Shlomo Hamelech tells us, 'Whoever gains in wisdom gains in pain' (*Koheles* 1:18). But I would add: It is worthwhile for a person to suffer pain, as long as he increases his knowledge."

◆§ A Host of Only Children

Once a man came to the *Netziv* and begged him to accept his son into the Volozhin yeshivah.

"Rebbe," he pleaded, "please accept him. He is an only child."

"Let me tell you something," the *Netziv* replied. "You have a single only child, while I have four hundred yeshivah students, each of whom is an only child to me."

◄§ *It Just Can't Be*

R' Chaim of Brisk once expounded a Torah thought. One of those present blurted out: "*Tosafos* at this and this place says differently."

"That isn't so," replied R' Chaim, "*Tosafos* doesn't say what you claim."

They took the volume of *gemara* down, and found that R' Chaim had been right.

"Don't imagine," said R' Chaim, "that I know what is written in every single *Tosafos*. That isn't true. However, it was logically impossible for *Tosafos* to have made a statement such as that."

◄§ *The Definition of a Lamdan*

R' Yechiel Meir of Gustinin would say: "Do you know who is a thief? Not a person who knows how to steal, but a person who actually steals. By the same token, do you know who is a *lamdan* (a learned Torah scholar)? Not one who knows how to learn Torah, but one who actually learns it."

◄§ *An Insane Asylum*

R' Yosef Yozl established the famed Yeshivah of Novarodok. His yeshivah had its students concentrate on their moral development by studying various *musar* (ethical) works.

Once, a man came to the yeshivah during the hour devoted to *musar* and found the students immersed in their studies — each in his own manner. One was pacing back and forth restlessly, another was beating his fist on his desk — it seemed like total chaos.

"Rebbe," said the man to R' Yosef Yozl, "this isn't a yeshivah, it's an insane asylum!"

"You're absolutely right," said R' Yosef Yozl, "whoever comes here insane leaves cured. . ."

◄§ Differences in Approach

When R' Meir of Lublin founded his yeshivah, *Yeshivas Chachmei Lublin,* he was asked, "What is the difference between your yeshivah and those in Lithuania?"

"The only difference between them," said R' Meir, "is the difference that existed between two yeshivah students.

"There were two yeshivah students, a *misnaged* and a chasid, who were studying Torah together, and they came upon the passage in the Talmud where we are told that 'it was said about R' Yonasan ben Uzziel that when he sat and learned the Torah, any bird that happened to fly overhead was immediately burned to a crisp' from the force of his studying (*Sukkah* 28a).

"Both students became immersed in thought. Finally the chasid broke the silence: "What are you thinking about?" he asked the *misnaged*.

"If the bird belonged to somebody, would R' Yonasan be required to pay for it?" the *misnaged* replied.

"And I was thinking," said the chasid, "about how holy R' Yonasan was and how great were his powers of learning."

◄§ Thieves to the Rescue

Yeshivas Chachmei Lublin attracted students from far and wide, and there was simply not enough room for them all to sleep in the yeshivah. To solve this problem, R' Meir made an agreement with the merchants of the city, whereby the yeshivah students would sleep in the stores each night, thus ensuring that each store had a built-in watchman.

It was then that R' Meir said, "The yeshivah students owe the thieves a debt of gratitude and should pray for them, for were it not for the thieves they would not have a place to lay their heads. . ."

ڡ True and False

R' Yaakov Maslianski would say: "If I ask a person why he doesn't spend time learning Torah and he tells me that it is because he doesn't enjoy it, I'm willing to leave him be. I presume that neither he nor his father nor the previous generations of his family enjoyed studying the Torah.

"If someone tells me, however, that he doesn't study Torah because he doesn't have the time, I can tell you that he is a liar. Had he wanted to, he would have found the time. . ."

ڡ Wasting Time

R' Eliyahu, the Gaon of Vilna, would spend all his time learning, and would not waste even a minute. He would mark the time spent away from study in a notebook: "On this-and-this day I wasted this number of minutes." On the day before *Yom Kippur* he would add up the total of minutes that he had wasted and would weep bitterly and confess his sin of having wasted time from learning Torah.

It was said that in the course of his whole life the entire amount of time he wasted in any *year* never exceeded three hours. . .

ڡ Respect for Torah

R' Efraim Zalman of Brody was known as a great Torah scholar and was very wealthy. He once happened to be in Stari, and visited R' Aryeh Leib, the author of the *Ketzos HaChoshen*. While they were speaking, R' Aryeh Leib said sorrowfully, "It is terrible to see how there is no respect for the Torah any longer."

"Rest assured," said R' Efraim Zalman, "there is still respect for the Torah. The proof of it is in the very fact that I've come to see you because of your learning."

"That's exactly the point," said R' Aryeh Leib. "Had you

yourself not been learned in Torah, would a rich man like you have come to visit someone as poor as I? It is only because you yourself are a scholar that you find it possible to humble yourself. . ."

◄§ Quarter Hours that Count

R' Yechezkel Benet would say: "If I am greater than my friends in learning, it is because of my quarter hours."

"What does that mean?" he was asked.

"It is customary for yeshivah students to stop studying fifteen minutes before the prayer time," said R' Yechezkel. "After all, one must prepare for the prayers. And one needs fifteen minutes to get ready for the meals.

"During those fifteen minutes I would continue studying. . ."

◄§ Yours Is Mine and Mine Is Yours

Someone once told R' Shmuel Shmelkis that a man was quoting R' Shmuel Shmelkis' original Torah, but calling it his own.

"As long as he quotes my interpretations and says they're his," said R' Shmuel Shmelkis, "I don't mind at all. I would be concerned if he gave his own interpretations and called them mine. . ."

◄§ The Time Limit

Once, R' Yaakov David of Slutzk, the *Ridbaz*, visited a yeshivah, and noticed that a number of the students were not studying the Torah.

"Tell me," he asked, "is there a limit as to how much Torah one is to learn?"

"Even the youngest of children knows the answer to that," they said. "The Mishnah specifically tells us that 'These are the matters that have no limit . . . and the study of Torah is equal to all of them' (*Peah* 1:1)."

"No," said R' Yaakov David. "There is a limit. One can only learn when he is alive. . ."

◄§ A Poor Memory

R' Meir Simchah of Dvinsk was once at a gathering of Torah scholars. They began mentioning different Torah giants and among them R' Yosef, the Rogachover.

"R' Yosef has the most remarkable memory," said one of them.

"That isn't so," said R' Meir Simchah, "he doesn't have a good memory at all."

"Meaning?" they asked in astonishment.

"It's just as I said," answered R' Meir Simchah. "A man who studies something and then remembers it some time later has a good memory. R' Yosef, however, who learns the whole Talmud daily, doesn't have any memory at all. . ."

◄§ Punishment for Torah Study

When R' Yosef, the Rogachover, lost his father, all the great Torah scholars came to comfort him during the seven days of mourning. While they were there, they began discussing Torah matters, and R' Yosef soon became involved in the discussion.

After the rabbis left, one of his close friends asked him, "Rebbe, isn't a mourner forbidden to study the Torah during the first seven days of mourning?"

"I know that I committed a sin," said R' Yosef, "and that I will surely be punished for it. But it is worthwhile being punished for the study of the Torah."

◄§ Closing a Yeshivah

R' Yosef Yozl of Novarodok established a yeshivah in a small town. When he found that the yeshivah did not turn out as he wished, he closed it down. He would say: "Whoever does not have the strength of character to close a yeshivah shouldn't open one."

⋖§ Five Minutes More

R' Meir Simchah of Dvinsk and R' Yosef of Dvinsk, the Rogachover, were among the greatest Torah scholars of their generation, but entirely different in nature. R' Meir Simchah was low-keyed and easy-going, while R' Yosef was always quick and hasty in his actions.

R' Yosef was accustomed to saying: "The only thing separating R' Meir Simchah and myself is five minutes. I answer immediately after hearing a question, while he replies after having considered his answer for five minutes."

⋖§ The Poor Rich Man

R' Yisrael Meir, the *Chafetz Chaim*, once tried to persuade a rich man to set aside regular periods for Torah study, but the rich man said, "Rebbe, I'm not able to. I'm kept extremely busy and never have any time."

"If that is so," said R' Yisrael Meir, "then you are the poorest of the poor. If you don't even have time, then what do you have?"

⋖§ True Concentration

R' Eliyahu, the Gaon of Vilna, was once studying with his students, when, suddenly, they heard a tremendous thunderclap overhead. All the students immediately interrupted their studies and recited the appropriate blessing. R' Eliyahu looked at them sorrowfully.

"Rebbe," they asked, "did we recite the wrong blessing?"

"No," said R' Eliyahu, "the blessing you recited was the correct one, but the way you were studying Torah was incorrect. Had you been studying the Torah properly, you wouldn't have heard the thunder."

☙ Why Have Yeshivos?

R' Yitzchak Elchanan once convened a meeting with the rich people of Kovno, trying to persuade them to help the yeshivos.

"But Rebbe," one of them asked, "why do we need so many yeshivos? How many rabbis can we use anyway?"

"That is a mistake," said R' Yitzchak Elchanan. "We do not establish yeshivos to produce rabbis who can *answer* questions in *halachah*, but rather laymen who will know when it is necessary to *ask* questions of a rabbi. . ."

☙ A Difficult Ruling by the Rambam

R' Yitzchak Elchanan studied all day and well into the night.

"Rebbe," someone asked him, "doesn't the *Rambam* himself rule that one must sleep eight hours each night?"

"Yes," said R' Yitzchak Elchanan, "that is indeed so, and you have no idea how many sleepless nights I have spent on that particular saying without being able to explain it satisfactorily."

☙ "How Do I Know I'll Wake Up?"

R' Yehoshua Leib of Brisk studied until midnight each night. Once, someone asked him, "Rebbe, according to the *kabbalah,* the best time to study the Torah is from midnight on. How is it that you only study until midnight?"

"How can I go to sleep early and then rise to study at midnight?" said R' Yehoshua Leib. "How do I know that I will still be alive by midnight?"

☙ Whatever You Wish

When R' Moshe Yitz'l became the rabbi of Ponivezh, the very first *Shabbos* in his new position he was scheduled to give a Torah discourse. As he went up to the *bimah*, he told the *shamash,* "Bring me a *gemara*."

The *shamash* ran to the book shelves and then realized that R' Moshe Yitz'l had not specified which volume, so he ran back and asked him, "Rebbe, which tractate?"

"Didn't I tell you to bring me a volume of the *gemara*?" R' Moshe Yitz'l said.

The *shamash* ran back to the book shelves, picked up the first volume that came to hand, and brought it to the rabbi.

R' Moshe Yitz'l opened the *gemara* and gave a brilliant Torah discourse that amazed everyone present.

⋙ New Fashions

R' Samson Raphael Hirsch was against the new breed of Jewish scholars who delved into *Tanach* but never looked at the *Mishnah* or *gemara*.

He would say: "Let me tell you the difference between previous generations and our generation. In previous generations, they would recite *Tehillim* and learn *gemara*. In our generation, they learn *Tehillim* and recite *gemara*."

⋙ True Modesty

R' Chaim of Brisk said about R' Akiva Eiger: "Had it not been for his saintliness and his modesty, R' Akiva would have been considered an even greater Torah giant. When he comes up with an absolutely brilliant analysis of a topic, he immediately has qualms and writes, 'Were I not in doubt. . .' "

⋙ Wasting the Most Precious Commodity

Once, R' Yosef Yozl of Novarodok visited a certain city, the home of one of his former students, who was reputed to have a brilliant mind. After greeting the man, R' Yosef Yozl asked him, "What do you do for a living?"

"I own a store," the student replied.

"What a pity," commented R' Yosef Yozl.

"Rebbe," the student told him, "I own a very large store, and am doing very well."

"Don't misunderstand me," went on R' Yosef Yozl. "I am not pitying you, but rather your talents. Even if you would have the largest of stores, you would only be using a *quarter* of your talents. What a waste of the other three quarters."

◆§ The Entire Torah in My Hands

The Gaon of Vilna held his student, R' Zalmele of Volozhin, in very high regard, for he knew all realms of the Torah and never stopped learning for an instant.

Once, the two sat learning throughout the night, until, just before dawn, R' Zalmele dozed off, and his head fell to the side. The Gaon arose, went over and supported R' Zalmele's head in his hands. Just then, one of the Gaon's other students entered the room. The Gaon motioned him to be quiet, and whispered, "The entire Torah is resting here in my hands."

◆§ A Question of Style

R' Yaakov of Lissa, author of the *Chavas Da'as*, was the student of R' Meshulam Igra of Pressburg. Sometimes, he would review what he had learned from his rebbe, and found that he could not understand it.

Once, R' Yaakov said to R' Meshulam, "I have a problem, Rebbe. When I learn what the *Rashba* says, I am able to fathom what he means. On the other hand, I often find myself unable to understand your Torah. Is it possible that your Torah is more profound than that of *Rashba*?"

"You are mistaken," R' Meshulam told him. "In truth, you don't understand what the *Rashba* really means either. However, the *Rashba* was so brilliant that he was able to clothe his thoughts in words that each person can understand in accordance with his ability. I, on the other hand, am not able to state what I want to say in a way that every student will be able to understand it according to his ability."

⋗ Short and to the Point

R' Leibele Katzenelenbogen of Brisk was considered to be one of the greatest Torah scholars of his generation. People from all over the world would send him their questions in *halachah*. He would answer all these questions personally, but, unlike the other great Torah scholars who always explained why they ruled as they did, he would simply give his ruling without any explanation.

Once, he was asked why he acted differently from the other great Torah scholars, and gave no reasons for his decisions.

"When a person asks a question in *halachah*," said R' Leibele, "he has three possible goals: He wants to show how great a Torah scholar he is, he wants to see how great the person answering him is, and he wants the decision. I see the person's ability in Torah from his question, and am not concerned with showing him my ability. All that remains, then, is for me to write what the *halachah* is."

⋗ *Warning Signs*

One of the *Chafetz Chaim's* close friends came to him and complained that there were more and more students in the *beis midrash*, and the expense of maintaining them was growing ever larger.

"Let me give you an illustration," the *Chafetz Chaim* told the man. "At the side of the road there are often signs warning people that it is dangerous to move any closer, for there is a ditch into which they may fall. Now these signs make the road even narrower than it would be otherwise, but if you take them away, the road becomes a much more dangerous one. Similarly, the more students we have, the safer the 'road' of Judaism becomes."

✍ Who Can Assess the Respect Due for One Masechta?

A man once came to R' Chaim of Sanz. R' Chaim treated him with great respect and had him sit at the front of the *beis midrash*.

"Rebbe," the man protested, "I am not a great Torah scholar. All I know is a single *masechta*."

"Is that so minor?" the rebbe asked him. "Do you know the respect due for a single *masechta*?"

✍ Proper Help

During World War I, one of the students of the Radin Yeshivah, founded and directed by R' Yisrael Meir, the *Chafetz Chaim*, was from Germany. Somehow or other, the authorities heard about him, and he was immediately seized and imprisoned, and charged with being a spy.

The *Chafetz Chaim* did everything he could to have the young man released, but all he was able to do was to arrange to have the trial postponed for a month. He himself then traveled to St. Petersburg to plead the student's case before Yisrael Grossenberg, a famous lawyer of the time. Traveling was extremely hazardous, with troops and armed robbers all along the way, and R' Yisrael Meir was already in his eighties at the time.

When R' Yisrael Meir arrived in St. Petersburg he immediately made his way to the lawyer, begging him to take the case. Grossenberg assured him that he would be able to have the young man cleared.

While they were talking, Grossenberg asked R' Yisrael Meir: "Rebbe, why did you have to come here yourself? Couldn't you have sent a messenger? Especially now, when the roads are so treacherous, and at your age and as frail as you are, was it necessary for you to put your life in danger?"

"I'm surprised at you," said R' Yisrael Meir. "What type of

questions are those? Don't you know that a rabbi who is a leader of Israel is not allowed to be frail or weak?"

~§ Shochet Versus Melamed

R' Meir of Lublin used to say: "What is the difference between the *shochet* and the *melamed* (teacher)? Before a *shochet* is accepted by the smallest of communities he is checked thoroughly and painstakingly. Did he receive authorization from a rabbi? Is he skilled? Is he pious? And in the end, all he is placed in charge of is animals and fowl. A *melamed*, on the other hand, is responsible for the souls of the children who are entrusted to his care, and he is not checked at all. Anyone who wishes may assume the title and go into business for himself."

~§ Forbidden Hebrew

R' Yehudah Leib Chasman was told that one of his students at the Hebron yeshivah had gone to hear a heretical lecture. R' Yehudah Leib invited the young man in, and began to lecture him on his conduct.

"Rebbe," the young man explained, "I only went there to learn how to speak Hebrew properly."

"That too," said R' Yehudah Leib, "is forbidden. It is as if a Torah scroll was burning and you used the flame to light a cigarette."

~§ What Came First?

R' Moshe Sofer, the *Chasam Sofer*, would say: "Why is it that Moshe the son of Amram is always referred to as *Moshe Rabbenu* (Moshe our Rabbi), while Moshe the son of Maimon (*Rambam*) is always called *Rabbenu Moshe* (our Rabbi Moshe)?

"Moshe became famous among our people before the Torah had been given, and therefore his name precedes his title, *Moshe Rabbenu*. Moshe ben Maimon, however, only became famous after his greatness in Torah became known, therefore we refer to him as *Rabbenu Moshe*."

◄§ *The Ordered Table*

R' Yaakov, the famous *Maggid* of Dubno, visited R' Eliyahu of Vilna frequently. Each time he would come with a different story or parable to illustrate various texts.

Once, before R' Yaakov had written his explanation on the Torah, R' Eliyahu asked him, "Why don't you arrange all your various speeches and comments according to the different chapters of the Torah and publish them?"

And as usual, the *maggid* answered with a parable.

"Let me tell you a story," he said. "Once there was a rich man who married off his son. He invited all his relatives and friends to the party. The poor of the city were also invited. Now, what was the difference between the rich and the poor at the party? The rich sat down and ate each course in its proper order: fish, followed by soup, then meat, and finally dessert. The poor, however, not knowing what would be next, grabbed whatever they could and ate as fast as they could; some dessert, a mouthful of bread, a cup of wine, a piece of meat.

"The great Torah sages who know the Torah well are able to interpret it in its sequence. I, however, who am poor in Torah knowledge, grab whatever I can to speak about — a quotation from the prophets, a verse from the Torah — without any order."

◄§ *Everything in Its Proper Time*

When R' Yitzchak Elchanan Spektor of Kovno was young, he was extremely poor. He once needed money to buy shoes and didn't have a coin to his name. He went to a rich man and asked, "Could you please lend me three guilders for a pair of new shoes?"

The rich man looked at him askance and answered, "Away

with you, young man! How long are you going to continue wasting your time studying? If you're willing to go out and work, I'm willing to even find you a job with me."

"I've come here," said the young boy firmly, "to arrange a loan to buy a pair of shoes, and not for advice."

The rich man became angry and ordered him out of his house.

A number of years passed and R' Yitzchak Elchanan became a world authority in Torah, and was appointed to be the Rabbi of Novarodok. It was during that time that he printed his work *Be'er Yitzchak*. While in Koenigsberg to supervise the publication of his work, a man approached him and said, "Rebbe, Hashem has been good to me, and I would like to help with the cost of your Torah work."

R' Yitzchak Elchanan looked at the man, and recognized the same rich man who had once refused to lend him three guilders for a pair of shoes.

"No," said R' Yitzchak Elchanan. "Once, you could have helped with three guilders. Now you can't do so for all the money in the world."

~§ The Carriage Driver Is Better

A carriage driver once came to R' Yisrael of Vizhnitz and said, "Rebbe, when we were children, we both studied with the same teacher. I, who was the son of a carriage driver, became one as well, while you, the son of a rebbe, followed in your father's footsteps."

"Well, you are more fortunate than I," said R' Yisrael. "You have taken up your father's trade, and are as good in it as he was. I, however, do not even begin to approach the learning of my father."

~§ The Loser and the Finder

Once, two young men came to R' Yitzchak Shmelkes of Lvov, both asking to be ordained by him. R' Yitzchak tested both young men, and then decided to ordain one but not the other.

"Rebbe," asked the one who had not been ordained, "my friend, too, didn't know all the answers and had to look up things in the *Shulchan Aruch*. Why was he ordained while I was not?"

"The difference was," said R' Yitzchak, "that when he went to look up something, he went as if looking for something that he had *lost*, while you went looking for things as if you wanted to *find* them."

⋖§ *Better*

It is said that the Vilna Gaon knew all of the Torah *better* than the average Jew knows the *Ashrei* prayer. But the average Jew knows *Ashrei* by heart. How can someone know something better than that? The answer is that if you give the average Jew a verse in *Ashrei* and ask him what the *preceding* verse is, he will have to think before answering, but the Vilna Gaon knew the entire Torah so well that he knew immediately, without having to think, what preceded any particular passage.

Prayer

◆§ A Reason to Pray Early (I)

R' Pinchas of Koretz would say: "I arise and pray at sunrise, before the world is full of foolishness and vanity."

◆§ A Reason to Pray Early (II)

R' Kalman of Doline would arise early to pray. When he was asked why, he said: "When a merchant doesn't have the best merchandise he arrives at the marketplace early, before anyone else arrives."

◆§ Prayer Versus Study

R' Yaakov Yosef, author of the *Toldos*, would say: "I find it easier to understand ten complicated explanations of the Talmud than to pray one prayer."

✒ Eleven Spices

R' Pinchas, author of the *Hafla'ah*, once gathered a *minyan* at his home for prayer. Even after there were ten men, he asked that another be brought, because he felt that one of the ten was not a believer in Hashem, and he did not want to include him in the *minyan*. That particular man sensed the reason for the rabbi's decision, and said: "Isn't it true that one of the ingredients of the incense that was offered in the Temple was galbanum resin, which is not the most fitting item, yet it was included with the others?"

"That is the reason," said R' Pinchas, "why the incense was made up of *eleven* ingredients and not *ten*."

✒ Our Father

R' Levi Yitzchak was once traveling and took lodging in an inn. At that inn there were a number of merchants on the way to a neighboring fair to buy goods. The merchants did not recognize R' Levi Yitzchak, and took him for another merchant.

In the morning they all arose, and since there was only one pair of *tefillin* in the whole group, each prayed hurriedly and then passed the *tefillin* on to his neighbor.

After they had finished praying, R' Levi Yitzchak called over two of the younger ones, and said, "I have a question. Ma, Ma, Ma, Na, Na, Na?"

"What's that you're saying?" the merchants asked.

R' Levi Yitzchak continued mumbling, "Ba, Ba, Ba, Ta, Ta, Ta."

Both looked at him as if he was crazy.

"What's the problem?" said R' Levi Yitzchak naively. "Don't you understand what I'm saying? Wasn't that exactly the way you prayed?"

"When an infant in its crib murmurs *ba* and *ma*, not even the greatest wise men in the world know what the infant is talking about," said one of the merchants. "Yet the child's parents immediately know what the child wants — whether it is hungry or thirsty or wet. We Jews are the children of Hashem, and Hashem understands what we are asking for and hears our prayers."

"You answered well. Our Father in heaven will surely hear the prayers of His children," said R' Levi Yitzchak and began dancing.

↝§ For Your Nation Are All Righteous

R' Levi Yitzchak of Berdichev once saw a wagon driver wearing *tallis* and *tefillin* and mumbling his prayers as he greased the axles of his wagon. R' Levi Yitzchak looked up to the heavens and exclaimed, "Lord of the universe! Which other nation is as holy as your nation Israel? Here we have a simple man who, even as he greases the axles of his cart, prays."

↝§ "Welcome Home!"

R' Levi Yitzchak once saw a man finishing his prayers. He went over to him and said, "Welcome home!"

"But Rebbe," said the man, "why this welcome? I haven't come from anywhere."

"While you were praying," said R' Levi Yitzchak, "you were in all the fairs and were making all kinds of deals in your mind. Now that you've returned, isn't it only proper that I greet you?"

↝§ Burning Prayer

R' Yaakov Yitzchak, the *Yehudi Hakadosh*, would pray very quickly. The *Chozeh* of Lublin once asked him: "Rebbe, why do you pray so fast?"

"The prayers are so precious to me," said R' Yaakov Yitzchak, "that I snatch at them and swallow them."

"And why is it," asked the *Chozeh*, "that I don't pray fast? Are the prayers less precious to me?"

"Your prayers," said R' Yaakov Yitzchak, "are like a burning flame, and whoever snatches a burning flame gets burned."

ᴥᔰ Express Prayer

R' Eliezer Yitzchak of Volozhin once saw a student who prayed very quickly. He called the student in and began speaking about how important it was to pray slowly, how prayer without concentration on the meaning of the words was like a body without a soul, and so on.

"Rebbe, let me explain myself," said the student. "Imagine a man traveling in a cart. If the cart goes too slowly, all types of creatures jump onto it. If the cart travels very fast, however, nothing can jump onto the cart. Similarly, when I pray slowly all types of foreign thoughts enter my head, whereas when I pray quickly I don't have that problem."

"I'm afraid, however," said R' Eliezer Yitzchak, "that when you pray as fast as you do, you yourself may be one of the 'creatures' that doesn't manage to jump onto the cart."

ᴥᔰ Late Prayers

R' Naftali of Ropshitz once saw a young man running into the study hall after noon. The man then put on his *tallis* and *tefillin* hurriedly, ran back and forth and before one could take a second glance had finished his prayers.

R' Naftali called him over and said: "Let me tell you a story. There was a man who would have black bread and a dish of barley each day for breakfast. Whenever he came home from his morning prayers his wife had the same meal ready for him.

"One day he came home, and found that there was nothing on the table. His wife called out to him from the adjoining room, 'Please wait, and I'll get your meal ready.'

"He waited patiently: One hour, two hours, three hours passed. He was really going to get a feast, he thought. Finally, after the three hours his wife walked in — carrying black bread and a dish of barley.

"'I'm amazed,' said the man to his wife. 'I thought that after all that time you would have something really special. If this is all you brought, you could have brought it early in the morning!'

"There are righteous sages who do not pray immediately. They need time to think their thoughts through and to compose themselves for prayer. Hashem wants their prayers and waits for them eagerly. But you, since your prayer is hurried anyway, you could have prayed in the early morning."

►§ Unhurried Prayer

R' Moshe Sofer, the *Chasam Sofer*, would pray very slowly. After he completed his prayers one day, one of his students asked: "Rebbe, why do you take so much time praying? After all, you could spend that time studying Torah."

"I'm not worried about that," said R' Moshe. "We are told that whoever takes his time praying has his days lengthened, and I will therefore have enough time left to study more."

►§ Pre-Prayer Preparation

A chasid asked R' Chaim of Sanz, "Rebbe, what do you do before the prayers?"

R' Chaim answered, "Before the prayers I pray."

►§ "I Believe with Perfect Faith"

R' Chaim of Sanz would take a long time saying the Thirteen Principles of the Faith formulated by the *Rambam*. He would say each one deliberately: "I believe with perfect faith that. . ."

After he had finished saying all thirteen once, he would say to himself, "Chaim, you still don't believe!" and would say the whole list again.

Then he would say to himself, "Chaim, you still don't believe with perfect faith!" and he would repeat the list.

⋅§ Hashem's Favor

R' Dov Ber, the *Maggid* of Mezritch, would say: "Hashem did us a great favor in that our very soul does not fly out of our body when we pray."

⋅§ Prayer Thoughts

R' Yaakov Yitzchak, the *Yehudi Hakadosh*, would say: "Whenever I get up to pray, I always imagine that there are ten Cossacks surrounding me with swords in their hands, ready to slay me on the spot if I don't pray properly."

⋅§ Passion in Prayer: With and Without the Rebbe

Some of the chasidim once came to R' Menachem Mendel of Lubavich and complained:"Rebbe, we were at an inn with the chasidim of Pshischa and we all prayed together. They immediately showed the proper fervor, while we, the chasidim of Lubavich, required much time to reach the proper fervor."

"The reason," said R' Menachem Mendel, "is that they reach their passion because of their rebbe, whereas with us, each one has to work up to it himself."

⋅§ The Logic of a Wagon Driver

R' Moshe Yitz'l of Ponivezh would say: "During my entire life no person ever vanquished me except for a wagon driver.

"I was once traveling by wagon. When the time came to pray, both the driver and I began at the same time, but he finished considerably before me.

" 'How is it,' I asked him, 'that you finished praying before me? Do you know the prayers better than I?'

" 'Yes,' he answered. 'There is indeed a simple explanation

for my knowing the prayers better than you. How long did it take you, Rebbe, to learn to pray?'

" 'Three months,' I answered, 'and after that I began studying the Torah.'

" 'And I,' said my driver, 'spent four years learning to pray. Therefore it is logical that I should know the prayers better than you do.' "

⊸§ The Prayer of Two Brothers

R' Chaim Tzvi Teitelbaum of Sighet would pray very quickly, and would end his prayers before the majority of the congregation.

"Rebbe," he was asked, "why is it that you pray so fast, while your brother, R' Yoel, is always the last one to end his prayers?"

"I'm not like my brother," he explained. "My brother is a great Torah scholar, and when he takes a long time, everyone assumes that he has lofty thoughts and thinks hidden meanings in the prayers. I, however, am not a Torah scholar, and were I to take my time in prayer, people would say that I don't even know how to read the words."

⊸§ Greater than Angels

R' Nasan Tzvi of Slobodka once summoned a student who was chronically late for prayers.

"Rebbe," the student protested, "human beings aren't angels."

"Indeed they are not," said R' Nasan Tzvi. "They are greater than angels."

⊸§ Praying with Kavanah

The mashgiach (the spiritual mentor of the yeshivah) came to R' Yosef Leib, the rosh yeshivah of Telshe, and complained that a student was praying without kavanah, the proper concentration.

"And who," R' Yosef Leib asked him, "does pray with *kavanah*? Had we really prayed with *kavanah*, how would we remember to add *ya'aleh veyavo* on *Rosh Chodesh* or *al hanisim* on *Chanukah*?"

The Haskalah – Heretics

⋅§ Let the Dog Pass Judgment

Once R' Chaim Rapaport, the Rav of Lvov, met a Reform Rabbi who was very knowledgeable in secular studies and adept in foreign languages, but knew very little Torah. This man mocked R' Chaim for knowing only Torah.

"What do you do," R' Chaim asked the Reform Rabbi, "if someone comes to you with a question about whether a piece of meat is kosher or not, as your Torah learning is not very broad?"

"I always rule that the meat is not kosher," the Reform Rabbi answered.

"Let me tell you a story," said R' Chaim:

A farmer lived in a small village very far from the city. During the winter, he would slaughter ducks and use their meat and fat. Sometimes, a question arose as to whether a particular bird was kosher or not, so he would harness his horse and gallop off to the nearest city to ask the Rabbi.

Once, the farmer had a visitor, who was a heretic. The farmer told him how difficult things were, and how he sometimes had to make a long trip on the coldest of winter days to ask the Rabbi for a ruling.

"Let me give you a simple solution," said the visitor. "The Torah tells us to throw non-kosher meat to the dogs. Whenever you find you have a question whether a duck is kosher or not, place it before your dog. If it eats the meat, you will know that the duck was not kosher; if it doesn't, you will know it was kosher."

The farmer was delighted. He no longer had to make those long trips.

A few days later, he slaughtered a duck and was unsure of its *kashrus*. He placed the duck before his dog, with his whole family standing by to see what would happen. The dog smelled the fresh meat, but, what with everyone standing about, it became afraid and did not touch the meat.

"It's kosher, it's kosher!" crowed the farmer with delight, and the family ate the duck without any qualms.

As time went on, the dog became accustomed to the ducks and the family presence. Every duck that was placed before him was devoured. There wasn't a single bird which was kosher.

The farmer saw he was in trouble. Finally, when a question arose about a duck, he harnessed his horse and raced off to the Rabbi.

"Why haven't I seen you for so long?" asked the Rabbi. "Have you stopped slaughtering ducks? Or didn't you have any questionable ones?"

"No, Rebbe, I'm still slaughtering ducks as before, but if I have had any questions, I have let my dog decide whether the meat was kosher or not," said the farmer, and explained what he had been doing.

"Well, why did you come now?" asked the Rabbi.

"The trouble, Rebbe," said the man, "is that my dog adopts too severe a position about what is kosher and what isn't."

◦§ A Different Approach

R' Yisrael Salanter said, "Had I lived at the time of the *Chasam Sofer* (when the Reform movement first began), I would have adopted a different approach. I would have spoken to their leaders and shown them where they had erred. If I emerged victorious, it would have been for the good. Had I not emerged victorious, I would have pretended to go along with them. 'If you want a synagogue with an organ, my friend,' I would have said, 'let us build one with an organ.' In that synagogue I would have placed ten Torah scholars to do nothing but study Torah, and in the end that synagogue would have turned into a *beis midrash*."

◦§ Start with Yourselves First

When the Russian government, during the reign of Czar Nicholas I, attempted to spread *haskalah* among the Jews of Russia, the Minister of Education, Ovarov, sent a Jew, Dr. Lilienthal, throughout the country, to try to persuade the Jews to accept the idea of *haskalah*.

Lilienthal's first stop was Vilna, because it was a very influential city. He summoned all the leaders of the community and began to praise the advantages of secular knowledge, and the tremendous favor that the government was offering the Jews by introducing it.

Finally, one of the leaders, Chaim Nachman Parnes, could not bear it and said, "I cannot accept your line of reasoning. If the government really feels that a secular education is so vital, why doesn't it start with the Russian peasants, the vast majority of whom are illiterate. Almost all Jews are literate, while the non-Jews don't even know the letters of the alphabet."

❧ I, Too, Am Lenient

R' Yoshe Ber of Brisk was accosted by one of the *maskilim* (freethinkers).

"I am sure, Rebbe," he said, "that you do not follow the course of the other Rabbis. They only know how to pile one severe ruling upon another; they are afraid to be lenient. You, though, are a great Torah scholar, and I am sure that you are lenient in many of your rulings."

"That is true," said R' Yoshe Ber. "I was indeed lenient in my book."

"In regard to what?" asked the *maskil*.

"Well," said R' Yoshe Ber with a smile, "there are Rabbis who rule that a man must recite the *Shema* at night before midnight, and if he does not do so by midnight, he has not fulfilled the *mitzvah*. I, though, rule leniently, that one may recite the *Shema* any time before dawn."

❧ It's Included in the Price

The *Netziv* was not only a great Torah scholar, but had a phenomenal knowledge of Hebrew grammar and wrote a very fluent Hebrew.

A *maskil* was amazed at the *Netziv's* command of *Tanach* and of the Hebrew language. "Rebbe," he said, "how do you know *Tanach* and the Hebrew language so well? We, the *maskilim*, spend all our time studying *Tanach* and Hebrew, and our study requires all of our effort. Yet you devote all your time to studying Torah. How did you manage to learn Hebrew so well?"

"Let me tell you a story," answered the *Netziv*:

There was once a storekeeper who came to the big city, Lodz, to buy goods. He stayed at an inn together with an important merchant, who had also come to Lodz to buy materials.

As he sat next to the merchant, the latter was going over his bills, and, unable to overcome his curiosity, the storekeeper looked at the bills: woven fabric, such-and-such a price; satin, such-and-such a price, and so on. All of these fabrics needed to be wrapped, yet there was no charge on the bills for the paper and string needed to wrap the fabric. Paper and string must be free in Lodz, he thought to himself. That being the case, he would take as much paper and string as he could carry, and bring it home, where he would be able to sell it for a fine sum.

He came to a wholesaler, and asked him for wrapping paper and string. The wholesaler brought him what he had asked, but also presented him with a bill.

"I don't understand," said the storekeeper. "I noticed that on the invoices of another merchant, there was no charge for the paper or string."

"Fool!" said the wholesaler. "If one buys material, the wrapping and the string are included in the price. You, however, did not buy any merchandise, but only the paper and string. You must pay for them."

"The Torah is our 'merchandise,' concluded the *Netziv*. "All the other studies and disciplines are but servants to the Torah, so as to enable us to understand the Torah better. They are the paper and string tied around the merchandise to protect it. If a person studies Torah, the other disciplines are given to him freely, without any effort. But that is not true for the *maskilim*. They do not study the Torah, but only other subjects. It is only proper, then, that they pay for them, that those other disciplines be acquired through effort."

⋙ Clothes — A Door to the Mind

People came to the *Netziv* of Volozhin to complain that a young man in the yeshivah was wearing the modern clothes of the *maskilim*, rather than the clothes normally worn by yeshivah students.

"Clothes don't make the difference," said the *Netziv*.

"But, Rebbe," they said, "we are told that one of the signs of the Jew is his distinctive garb."

"You misunderstood me," said the *Netziv*. "If a watch stops, its hands cease to move. This does not mean that the trouble lies in the hands. But if the hands do not move it indicates that the inner works of the watch are defective. When a Jew begins wearing clothes different from those worn by the other Jews, it is a sign that the inner workings of his mind are defective."

↵§ The Purpose of the Theater

A man who loved to go to the theater came to R' Moshe Mordechai Epstein of Slobodka and said to him, "I have a complaint against you religious Jews. You forbid people to go to the theater. Everyone knows that the entire purpose of the theater is to have people think about the play and work to better themselves."

"Let me tell you a story," said R' Moshe Mordechai:

There was a man who spent his entire life going to the theater. When he died, he came to Heaven and said, "Prepare me a place in the Garden of Eden."

"Why do you deserve a place?" he was asked.

"I helped the public," he said, "for I spent my entire life with the theater, and made people better themselves."

"Wait," they told him, "at the entrance to the Garden of Eden until someone comes who was bettered as a result of going to the theater, and then you can both together enter the Garden of Eden."

And that man is still waiting at the entrance to the Garden of Eden, R' Moshe Mordechai concluded.

↵§ Why He Did Not Fall

When R' Meir was the Rav of Premishlan, the only *mikveh* that was available was on the steep slope of a hill. The members of the community would make their way very slowly up the side of the hill to reach the *mikveh*. But R' Meir would scamper up the mountain, immerse himself, and then scamper down the mountain again, whether it was summer or winter.

Two young men who had leanings toward *haskalah* decided that if R' Meir could be so nimble, then so could they. One wintry day they tried to emulate him, but slipped on the icy cliff and hurt themselves in falling.

"One who is tied to Heaven does not fall," said R' Meir.

◦§ Beyond the Grave

A chasid came to R' Ben Zion of Bobov, and asked for a blessing that his son be accepted in a particular school.

"Why," R' Ben Zion asked him, "do you want to send your son to study secular subjects, rather than to a yeshivah to learn Torah?"

"Rebbe," the chasid answered, "once my son graduates from the school, I'm sure he'll be able to support me until I am one hundred and twenty."

"Nu," R' Ben Zion asked, "and what happens after the one hundred and twenty years?"

◦§ Are You Really Sure?

A famous Jewish heretic, who had once studied Torah and then left the faith, would travel from one Torah sage to another and argue with them about religion. He finally visited R' Levi Yitzchak of Berdichev. "My son," said R' Levi Yitzhak, "a number of great Torah sages have argued with you, and you have refused to budge. No one can force you to believe this and not believe that. However, you are obviously still unsure of your position, for otherwise you would not continue your debates. After all, maybe there is a G-d and there is reward and punishment. Maybe there is *gehinnom* and the Garden of Paradise. What, then, will you do on the day of final reckoning?"

◦§ The Muddy Convert

When Moses Montefiore, the great benefactor, was in Vilna, both Jews and non-Jews from all over the city came to visit him. Montefiore was very gracious, and received everyone who came to see him.

A Jewish convert to Christianity asked to see him, but Montefiore refused. Those who were there were astonished, because they knew that he met with non-Jews quite freely.

"We know," he said, "that Israel is compared to dust ("your seed will be as the dust of the earth" — *Bereishis* 28:14). The other nations are compared to water ("the rushing of nations, that make a rushing like the rushing of mighty waters" — *Yeshayahu* 17:12). Now dust by itself is fine, and water by itself is fine. Once water is placed on dust, though (i.e., the baptism), all that one gets is mud, and I can't stand mud."

◆§ What Came First?

One of the students of R' Chaim of Brisk would always ask questions about the most fundamental precepts of the Torah. Eventually, he became a heretic.

Years later, R' Chaim met his former student and he asked, "What came first in your case? Was it your questions that made you become a heretic, or was it your heresy which made you ask questions?"

"I must admit," answered the former student, "that my heresy came first."

"So," said R' Chaim, "you were not asking questions, but were giving excuses for what you wished to do."

◆§ Minimizing the Damage

When an assimilationalist Jewish school was opened in Neitra, R' Yechezkel, the Rav of the town, called in the teacher who had been engaged and spoke to him at great length. When the teacher was leaving, R' Yechezkel asked him to come back whenever he wished to. And whenever he came, R' Yechezkel spent a great deal of time with him.

Once, the teacher of the local Talmud Torah came to see R'

Yechezkel, and in a very short time R' Yechezkel sent him on his way.

"Rebbe," someone asked R' Yechezkel, "why is it that you show such respect and spend so much time with the school teacher, while you have almost no time for the Talmud Torah teacher?"

"There is a simple explanation," answered R' Yechezkel. "The former teaches his students all types of heresies, and the more I waste his time, the less the children receive from him. The Talmud Torah teacher, on the other hand, is teaching his students Torah, and every minute I detain him is a minute wasted from learning Torah."

☙ It's All a Question of Time

When R' Shimon Sofer of Cracow was young, he told his father, the *Chasam Sofer*, "Father, yesterday a heretic asked me this question, and I was unable to answer him." And he repeated the question.

The *Chasam Sofer* said nothing then, but a few days later he summoned his son and showed him that the question was easily answered.

"Father," R' Shimon asked, "if you knew the answer when I asked you, why did you wait a few days before telling it to me?"

"I wanted to teach you," said the *Chasam Sofer*, "that in questions of faith, one does not have to worry if he does not have an immediate answer. If he doesn't have an answer today, he will have it tomorrow. Meanwhile, there is no reason to lose faith."

Eretz Yisrael

⊷§ For Love of Eretz Yisrael

R' Baruch of Mezhibozh loved *Eretz Yisrael*, and was very interested in settling in it. At the time, there were very few Jews in the country, and they all lived in the greatest of poverty. The trip itself was a hazardous one, which took months.

In order to encourage his chasidim to live in *Eretz Yisrael*, R' Baruch sent R' Velvel of Zbarzh. After many long months of traveling, R' Velvel and his wife reached *Eretz Yisrael*, and settled in Tiberias (*Teveriyah*).

A year passed, and a second, and there was no word from R' Velvel; in those days, there was no such thing as mail service. R' Baruch then sent R' Yaakov Shimshon, the Rabbi of Shpitevka, to *Eretz Yisrael*, to see what was happening.

R' Yaakov Shimshon finally arrived in Acre (*Akko*) by ship. From there, he rode on a donkey to Tiberias. When he reached R' Velvel's home, he saw a woman in the courtyard, washing linens. He recognized R' Velvel's wife. He immediately tried to return to Acre, because he could not bear the suffering of so righteous a woman.

R' Velvel's wife, though, saw him, and said, "Rebbe, I want you to know that the wash is not my own, but that of other people. This is *Eretz Yisrael*, and it is worth suffering in order to live in it."

R' Yaakov Shimshon burst into tears, dismounted the donkey, and entered R' Velvel's home.

⏜§ *Wherever I Travel*

R' Nachman of Breslov would say: "Wherever I travel, my destination is always *Eretz Yisrael*."

⏜§ *From Those Days*

He would also say: "Whatever life there is within me comes from the time that I spent in *Eretz Yisrael*."

⏜§ *The Good Side*

The Rebbe of Koretz once explained: "When Moshe said: 'Let me pass over, I pray You, and see the good land,' (*Devarim* 3:25) what he meant was that he did not want to imitate the *meraglim* (the spies) who had seen only the negative aspects of *Eretz Yisrael*. He wanted to see its good qualities."

⏜§ *One Brick at a Time*

R' Naftali of Ropshitz would say: "By our service to Hashem, we build *Yerushalayim* each day. One of us adds a row of bricks, another a single one only. When *Yerushalayim* is completed, the redemption will come."

This World and The World to Come

⊷§ *I Will Not Budge*

R' Pinchas of Koretz would say: "If I am taken immediately to the World to Come, that will be fine. However, if first I am taken to *Gehinnom* before I am taken to the Garden of Eden, I will refuse to budge from there as long as a single Jew remains."

⊷§ *You Have to Work for It*

Late one night, as R' Pinchas, author of the *Hafla'ah*, sat learning, he heard someone knocking on the window. From the freezing cold and raging snowstorm a voice cried out, "Take pity on a Jew and allow me in."

R' Pinchas immediately opened the door, and a man covered

with snow and close to exhaustion stumbled in. R' Pinchas sat him down near the fire, and the man began to recover.

He asked R' Pinchas to excuse him for having bothered him in the middle of the night and having disturbed his learning. He was a merchant, he said, from a distant town who was on his way to the fair. In the snowstorm he had lost his way and had finally stumbled on this village. As R' Pinchas' was the only light in the village, he had knocked on the window and asked for shelter.

"Rebbe," he said, "what are my chances of going to the Garden of Eden? In this world, I am constantly forced to wander about to make a living, and one can hardly call it life."

"Do you set aside time every day to learn?" asked R' Pinchas.

"No," replied the man. "My day is much too busy to set aside time for learning Torah."

"Well," said R' Pinchas, "if in this world, where you labor and work so hard, you have nothing, then what do you expect to receive in the Garden of Eden, for which you are doing nothing?"

⋅§ For What One Must Be Accountable

R' Zushia of Hanipol said: "In the World to Come, Zushia will not be held accountable for not having attained the level of the Baal Shem Tov. He will be held accountable for not having attained the level of which Zushia was capable."

⋅§ Nothing with Which to Live

R' Moshe Sofer, the Chasam Sofer, would say: "I have heard many people complain that they have nothing with which to live. I have never heard anyone complain that he has nothing with which to die."

◆§ Facing Your Horse

R' David of Lelov saw a wagon driver whipping his horse mercilessly. "Let me ask you," said R' David, "after your death, your horse will appear to testify against you in the World to Come. Won't you be ashamed to defend yourself against a horse?"

◆§ A Jew Has Arrived

R' Moshe of Kobrin would say: "If I knew that after my death they would say in the World to Come, 'a Jew has arrived,' I would not have anything to worry about."

◆§ With Great Mercy

A Rabbi, while speaking to R' Avraham Mordechai of Gur, asked about a particular individual. R' Avraham Mordechai didn't have the heart to tell him the man was dead, and said, "That man needs great mercy."

The next day, the Rabbi heard that the person he had asked about was indeed dead. He came back to R' Avraham Mordechai and said, "Rebbe, you didn't tell me the truth. I'm surprised at you."

"What I said was absolutely true," replied R' Avraham Mordechai. "The dead, too, need great mercy, as we say in the Shemoneh Esrei: 'He revives the dead with great mercy.' "

◆§ Who Says It'll Be Better?

A chasid came to the Rebbe of Gur and complained about how terrible his life was: "Rebbe, I have troubles without end," he said. "I wish I could leave this world and put an end to all my troubles."

"Who said that things will be better for you in the World to Come?" asked the Rebbe.

~§ If Not Now, When?

R' Hillel Lichtenstein became extremely ill. His doctors ordered him not to study Torah, but he ignored them.

When R' Moshe Sofer, the *Chasam Sofer*, heard of this, he sent a message to R' Hillel: "Why are you disobeying the doctors at a time when your life is in grave danger?"

"That is exactly the point," replied R' Hillel. "If I do not learn now, then when?"

$\mathcal{M}ashiach$

◆§ *The Fallen Tefillin*

R' Levi Yitzchak of Berdichev would say: "Lord of the universe! Why don't You act with Your children the way the simplest Jew acts? I once saw a Jew, the simplest of the simple, who accidentally dropped his *tefillin* on the ground. He immediately picked them up and kissed them. Yet we, Your nation, are Your *tefillin* (*Berachos* 6). You threw us down, and for close to two thousand years we have been rolling about in the lowliness of exile. The time has come, our Father in Heaven, to raise us up from the ground and to send us *Mashiach*."

◆§ *The Invitation*

When R' Levi Yitzchak of Berdichev sent out the invitations to his grandson's wedding, he wrote as follows: "The wedding will, please Hashem, take place in Yerushalayim on this-and-this date. If, Heaven forbid, the *Mashiach* has not arrived by this date, it will take place in Berdichev."

✑ Always Ready

Before R' Bunim of Pshischa went to sleep — even if it was only for a short nap — he always saw to it that his *tallis* and *tefillin* were right at hand.

"If I am awoken and told that *Mashiach* has arrived, they will be there," he said. "For how can a Jew set out on the road without his *tallis* and *tefillin?*"

✑ The Unbelieving Dogs

Once R' Shmuel Elye of Bilgoray came to an inn where there was a group of freethinkers. They began laughing at the idea of *Mashiach*.

"Let me tell you a story," said R' Shmuel Elye:

Once there was a fox who saw a bird perched on top of a tree. He was very hungry, so he said to the bird, "Why don't you come down and keep me company?"

The bird refused. "I know," it said, "why you have invited me. You are hungry and want to eat me."

"Heaven forbid," said the fox virtuously. "*Mashiach* has come, and now we have the fulfillment of the verse: 'The wolf will dwell with the lamb' (*Yeshayahu* 11:6). No animal will harm any other."

As they were talking, they suddenly heard the baying of hounds and the sound of trumpets.

"What do you see from where you are?" asked the fox.

"It's nothing," replied the bird. "Just some hunters and their dogs."

The fox became terrified and began to run away.

"Why are you running away?" asked the bird. "After all, *Mashiach* has come, and no creature will hurt any other."

"You are right," said the fox, as he ran for his life. "But these dogs don't believe in *Mashiach*."

⋙ Even After Death?

A chasid once came to R' Menachem Mendel of Kotzk and asked him for permission to go up to *Eretz Yisrael.*

"Why do you wish to go?" asked R' Menachem Mendel.

"I want to," said the man, "because our Sages tell us that when *Mashiach* comes, all the bodies of those buried outside *Eretz Yisrael* will have to roll in underground tunnels all the way to *Eretz Yisrael.* I want to save myself that torment."

"Is your body so important to you that you are even worried about it after your death?" said R' Menachem Mendel.

⋙ Changes of Perspective

R' Yaakov Taub of Neustadt would say about the birth pangs during the times right before the coming of the *Mashiach*: "In previous generations, people were afraid of the *Mashiach's* time, but nowadays people no longer fear it. Why? Imagine a man who walks along the road and sees a forest which appears to be thickly wooded and impenetrable far in the distance. As he gets closer, though, he can see that there is room between the trees, and that a person can make his way through the forest."

⋙ Check First

Whenever R' Zundel of Salant got to the blessing of *Es Tzemach David* in the *Shemoneh Esrei*, the blessing dealing with the coming of *Mashiach*, he would first open his eyes and look about before continuing with the prayer.

When he was asked why he did this, he said, "I want to see if *Mashiach* has indeed arrived. If he has and I recite the blessing, I will be guilty of pronouncing a blessing in vain."

⋙ Simple Proof

R' Chaim of Brisk was traveling by train. He sat in a corner learning, while those with him talked about this and that. In the car was a missionary, who tried to persuade the Jews that his god had been *Mashiach*.

"The *Tanna'im* who lived in his time knew him better than all the later generations, and they believed him worthy of the death penalty," said one of the Jews.

"The *Tanna'im*, too, could make a mistake," said the missionary. "Didn't R' Akiva believe that Bar Kochba was the *Mashiach*?"

They had no answer.

At that point, R' Chaim looked up and asked the missionary, "Why do you feel that R' Akiva was wrong and that Bar Kochba was not the *Mashiach*?"

"That's obvious," replied the missionary. "Bar Kochba was killed."

"Indeed?" said R' Chaim, "You, too, agree, then, that a *Mashiach* that is killed is not a *Mashiach*."

◆§ Who Listens to Whom?

R' Chaim of Volozhin was sitting with his disciples and discussing the ultimate redemption and the coming of *Mashiach*. One of them said, "Rebbe, I read the *Avkas Rochel*, describing all the terrible troubles that will befall the Jews in *Mashiach's* time, and I wonder if Israel will be able to bear them."

"Do you think," said R' Chaim with a smile, "that in *Mashiach's* time Hashem will leaf through the *Avkas Rochel* page by page?"

◆§ Avkas Rochel

Once R' Menachem Mendel of Kotzk studied the *Avkas Rochel*, describing all the troubles which will occur at the time of *Mashiach*. He exclaimed with a smile, "It is true that an author must obey what Hashem tells him. However, Hashem need not obey what an author tells him."

Between Man
and His
Fellow Man

Helping Others

⊷§ Others Should Also Be Able to Help

Before R' Yechezkel Landau, the *Noda BiYehudah*, became the Rav of Prague, he lived in Brody. He was a very wealthy man and held no official position.

While there, two great Torah sages came to him for a donation in order to ransom people who had been seized by the government.

"How much do you need?" he asked them.

"We need three hundred rubles," they replied.

R' Yechezkel left the room and came back with a pile of money. "Here are two hundred and ninety rubles," he told them. "You can collect the rest in town."

"Why only two hundred and ninety?" they asked. "If you have given us so much, why not add another ten rubles and spare us going through town like beggars and being humiliated in the process?"

"The *Mishnah* says: 'One who gives, but does not want others to give, has an evil eye for others' (*Avos* 5:16), because he doesn't want them to share in the *mitzvah*," said R' Yechezkel. "I want others, also, to have a chance to participate in the *mitzvah*."

ᴈ§ Take Before Eating

R' Meir of Tiktin would never eat on any day until he had helped at least one Jew in some way.

Once, the entire day passed, and R' Meir hadn't found anyone to help. Evening came, and then night — and still there had been no one to help. R' Meir was still fasting and feeling very depressed.

At midnight, he went to the market, to see if he could find someone to help. In the market stood a wagon with a load of lumber. The non-Jewish driver was standing by the wagon. R' Meir ran to the town carpenter and told him about the lumber. The carpenter came and saw that the lumber was of excellent quality and reasonably priced.

"Rebbe," said the carpenter said. "I really appreciate what you did for me, but I simply don't have enough money to pay for the lumber."

"That's no problem," replied R' Meir, "I'll lend you what you need."

He immediately ran home and came back with the amount the carpenter was lacking.

Only then did R' Meir return cheerfully home to eat.

ᴈ§ Onions and Garlic

Once R' Yaakov, the *Maggid* of Dubno, went out to raise money for the ransoming of captives. He came to a man who was very wealthy and a Torah scholar. The man greeted him warmly, and they began speaking in learning. R' Yaakov, looking for a contribution, gave a short talk on charity, and the man matched it with a talk of his own on the same topic. R' Yaakov then spoke on the topic of ransoming captives, which was again matched with a talk by his host on that topic. R' Yaakov saw that things were going nowhere, so he said to the rich man, "Let me tell you a story:

A man wandered to a faraway country, where the people had never seen onions in their lives. He took out some onions from his knapsack and gave it to the people of this country. They were delighted at this new vegetable, and gave him their weight in gold.

Having seen how well he had been rewarded for bringing onions to the country, the man returned the next year, this time with another vegetable they had never seen — garlic. Again the people were delighted, and paid him with their most valuable item; they gave him, not their weight in gold, but in onions!

"We have been trading Torah thoughts with one another," said R' Yaakov. "I gave you a Torah thought of my own, and you repay me with a Torah thought of yours. But, what I need is money."

๛ Not Overnight

After obtaining his bare necessities, R' Mordechai of Lechovich would take care to donate all the money he had left over to the needy. Furthermore, he made a point of donating all he had left each day before the end of the day. He would say, "If I go to sleep and there is a copper coin left in my pocket, I can't sleep the whole night. That one coin in my pocket makes me feel as if I am lying down on a hard rock rather than a bed."

๛ The Miser

When R' Yom Tov, the author of the *Tosafos Yom Tov*, was the *Rav* in Cracow, an extremely wealthy man, Shimon by name, who was known to be a miser of the worst sort, lived there. He would never give any money for any cause, no matter how worthy.

On the other hand, there were two tradesmen in the city, one a blacksmith and the other a baker, who gave very generously to charity whenever they were asked. They secretly supported a few families, and did good deeds constantly.

Shimon the miser died. He was given a miserly funeral, as he deserved, and was buried in the least honorable place in the cemetery, among the most worthless people.

Suddenly, with his death, the blacksmith and baker ceased being generous. Both stopped giving charity. They turned down requests which they had answered so readily earlier.

The rabbi summoned the two and asked them why they had changed so radically. They finally confessed. Whatever they had given had not been theirs, but Shimon's. He had sworn them to secrecy so that he would not be honored for his charity.

When R' Yom Tov died, his will specified that he wished to be buried next to Shimon the 'miser'.

⊷§ No Reason to Be Jealous

The Baal Shem Tov and his young son visited a very wealthy man. In the house, inside a glass case, they saw a beautiful collection of silver pieces.

After they had left, the Baal Shem Tov asked his son, "Are you jealous of that man? After all, your father has no silver pieces."

"I am," answered the child.

"Know, my son," said the Baal Shem Tov, "that if I had money to buy silver pieces, I would not buy them but would distribute the money to the poor."

⊷§ Knowing the True Worth

Once a poor man asked R' Shmelke of Nikolsburg for charity. R' Shmelke could not find any money, but saw a ring lying on the table and gave it to the poor man.

When R' Shmelke's wife found out about it, she became upset and said, "Do you know what you did? The ring has a precious stone in it, and is worth a lot of money."

R' Shmelke sent his *shamash* to fetch the poor man. When the man arrived, R' Shmelke told him, "I want you to know that that is a very valuable ring. Don't sell it for less than it's worth."

⇜ One Must Always Try Again

R' Levi Yitzchak of Berdichev went on a mission to raise money for the ransom of captives held by the government. He went from town to town, but was singularly unsuccessful.

"I have wasted my time," R' Levi Yitzchak thought to himself. "I wasted time that I could have used for studying Torah or praying, and I have nothing to show for it."

Shortly after his musings, R' Levi Yitzchak found himself in a town in which a Jew was caught stealing. The man was beaten thoroughly, and thrown into jail. R' Levi Yitzchak went to visit him and said, "See, my son, what you brought upon yourself. I am sure that you will never repeat your crime."

"Why not?" replied the man. "If I didn't succeed today, I may succeed tomorrow."

"I have learned a lesson," thought R' Levi Yitzchak to himself. "I, too, will continue. If I didn't succeed today, I may succeed tomorrow."

⇜ Honesty Pays

R' Eliezer Lipa was involved in ransoming those who had been seized by the authorities, and spent large sums of money to gain the release of Jews who had been seized by nobles for non-payment of debts.

Once he heard that a noble had seized a Jewish tenant for not having paid his rent. The debt owed was a few thousand thalers, and R' Eliezer Lipa only had a thousand. He went to the noble and begged him to take the thousand thalers and release the tenant.

"What will you gain," he asked the noble, "if you keep this poor Jew in prison? Even if you kill him, that won't add a single penny to your income. My way, at least you will receive a thousand thalers."

The noble understood the logic, took the thousand thalers, and freed the Jew.

As R' Eliezer Lipa was about to leave, the noble called him back and said, "I can see that you are a trustworthy person. My brother-in-law, who is also a wealthy noble, lives not far from here. He has flax to sell, and is looking for an honest merchant. I will give you a letter asking him to sell his flax to you."

"Your excellency," said R' Eliezer Lipa, "I cannot buy the flax. I spent my last money paying the debt of your tenant."

"Well, then," replied the noble, "I will give you back the thousand thalers, and use that to buy the flax."

R' Eliezer Lipa took the money and letter and went to the brother-in-law who read the letter and agreed to have R' Eliezer Lipa buy the flax. He sent along one of his servants to show him the merchandise, and on the way R' Eliezer Lipa heard someone crying bitterly.

"Who is crying?" he asked the servant.

"It's a Jew who was seized for not paying his debt," said the servant, "and the noble is going to starve him to death in punishment."

R' Eliezer Lipa went back to the noble, paid this Jew's debt, and had him set free. He then prepared to leave.

"But what about our business deal?" asked the noble.

"Your excellency," replied R' Eliezer Lipa, "I will tell you the truth. I cannot have business dealings with you, because of the way you treat people."

The noble was very affected by these words, and told R' Eliezer Lipa, "I promise you that I will never again do such a deed. As to the money which you gave me for the ransom, I will apply it to the purchase of the flax. We will do business, and both of us will benefit."

R' Eliezer Lipa bought the flax and earned a sizable amount.

৶ The Best Investment

When R' Menachem Mendel of Lubavich, the *Tzemach Tzedek*, married, his wife brought a dowry of two thousand rubles to the marriage. After the wedding, his grandfather, R' Shneur Zalman of Liadi, asked him, "Mendel, what are you going to do with the dowry?"

"I will invest it with so-and-so."

"Do you trust him?"

"What do you mean? I know that he is very wealthy and is an honest man."

"True! He is rich now. But what happens if he loses all his money, leaving you with neither the principal nor the profit?"

"What would you suggest instead?"

"I will give you good advice. Invest your money here" — and he pointed to the *tzedakah* box — "and your money will be protected."

R' Menachem Mendel thought that his grandfather was joking and smiled.

"You are wrong," said R' Shneur Zalman. "I was not joking, and meant every word I said. If you give your money to charity, both the principal and profit are guaranteed."

R' Menachem Mendel remained silent; he could not spend every last penny he owned on charity. Instead, he invested it with the wealthy man.

Some time later, there was a major fire that destroyed the rich man's home, and with it all his merchandise. He was left penniless, and had to beg to support himself.

R' Mendel, too, lost everything he had owned.

"You see what I said," his grandfather told him. "Now you have neither the principal nor the profit. Had you listened to me and given all your money to charity, you would have had both."

৶ Give Charity, Not Pity (I)

A poor man came to R' Menachem Mendel of Rimanov and told him of the bitterness of his lot and how he was in need of money for even the most basic necessities. The Rebbe was very touched and gave him a sizable gift. After the poor man had left, R' Menachem Mendel asked that he return and he gave him an additional sum of money.

"Rebbe, why did you give him money twice?" asked those who were close to him.

"When the poor man came to me and told me all his woes, I was very moved and gave him money," said R' Menachem Mendel. "That, however, was not charity. It only helped alleviate my distress. I therefore called him back and the second time I gave him charity."

◈§ Give Charity, Not Pity (II)

R' Bunim of Pshischa passed through the town of Sheps on his way home from Danzig. A man named R' Zalman Chasid lived there. He was a very great and righteous Torah scholar, who was exceptionally poor. When R' Bunim entered the local inn, he asked R' Zalman to visit him. R' Zalman came, dressed in tatters and this in the midst of the bitter winter.

"I would like you to do me a favor," said R' Bunim. "I would like you to prepare a lavish dinner for me." He took out a sizable amount of money, which he did not bother to count, and handed it to R' Zalman.

R' Zalman went to the market, and bought all that was needed for a banquet and still there was money left over.

R' Zalman left and R' Bunim called a tailor and ordered him to sew a coat and hat for R' Zalman. He also sent for boots and whole outfits of clothing for R' Zalman and the members of his family. Before the meal, he had his *shamash* bring all the clothes to R' Zalman's home. He himself came to the house, sent everyone else away, dressed R' Zalman from head to foot and saw to it that the others were dressed also. Everyone sat down to enjoy the feast. During the meal, R' Bunim again reached into his pocket and took out a pile of money which he did not count, and asked R' Zalman to go and buy more drinks.

When R' Bunim was ready to leave Sheps, R' Zalman came to thank him for everything he had done. R' Bunim then took out a gold coin and gave it to R' Zalman.

"But Rebbe," R' Zalman protested, "I still have money left over after buying the food and buying the wine."

"One who gives charity because he cannot stand another's suffering has not fulfilled the *mitzvah* of *tzedakah*. He is not helping the other person but himself; he wishes to relieve the pain of his heart. Whatever I gave you until now was because of compassion. I was unable to suffer your pain and that of your family. Now that you are dressed properly, and are not destitute, I wish to observe the *mitzvah* of *tzedakah*."

◄§ It's Not Your Fault

A poor Torah scholar came to R' Reuven Leib Himelstein of Warsaw, and asked for a donation. R' Reuven Leib gave the man a sum of money, and they began talking in learning. As the man was ready to leave, R' Reuven Leib reached into his pocket and took out some more money.

"Rebbe," the man asked, "why are you giving me more money?"

"In the time we spent talking, you could have been seeing others. Just because I enjoyed our conversation is no reason why you should lose money."

◄§ Needing More

A man who had lost everything he owned came to R' Akiva Eiger and asked to borrow fifty rubles. R' Akiva took his silver goblet and told the man, "Go and borrow fifty rubles, and leave this as a pledge."

The man borrowed a hundred rubles rather than fifty. Time passed, but he never paid back the loan, and left the pledge in the lender's hands.

"Rebbe, see how disgusting this man's actions are," R' Akiva Eiger was told. "Not only did he not redeem the pledged object and return it to you, but he borrowed a hundred rubles against it rather than fifty."

"Indeed?" said R' Akiva Eiger in surprise. "He needed a hundred rubles and only asked for fifty because he was embarrassed. From now on, whenever anyone comes to borrow money, I must be sure to ask him if he needs more than what he asked for."

◦§ Public as Opposed to Secret Acts

R' Mordechai Benet once came to a very wealthy man, who was known to be lax in his observance of the *mitzvos*, in order to ask him to give money for a certain charity.

"Rebbe," said the man, "it is my custom to give my *tzedakah* privately, not in public."

"That is very interesting," said R' Mordechai, "because all the sins you commit in private are known to everyone in town, whereas the *tzedakah* which you give privately is unknown to anyone at all."

◦§ Who Is Really to Blame

When R' Bunim of Pshischa was a young man and lived in Bendin, a poor young man of good family came to the town to collect money for *hachnasas kallah* — to pay for the costs involved in getting married. R' Bunim gave him a sizable contribution, and told a friend of his, who was in charge of a charity fund in their *beis midrash*, to give some money from the fund to this poor young man. When this became known, a storm erupted in the town. The elders of the *beis midrash* all met in order to decide how to punish R' Bunim's friend. R' Bunim also came to the meeting. At the meeting, each rose and described how a terrible sin had been committed, and what punishment should be meted out for this serious crime of giving money from the charity fund.

Finally, R' Bunim got up and said, "My friends, I would like to tell you a story:

Once there was a plague in the forest, and thousands of animals died. All the animals gathered to see what they could do to stop the plague. The elders got up and said, "We have been taught that plagues comes upon the forest because of sin."

They all decided that the king of beasts, the lion, and his ministers would sit as a court, and each animal would confess its sins.

The leopard got up and confessed. "My lord the king, and honored ministers," he said, "I was once very hungry. I saw a man. I killed him and ate him.'

The judges debated the case and ruled, "The leopard is perfectly guiltless. He only killed because he was hungry. And that is how a leopard acts."

The wolf got up and confessed. "My lord the king, and honored ministers," he said, "I was once very hungry. I had not eaten anything that entire day. Towards evening I saw a cow and a calf grazing. I killed the cow and her calf and ate them."

The verdict came down, "The wolf is innocent. It only killed because of its hunger. And that is how a wolf acts."

The court acquitted each animal in turn. The last animal to confess was a lamb. It got up and said, "My lord the king, and honored ministers, once, on a very cold day, my master took pity on me and brought me into his home. That night, I saw some straw that my master had pushed into his shoes. I was very hungry, and I pulled out the straw and ate it. The next day, my master walked about without straw in his shoes."

"You wicked animal!" they all shouted. "It was because of your sin that the plague came to the forest." They attacked the little lamb and within an instant, it was killed and devoured.

"Of those sitting in judgment," concluded R' Bunim, "there is one who is guilty of taking interest, others who have false weights, and some who underpay their workers. All of you, though, have reasons for your behavior and are innocent. The only one who has committed a sin among us is this young man in charge of the charity fund."

◄§ Why There Is No Blessing

R' Zvi Elimelech of Dinov would say, "Why didn't our Sages institute the reciting of a blessing before giving *tzedakah*, just as they instituted blessings before so many other *mitzvos*?

"The answer is that if giving *tzedakah* would have required a blessing in advance, the poor would die of hunger. A poor man would come along and ask for *tzedakah*. The person who had been asked would first go to wash his hands before the blessing, and possibly then go to the *mikveh*. He would then pronounce a *L'Shem Yichud* before the blessing and finally the blessing itself. By that time, the poor man would have died."

◄§ Eat Meat and Drink Wine

A wealthy chasid came to R' Yitzchak of Vorki. The chasid was known to be extremely miserly. He did not even spend money on himself and lived on little more than bread and water.

R' Yitzchak rebuked him and said, "If Hashem has blessed you with wealth, you must live well, eat meat and fish, and drink wine."

The chasidim present were astonished. When the man left they asked, "Rebbe, why did you rebuke him in this fashion? What difference does it make if he doesn't eat meat and drink wine?"

"It's not for him that I said what I said," explained R' Yitzchak, "but for the poor. If he eats meat and drinks wine, he will give the poor some bread to eat. However, if he himself eats only bread, what will there be left for him to give to the poor?"

◄§ Distant Relatives

R' Menachem David of Amshinov came to a rich man to persuade him to help a relative who was deeply in debt. The rich man turned him down. "What do I have to do with him?" he asked. "We are only distant relatives."

"Excuse me," R' Menachem David asked, "do you pray every day?"

"What? Do you think that I am not observant?"

"Well, if you do pray," R' Menachem David went on, "could you tell me how the *Shemoneh Esrei* begins?"

The man bristled. "A school child can answer that," he said. "It begins with the blessing of *Avos* which mentions Avraham, Yitzchak and Yaakov."

"Well, who are Avraham, Yitzchak and Yaakov?" persisted R' Menachem David.

Now the man was really angry. "Those are obviously our forefathers!"

"When did our forefathers live?" went on R' Menachem David.

"Thousands of years ago," answered the rich man.

"Well, let's see now," said R' Menachem David. "They are extremely distant relatives of yours, who lived hundreds of generations ago, yet you mention them three times a day and ask to benefit from their good deeds."

◆§ Giving and Taking

R' Yisrael of Ruzhin would say: "A folk proverb says that a fool gives while a wise man takes. This refers to those who give *tzedakah*. A fool who gives *tzedakah* thinks that he is giving, while a wise man who gives charity knows that by his giving he is in reality taking."

◆§ The Proper Way to Give Tzedakah

When the *Malbim* was the rabbi in Mohilew, he devoted a good part of his time to looking after the needs of the poor.

Once, a woman came to him, crying bitterly. "Rebbe, my husband and provider died, and I have no source of income," she said.

"What did your husband do for a living?" asked the *Malbim*.

"He drove a wagon. It was the hard work and our dire poverty which made him die before his time," she replied.

"Do you have any skills?" he asked.

"Yes, Rebbe, I know how to bake cakes well. Had I the money, I would have gone into business myself, buying the finest ingredients and making a living from my cakes."

"If that is so," said the *Malbim*, "let us be partners. I'll give you the money, and you'll supply the labor, and Hashem will give us His blessing." The *Malbim* rose, went into the adjoining room, and came back with a hundred rubles. "This is my share in the partnership," he told the woman.

The woman took the money and her eyes were again filled with tears, but this time of gratitude.

"You must stop crying," said the *Malbim*, "because if you cry, I will withdraw from this partnership. Hashem only brings blessing upon those who are joyful."

The widow rented a place, bought the finest ingredients, and began baking cakes. As she was indeed very skilled, her name soon spread throughout the town, and all came to buy her products. Soon she was earning a good living.

The woman also kept scrupulous records.

After six months had elapsed, the ledger showed a profit of hundreds of rubles. The woman took the ledger, plus half the profits, and came to the rabbi to give him his share.

"Rebbe," she said, "here is the ledger and this is your share of the profits."

The *Malbim* pretended to check the figures; then he counted the money she had brought him. He then returned both the ledger and the money to the woman and told her, "The accounts are perfectly in order. As to dividing up the profits, that isn't done when a business is successful. I would like my share to remain invested in the business."

⋅⋟ Keep the Door Open

Once R' Zundel of Salant was seen bent over at the door of his home, with hammer, screwdriver and pliers.

"Rebbe," he was asked, "what are you doing?"

"The lock broke and I am removing it," said R' Zundel. "Otherwise, the door locks by itself and prevents the poor from coming in."

◆§ This Game Is for the Poor

All his life R' Nachum of Horodno collected money for the poor and helped whoever needed help. He would go from house to house and from store to store to collect money for those in need.

It was also his custom to visit the different inns and taverns late at night. It was there that people would gather to gamble at cards. R' Nachum knew that gamblers spent their money freely, and they were generous when asked to help the poor.

He would enter a tavern and see a group playing cards. He would walk over to the group and say, "Play, my children, but the money of this round will be for the poor."

The players knew R' Nachum, and were good-natured about it. They would immediately give him all the money of that game, and would add more of their own.

Once, R' Nachum came into a tavern and saw a card game going on. As usual, he went over and asked for the money of the round for charity. These people, though, did not know R' Nachum, and began to ridicule him. R' Nachum, though, did not let them be and remained insistent. Finally, one of the players got up and slapped R' Nachum.

R' Nachum rubbed his cheek and said gently, "That was what you gave *me*, and what will you now give to the poor?"

They were amazed, begged his forgiveness, and gave him a handsome sum.

◆§ Repaying Good for Bad

R' Nachum of Horodno once approached a prominent Jewish lawyer for a donation for the poor. The lawyer, an assimilated Jew, had little time for Jews or things Jewish. He also had a vile temper, and let R' Nachum feel the full brunt of it. "Who put you in charge of collecting charity? All you do is go from door to door and steal from everyone. I won't give you a kopek. Get out!" he yelled.

R' Nachum realized with whom he was dealing. He did not say another word, but turned around and left.

Some time later, the lawyer was accused of a crime. He knew that if he was convicted, it would mean a prison sentence. He hired the best lawyers, but they could not keep him out of jail, and he was sentenced to two years in prison. His legal expenses had cost him everything he had; he left his wife and children destitute when he entered prison.

When R' Nachum heard about the case, he went to see the lawyer's wife. He found her deeply depressed. She began pouring out her soul to R' Nachum. "I am in terrible straits. My husband has been locked away for two years and I am like a widow and my children like orphans. Our legal costs took away all our money, and now I am penniless," she said.

R' Nachum assured her that things would be better and gave her encouragement. As he was speaking, he asked her how much she needed for her living expenses.

"We were living on twenty-five rubles a week," she said. In those days, that was considered a princely sum.

R' Nachum handed her twenty-five rubles and told her not to move out of her beautiful home, not to sell any of her possessions, and to have her children enjoy the same standard of living they had had until then.

Each week, from then on, R' Nachum would bring her twenty-five rubles. This continued for the full two years.

The lawyer finally returned home, and saw that everything was as it had been. The same beautiful home, the same beautiful possessions. His children, too, were in the best of health, with shining faces. He was amazed and asked his wife, "How did you support yourself during the past two years?"

"The old man who goes from door to door collecting charity would leave twenty-five rubles for me each week," she said. "Had it not been for his help, who knows what would have become of me and our children."

When the lawyer heard this, he ran to R' Nachum. With tears in his eyes, he asked his forgiveness for the insults he had heaped on him, thanked him over and over for what he had done, and promised to use his first earnings to repay the amount that R' Nachum had advanced. He also promised a sizable donation for the poor.

From that time on, the lawyer was a different man. He drew closer to his fellow-Jews and his home was always open to anyone in distress.

⋑ Wait Until You Get to Warsaw

Whenever he was invited to be a *sandak* at a *bris*, R' Nachum of Horodno would investigate the financial position of the family which had honored him. If he found that the family was poor, he would pay all of the family's expenses for the first week after the birth.

Once, a storekeeper who had a reputation of being wealthy asked R' Nachman to be *sandak*. R' Nachum checked and found that the storekeeper was in reality in deep financial trouble.

R' Nachum realized that the storekeeper would never take a gift from him. He, therefore, approached the man and asked, "When will you be traveling to Warsaw?"

"What do you need in Warsaw, Rebbe?" the man asked in return.

"One of my friends," said R' Nachum, "is in a hospital in Warsaw. I want to send him thirty rubles and cannot send it by mail, because I don't know the exact address. I would appreciate if you could take the money, and the next time you're in Warsaw for business, please look him up and give him the money."

"Rebbe," the man stammered, "I don't know. . . I'm not sure when I'll be in Warsaw next."

"That's no problem," replied R' Nachum. "There's no rush. Please take the money now, and the next time you're in Warsaw you'll give a similar sum to my friend."

The storekeeper took the money from R' Nachum, and that took care of the expenses of the first week and the *bris*.

When R' Nachum came to the *bris*, the storekeeper said, "Rebbe, you left out the most important detail. What is the name of your friend in Warsaw?"

"I forgot it myself," replied R' Nachum, "but I have it written down at home."

Time passed. Each time the storekeeper met R' Nachum, he asked him for the name, and each time R' Nachum told him that he hadn't had time to look it up. Eventually, the storekeeper's finances recovered, and he paid R' Nachum back.

∽§ This Is My Occupation

In his old age, R' Nachum of Horodno was sickly and in great pain. That did not stop him from going about, day and night, to collect *tzedakah* for the poor who depended on him.

One night, as he was on his way to collect some money, his sickness got the better of him and he fell down in great pain. It was after midnight and pitch dark. R' Nachum lay groaning, but not another soul was around. A Jewish wagon driver passing by heard the groans and found R' Nachum lying on the ground, half dead. He picked him up, placed him in the wagon, and started driving him home. R' Nachum turned to the wagon driver and asked him to stop. He wanted to get off.

"Why, Rebbe?" asked the wagon driver. "I am quite willing to drive you home."

"I'm sorry," said R' Nachum, "I have things to attend to. I have to collect money for the poor."

"Rebbe,' said the wagon driver, "you're sick, and it's late at night."

"Tell me," said R' Nachum, "would you have been about at this time of night if you didn't have work to do?"

"What can I do, Rebbe? This is my occupation, and I have a wife and five children to support."

"Well, that's exactly the point," said R' Nachum. "If you, who only have six to support, are working at this hour, then I, who have hundreds of people depending on me, must certainly work now."

∾§ Don't Make the People Liars

The *Netziv* once came to a town to collect money for his yeshivah. In that town lived an extremely wealthy man who was known to be very miserly. When the *Netziv* asked him for a donation, he gave a small sum.

"It's wrong," said the *Netziv*, "to cause people to lie."

"What do you mean?" asked the man.

"Every person has a certain reputation," said the *Netziv*. "I am thought to be a *rav* and *rosh yeshivah*. I do everything in my power so that this will be at least partially true. I give Torah discourses, send replies to halachic questions and maintain a yeshivah. You have a reputation of being a wealthy man. That means you should act like a wealthy man. You should be the first to offer financial support for every worthy cause, and donate generously when called upon to do so. If you don't do so, you cause people to be liars."

∾§ For All or for None

The community of Brisk supplied R' Chaim, their *Rav*, with basic necessities, including wood to heat his home in the winter.

The community leaders discovered that the cost of the rabbi's firewood was five hundred rubles per year. Even the richest person never used more than fifty rubles of firewood in any year. They checked and found that the firewood was kept in an unlocked shed behind R' Chaim's house, and that the poor had been coming in and taking firewood whenever they needed to. The leaders then put a lock on the shed and gave the key to the *shamash*.

R' Chaim had the lock removed, and again the poor came to take firewood.

The community leaders came to R' Chaim to complain. "Rebbe," they said, "the community cannot afford to supply firewood to all the poor in town."

"Then I want you to stop heating my house as well," said R' Chaim. "How can I sit in a warm house when all the poor are sitting in the cold?"

৵ "It's up to You"

R' Chaim of Brisk once collected money for a worthy cause. He very much wanted a wealthy man, who was known to be miserly, to contribute, and he sent for the man without telling him why. When the man heard the rabbi wanted to see him, he came immediately. When he was told why he had been called, he rebuked R' Chaim. "Common courtesy requires a man who wants a favor to go to the one from whom he wants the favor," he said.

"I was afraid," said R' Chaim, "that I might be wasting my time."

"Is that fair?" exclaimed the man angrily. "Why are you worried about wasting your time and not about wasting my time?"

"Well," said R' Chaim, "whether your time has been wasted by coming here is strictly up to you. If you donate to this cause, you obviously will not have wasted it."

৵ You Have to Experience It

R' Elye Chaim of Lodz was always involved in raising money for the needy and for worthy causes. In order to do so, he would visit various wealthy individuals.

Once, the winter was a particularly severe one and as a result, the price of firewood shot up. R' Elye Chaim began to make the rounds of the rich, to have them donate money for firewood for the poor.

His first stop was Kalman Poznanski, the richest man in the city. When R' Elye Chaim came to the door, Poznanski's servant ran to tell his master that the rabbi had arrived.

Poznanski immediately came to the door, still dressed in his shirtsleeves. He greeted the rabbi and invited him in, but R' Elye Chaim remained standing at the door and began to discuss all types of topics of concern to the city. Poznanski was too respectful to say anything and stood listening, but he began to feel the full force of the cold. R' Elye Chaim, for his part, discussed one topic after another, speaking at leisure like a man sitting on a couch in someone's living room. Finally the cold was too much for Poznanski, and he said, "Rebbe, would you mind stepping inside? I'm freezing."

"Now," said R' Elye Chaim without moving an inch, "I will tell you why I came. This is a very bitter winter. Prices of firewood have risen drastically, and the poor are all freezing. I came to ask you to contribute money toward firewood for the poor."

Poznanski unhesitatingly gave him a large donation for firewood.

At that point, R' Elye Chaim entered the house and both sat down in the living room.

"Excuse me, Rebbe," Poznanski finally blurted out "but why did you stand at the door so long without entering the house? It doesn't seem proper for a rabbi to stand on the doorstep."

"My reason for doing so was simple," said R' Elye Chaim. "There is a folk proverb that 'a person who is full cannot fathom the suffering of one who is hungry.' I came to let you know of the suffering of the poor who have no wood with which to warm their homes. Had we been sitting in your beautiful warm living room, could I have depicted to you even a thousandth part of what the poor are suffering? When we stood at the front door for quite a while, you felt the cold in your bones; you were able to appreciate, somewhat, what it is like in the homes of the poor, and you contributed handsomely."

‏‏‏ *A Lesson from a Beggar*

R' Meir Shapiro of Lublin would say, "I learned how to collect *tzedakah* from a beggar.

"A beggar came to my door and asked for *tzedakah*, and I gave him half a *zloty*. He asked me if I could give more.

"One of those present told the beggar, 'I am surprised at you. When you are given a *groszy* ($^1/_{100}$ of a *zloty*), you accept it without an argument. Here, where you were given half a *zloty*, you argue for more.'

"The beggar replied, 'If I am given a *groszy* it doesn't pay to argue, because even if they give me more, how much more will they give me? Another *groszy*. However, when I am given half a *zloty*, it is worth arguing, because they may add another half *zloty*.'

"Whenever I ask a donation from a wealthy man and he gives me a sizable sum, I tell him that story."

~§ The Rich American Uncle

R' Meir Shapiro of Lublin came to the United States in order to raise money for the yeshivah which he had founded, *Yeshivas Chachmei Lublin*. When he went to the home of a rich man to ask him for a donation for his yeshivah, the man said, "Rebbe, your yeshivah is so large and the upkeep is tremendous. I don't understand why you built it in Poland, which is such a poor country."

R' Meir replied, "Poland is the best place for such a yeshivah because it has so many outstanding students. As for the upkeep, let me tell you a story":

A chasid came to his rebbe to ask him whether he should invest in the stock market. On the one hand, one can get a tremendous return on one's money by investing it in the stock market, but on the other, one may lose everything. His rebbe said, "If your family is wealthy and you can count on them supporting you financially if you're in trouble, you may invest in the stock market. Otherwise, don't take the risk."

"We, in Poland," said R' Meir, "have relatives in America, and we can always count on them."

◆§ Worse than Haman

R' Meir Shapiro of Lublin asked a wealthy man for a contribution for the yeshivah. The man turned him down and said, "Neither I, my children nor grandchildren need yeshivos."

"I am surprised," said R' Meir, "that a Jew can wish to be worse than Haman."

"What do you mean?" asked the man.

"Our Sages tell us that Haman's grandchildren studied Torah in Bnei Brak," said R' Meir. "Yet you are positive that your descendants, for all eternity, will never study in a yeshivah."

The man changed his mind and gave R' Meir a large sum.

◆§ My Part in the World to Come

Once, when R' Meir Shapiro of Lublin approached a man for a donation to his yeshivah, the man told him, "Rebbe, I will give a generous donation for your yeshivah, but under one condition."

"And what is that?" asked R' Meir.

"If you give me your share in the World to Come," said the man.

"I agree," said R' Meir, "and am willing to give you my entire share in the World to Come except for one small part."

"And what part is that?" asked the man.

"The part," replied R' Meir, "which I will receive in the World to Come for having given away my part in the World to Come in order to receive a contribution for my yeshivah."

◆§ An Argument for the Sake of Heaven

R' Zalman, the son of R' Uri of Vilna, was a very learned and wealthy man. He made a point of helping others by giving them interest-free loans. Small merchants, storekeepers and tradesmen would come to him when they needed money, and he would happily lend them what they needed, and would allow them to pay back their loans bit by bit.

A man once came to him for a loan. He needed three hundred rubles for ninety days. R' Zalman had never seen the man before and asked, "Do you have anyone that can act as a guarantor?"

"No," said the man, "I am new here."

"I'm sorry," said R' Zalman, "I need a guarantor for the money."

Tears started running down the man's face as he turned to leave.

"Just one second," said R' Zalman. "Isn't there a single person in the entire city who can serve as a guarantor for you?"

"No," said the man. "My only guarantor is Hashem Himself."

"Well, if that's the case," said R' Zalman, "we couldn't ask for a better guarantor than that."

He took a piece of paper and wrote on it: "He that has pity upon the poor lends to Hashem" (*Mishlei* 19:17). He placed this paper among his loan documents, and gave the man three hundred rubles.

Ninety days later the man returned and told R' Zalman:

"Hashem helped me in my business venture, and I have come to pay my debt."

"I'm sorry," said R' Zalman, "I can't take the money. The debt has already been paid."

"By whom?" asked the man in astonishment.

"By your guarantor," replied R' Zalman. "He paid me what I had given you. That very day when you were here, after you left, a business deal presented itself to me and I made a profit of exactly three hundred rubles."

The man, though, was adamant in insisting on repaying the loan. In the end they agreed that the money would remain with R' Zalman to be used for loans to others, and that the future *mitzvah* would be considered as belonging to both of them.

~§ A Court Case

R' Motel of Shavel was out walking in the market area when he saw a man crying. He went over and asked, "Why are you crying?"

The man began pouring out his tale of woe. "I am a storekeeper in a village nearby. I left my home with a hundred rubles in order to buy goods for my store. After arriving here, though I looked in all my pockets, I could not find the money. Now I am lost, because I cannot buy goods, and I have no way to earn a living."

"Don't worry," said R' Motel, "I found your money. Come to my home and I will return it."

R' Motel took the man to his home, and gave him a hundred rubles.

The man's eyes lit up, and he thanked R' Motel profusely. He took the money and bought all the goods that he needed for his store.

As soon as he arrived home, his wife said jokingly, "Why are you always so absentminded? You may have gone to buy goods, but you forgot the money at home."

He realized what had happened; R' Motel had given him a hundred rubles.

The next morning the man returned to Shavel, immediately went to R' Motel, and told him, "Rebbe, you fooled me. I never lost anything and you never found anything. I had forgotten my money at home."

He then placed the hundred rubles before R' Motel.

"I cannot accept the money," said R' Motel. "I gave it to you as a gift."

"But I don't want gifts," said the storekeeper.

Each was adamant. They finally decided to go to the *beis din* to determine who should have the money.

The *beis din* found this an interesting case. Each claimed that he did not want the money, and that the other should receive it.

In the end, after hearing both sides, the *beis din* ruled that R' Motel was to keep the money in his possession to be used for charitable purposes, and that whatever *mitzvah* would come of the use of the money would be considered as done by both of them.

⋑ Found Money

R' Yosef Rivlin was walking through the streets of Yerushalayim just before *Shabbos*, when he saw a woman crying bitterly.

"I am in such trouble, what will I do this month?" she kept repeating.

R' Yosef asked her what had happened. "I had just received my monthly allocation, a gold napoleon coin, when it slipped out of my hands and I lost it. I have searched and cannot find it," she said.

R' Yosef took a gold napoleon from his pocket and told her, "I found what you lost. Here, take it."

The woman was overcome with joy and thanked R' Yosef over and over again. She then ran off to prepare for *Shabbos*.

"Rebbe, why did you tell her that you had found her coin, rather than tell her the truth — that you were giving her your own coin as a gift?" they asked R' Yosef.

"Had I told her that I was giving her my coin as a gift, she would still seek to find her lost coin," said R' Yosef. "Now that I told her that this coin was the one she lost, she felt relieved."

⋑ Observing the Mitzvah to Remain Silent

A wealthy man lived in Berdichev, when R' Levi Yitzchak was the *rav* there. The man was as miserly as he was wealthy and never gave money to any cause or any poor people. But, he was scrupulous in the observance of the *mitzvos* between man and Hashem.

R' Levi Yitzchak once asked him to contribute to some charitable cause. Not only did the man turn him down, but he told him, "Rebbe, please do me a favor. Don't bother coming to me for charity. I know I won't give you anything, and you will be causing me to violate the *halachah* which forbids one to disregard the rabbis."

Some time later, the brother of the wealthy miser appealed to R' Levi Yitzchak for help. This man was extremely poor and had many children. "Rebbe," he said, "I have a daughter who is about to get married and I have no money to pay for all the expenses. Could you please speak to my brother? He ignores all my requests."

That day, R' Levi Yitzchak came to the rich man's home and sat done for a full hour without uttering a word. The next day he did the same. The wealthy man, out of respect for R' Levi Yitzchak, did not ask what or why.

Finally, on the third day, the wealthy man could not overcome his curiosity and asked, "Rebbe, why do you just sit here without saying a word?"

"We are told by our Sages," explained R' Levi Yitzchak, "that just as it is a *mitzvah* to tell a man something one knows he will obey, it is a *mitzvah* not to tell him something he will not obey.' Now, I have always been able to fulfill the first part of this saying, thank G-d, because when I speak to the people they are all eager to obey what I tell them. As to the second part of the saying, not to tell someone something he will not obey, I have not been able to fulfill it until now, because there was never anyone who would not obey me. All my life I sought an opportunity to observe this saying, and here, in your home, I finally found the opportunity I was looking for."

The wealthy man turned all shades of red, and he begged R' Levi Yitzchak to tell him why he had come. R' Levi Yitzchak told him about his brother's problems, and he consented to help.

◄§ *A Good Reason to Boast*

A rabbi who was collecting money for *hachnasas kallah* (funds to help couples about to be married set up their homes) came to R' Akiva Lehrn of Amsterdam and asked him for a donation. R' Akiva discovered that he was a great Torah scholar, and they spent much time talking in learning. Finally, R' Akiva gave the man a very generous gift, and said, "I want you to promise me that when you reach Frankfurt you will see Baron Rothschild and tell him how much R' Akiva of Amsterdam gave you."

The rabbi was astonished at this request, for he couldn't understand how a man as righteous as R' Akiva could be conceited. R' Akiva, though, insisted on this condition, and would not let him go until he had promised to fulfill it.

The rabbi arrived in Frankfurt and met Baron Rothschild.

"Excuse me, sir," he said, "but R' Akiva Lehrn insisted that I promise to tell you what I would have preferred not mentioning." He then told the baron of the amount that R' Akiva Lehrn had given him.

"Do not worry," said the baron. "R' Akiva and I have an agreement. He knows that I am very busy and am unable to take the time to find out whether those who come to me represent worthy causes or not. R' Akiva has taken it upon himself that whenever he finds someone worthy he will let me know how much he gave, and I will give the man ten times that amount."

৵ Everything Counts

While on a visit to a certain town, R' Yisrael of Ruzhin lodged in the home of a wealthy local resident. The whole town was agog, and everyone ran to receive a *brachah* (blessing) from the rebbe. It was at the height of the winter. The streets were wet with slush and those who came to see R' Yisrael tracked in a good deal of mud and dirtied the clean floors. R' Yisrael's host became very upset, and scolded those who came in with mud on their boots. When the rebbe heard about this, he asked the man to come in, had him sit down, and told him a story:

There was an innkeeper who lived in a small village, and who barely earned a living from the few travelers who came through the village. On what he earned, he had to support his wife and six children, as well as his father and mother.

One year, there was a very severe winter, with snow piled high on all the roads. People stopped traveling altogether, and the innkeeper's income ceased. He and his family faced constant hunger.

Pesach was around the corner and he had no money to buy the essentials. He therefore decided to make his way to the big city. There, he might earn some money and have enough for the festival needs.

While driving to the city, he saw a peasant leading a cow.

"Would you sell me your cow?" he asked the peasant.

The peasant was happy to do so. The innkeeper brought the cow to the local fair, where he sold it at enough of a profit to buy wheat for *matzos*. He went to the local baker to have his *matzos* baked, but was told he would have to wait until all the rich people had finished with their baking. By the time he had his *matzos* baked, it was very dark.

The road home was filled with potholes and thick with mud. His wagon fell into a deep, muddy ditch and he could do nothing to get it out. He stood there weeping bitterly.

Just then, a wealthy man passed in his carriage, heard the sobbing and sent his servant to find out what had happened. The servant returned and told his master about the unfortunate innkeeper.

The wealthy man ordered his servant to unhitch the horses and they soon pulled the wagon out of the ditch and onto the road.

His rescuer, seeing that the innkeeper was exhausted and famished, gave him food and accompanied him home.

When they entered the innkeeper's home and he saw the poverty in which he lived, the wealthy man was very moved and gave him five hundred rubles. "I want you to buy everything you need to celebrate *Pesach* properly," he said. "After *Pesach*, build yourself a winery and sell wine.'

It was that help which changed the poor innkeeper into a prosperous man.

Some time later, the wealthy man died and came to be judged for his life on earth. All his merits were placed on one scale, and all his sins on the other. The sins very clearly outweighed the merits, and the man stood in shame and trembled at what lay in store for him. As he stood there, a massive amount of merit was added. That was the *mitzvah* he had performed in helping the innkeeper; that action had kept ten people alive.

But still, the sins outweighed the merits.

An angel then flew off and brought back the ten people whose lives had been saved. He placed them on the balance pan of merits, but even that was not enough. The angel brought the horse and wagon, and even that was not enough.

Finally, the angel flew and brought back the mud in which the wagon had been mired — and that tipped the scales. The merits outweighed the sins.

"Mud can be what tips the scales in the future and saves a man from being sent to *Gehinnom*," concluded R' Yisrael.

◄§ One Favor Is Enough

R' Yoshe Ber of Brisk came to the home of a wealthy man to ask for a donation for *tzedakah*. The man received R' Yoshe Ber very graciously and gave him a sizable amount of money.

"But, Rebbe," said the man, "I don't understand why you had to come to my house. I would have been most honored had you invited me to your home."

$Proper$ $Conduct$

⋈ Learning From Everyone

R' Zushia of Hanipoli would visit his rebbe, the *Maggid* of Mezritch, twice a year, once in the summer and once in the winter. Each time he would remain for three months and learn from him how to conduct himself properly.

Once, in the winter, he came to the *Maggid* on a Friday morning, as the *Maggid* was going over the weekly *parashah*. R' Zushia waited for him. When the *Maggid* had completed his review, he greeted R' Zushia and said, "Zushia, my son, I am ordering you to return to your home today."

"Rebbe," R' Zushia pleaded, "I have just arrived, and want to remain for three months in order to learn how to act properly. I am willing to accept your order if you will teach me today what I would have learned by staying here for three months."

"I agree to your condition," said the *Maggid*. "I will teach you three things one should learn from an infant, and seven one should learn from a thief.

"There are three things one should learn from an infant:

1) An infant is always happy, and is never overcome by depression.

2) An infant does not remain idle for even an instant.

3) When an infant wants something from his father, even if it is the most insignificant thing, he cries.

"There are seven things one should learn from a thief:

1) A thief works mainly at night.

2) If a thief does not succeed one night, he tries again the following night.

3) A thief loves his friends as himself, and is willing to give his life for his friends.

4) A thief is willing to give his life for even the most insignificant matter, even if there is doubt involved.

5) In the morning, the thief sells whatever he has at a fraction of its worth, so as not to remain with anything in his hands.

6) A thief does not confess to his theft, even if whipped. He always states, 'I do not know.'

7) A thief loves his trade and will not exchange it for any other in the world."

⋑ Ask Zushia

The brothers R' Shmelke and R' Pinchas asked their rebbe, the *Maggid* of Mezritch, "Rebbe, teach us how a person can fulfill the words of the *Mishnah:* 'A person must thank G-d as much for the bad as for the good.'"

"Go and ask Zushia about this," said the *Maggid*. Zushia was a great man who was poor, sick, and had a shrewish wife, who caused him all sorts of agony.

They went into the *beis midrash* and found R' Zushia of Hanipoli. They told him why the *Maggid* had sent them.

"I am amazed that the rebbe sent you to me," said R' Zushia.

"This is the question that one asks a person who has had bad befall him. Never in my life has anything bad ever happened to me, but only good."

⋰§ Regards to My Father

R' Elimelech of Lizhensk met a group of people traveling to Warsaw, and said, "Please do me a favor, and send regards to my Father."

"Who is your father?" they asked him.

"My Father," replied R' Elimelech, "is your Father — Our Father in the Heavens."

⋰§ No One Seeks

R' Yechiel Michel, the grandson of R' Baruch of Medzhibozh, grew up in his grandfather's home.

When he was a little boy, he was playing hide-and-seek with a friend. He hid, and waited for his friend to find him. The time dragged on, but his friend did not find him. He finally left his hiding place, looked around, and saw that his friend had left. He came crying to his grandfather.

"Why are you crying?" R' Baruch asked him.

"I hid," the little boy sobbed, "and no one came to look for me."

R' Baruch sighed and said, "Hashem says the same thing: 'I hide and no one comes to seek Me.'"

⋰§ The Care One Must Take

R' Chaim of Volozhin wrote a letter to his daughter in Lida. After writing and signing the letter, he gave it to a messenger.

Immediately after the messenger had left the house, R' Chaim caught himself, ran out, and called him back. He then rewrote the entire letter.

R' Chaim's son, R' Yitzele, saw that the two letters seemed to be identical, and he asked R' Chaim, "Father, why did you rewrite the letter? After all, the two letters seem to have been identical."

"In the first letter," said R' Chaim, "I was not careful in the spelling of your sister's name. I was afraid that people might think that this is the proper way to spell the name, and might use that spelling in a divorce. That would invalidate the document. I therefore rewrote the entire letter with the proper spelling."

◆§ Whom to Pity

R' Akiva Eiger was told about the terrible plight of a poor but fine man who had eaten nothing but bread and a little onion for supper. He had said the *Shema* before sleeping, and had then gone to bed. Everyone thought the man was unfortunate.

"Why do you call him unfortunate?" R' Akiva Eiger asked. "The man who has chicken fried in butter for supper, and who does not say the *Shema*, and then goes to bed is the unfortunate one, because he has no one in whom to trust and hope."

◆§ An Old and Foolish King

R' Yisrael of Ruzhin was imprisoned for some time as the result of false accusations made against him. When he left the prison, he said, "All my life, I never understood why the *yetzer hara* — the Evil Desire — is referred to by our Sages as an old and foolish king (*Koheles* 4:13). I understood that he is a king — because he rules man. He is old — because he has been with man from the earliest stages of Creation. But why foolish? After all, doesn't he always come up with new ways to persuade the person to sin? When I was in prison, though, I finally understood this. Even there, the *yetzer hara* never left me for an instant. 'You are nothing but a fool, and deserve to be called such,' I said to him. 'I, unfortunately, am forced to remain in prison and cannot see the light of day. But you, why should you remain here?'"

৵§ The Fast

R' Alexander Ziskind, the author of *Yesod VeShoresh HaAvodah*, would make a point of breaking every fast with a little fish containing many bones, so that he would be forced to eat slowly and not give in to his desire to eat.

৵§ An Extra Mitzvah

A man who was collecting donations for a yeshivah stayed with R' Yoshe Ber. Just before *Shabbos* began, R' Yoshe Ber said to his guest, "Would you mind lending me five kopeks?"

The guest was surprised at the request for a loan of so small a sum, but he immediately took out a five-kopek piece and gave it to R' Yoshe Ber. Immediately after *Shabbos*, R' Yoshe Ber returned the same exact five-kopek piece. Again the guest was astonished, but out of respect for his distinguished host, he did not say a word.

R' Yoshe Ber had reasoned that a man who traveled from place to place would never be asked to lend money, and could not, therefore, fulfill the *mitzvah* of *gemilus chasadim* by helping his fellow man. By borrowing this money and returning it, R' Yoshe Ber had enabled him to fulfill the *mitzvah*.

৵§ How Are You Doing?

While R' Yoshe Ber was the *Rav* of Slutsk, he visited Minsk. All the great Torah sages of the city came to meet the distinguished *rav* and hear him speak in learning.

One of them was a former student of his, now a wealthy merchant in Minsk. When R' Yoshe Ber saw the man, he greeted him very warmly and asked him, "How are you doing?"

"Thanks to Hashem," the former student replied, "I am well, and I have a decent income."

They talked about this and that, and a few moments later R' Yoshe Ber again asked, "How are you doing?"

"Thanks to Hashem," the man answered, "my family is well and I am doing well."

Again they talked about this and that, until a short while later R' Yoshe Ber again asked, "How are you doing?"

"Excuse me, Rebbe," the merchant said, "but that is the third time you're asking me the same question. Thank to Hashem, we are well."

"You have not been answering my question," R' Yoshe Ber told him. "I asked you, 'How are you doing?' and you answered that you are well and are doing well. That is not your doing, but Hashem's doing. I want to know what *you* are doing: Do you have fixed times for Torah study? Do you help others through charity? How are you doing as a Jew?"

◆§ Ulterior Motives

When R' Zundel of Salant learned in the Volozhin yeshivah, the other students would see him take a walk every morning in the non-Jewish section, smoking a pipe. This was hardly fitting conduct for a yeshivah student. They therefore informed the *rosh yeshivah* of R' Zundel's strange conduct. The *rosh yeshivah* called R' Zundel and asked, "Zundel, I have heard that you take a walk every morning in the non-Jewish section. Is this true?"

"It is true," admitted R' Zundel. "You see, Rebbe, I heard that there are Jews in this city who buy bread from non-Jewish bakers. As I walk about, I stop by at the different bakers and ask for permission to light my pipe. In the process, I throw a small wood chip into the fire, and with that, the bread that is baked gains the status of bread baked by a Jew."

◆§ Trustworthiness

R' Yisrael Salanter stayed at a village inn. The innkeeper looked at him and saw a distinguished-looking man, and asked, "Are you by any means a *shochet*?"

"Why?" asked R' Yisrael.

"I have an animal to be slaughtered, and it's a real nuisance to bring it to the city to be slaughtered," the man replied.

"No," said R' Yisrael, "I am not a *shochet*."

A few minutes later R' Yisrael said to the innkeeper,

"Would you mind lending me a ruble?"

"I can't lend you any money," said the innkeeper. "I don't know you at all."

"Listen to what you've just said," R' Yisrael told the man. "You are not willing to trust me with even a ruble, yet you would have trusted me without any qualms to slaughter an animal, an act which involves many Torah laws and prohibitions."

⋖ As Long as the Candle Burns

R' Yisrael Salanter brought in his shoes for repair. It was getting late, and the shoemaker was working by the light of the stump of a candle, which was beginning to burn out.

"It's a pity," said R' Yisrael. "You won't have time to complete the repair."

"Don't worry, Rebbe," the shoemaker told him. "As long as the candle burns, there is still time for repairs."

"What a marvelous sentiment," said R' Yisrael, and, rocking back and forth, he sang, in the melody used in studying *mussar* (ethical works): "As long as the candle of the soul burns, there is still time to mend our ways."

⋖ Careful Speech

R' Leibele of Kelm was very careful never to say anything which was forbidden or improper.

A young man came to discuss something. After they had spoken for some time, the young man rose and said, "I'll leave now. I'm sure you must be busy."

"How do you know that?" asked R' Leibele.

"I assumed so," the young man replied.

"But you said you were *sure*," R' Leibele rebuked him. "A person must be very careful as to what he says."

◄§ The Punishment for Lying

R' Moshe Yitzchak of Kelm would say: "The liar's punishment is worse than that of the thief or the armed robber. A thief steals at night but not during the day. An armed robber steals both by day and night, but from individuals, not from an entire community. A liar, though, lies both at night and during the day, both to an individual and to an entire community."

◄§ Each Day Anew

Before going to sleep each night, R' Levi Yitzchak of Berdichev would review everything he had done during the day. If he found that he had done something wrong, he would say, "Levi Yitzchak won't do that any more."

Then he would catch himself and say, "Levi Yitzchak, you said the same thing yesterday."

And he would answer, "Yesterday I wasn't telling the truth, but today I am."

◄§ Fulfilling His Obligations

R' Levi Yitzchak of Berdichev was the great defender of Israel, seeking out their merits and demanding compensation from Hashem.

R' Baruch of Medzibozh said about him: "According to R' Levi Yitzchak, Hashem has not yet fulfilled His obligations to a single Jew."

◄§ The Great Fair

When he was young, R' Moshe Leib of Sasov and his family lived in dire poverty. R' Moshe Leib's neighbor, a merchant who traveled to different fairs, took pity on him, and said to him, "If you come with me to the fair and guard my goods, I will pay you a week's wages."

R' Moshe Leib accepted the offer.

As soon as they came to the fair, R' Moshe Leib went to the synagogue, prayed *shacharis* at length, learned Torah, and by the time he returned, it was already the end of the day. Of course, he was paid nothing.

When he entered his home, his children fell upon him and said, "Father, what did you bring us from the fair?" R' Moshe Leib burst into tears.

"Why are you crying"? they asked.

"Woe, woe," he sighed. "After I came back from the fair, which lasted only a single day, I was asked, 'What did you bring with you?' When I return from the Great Fair of Life, how much more so will they ask me, 'What did you bring with you?'"

⋅⋖ *The Common Man*

R' Yaakov Yitzchak, the *Chozeh* of Lublin, said to a simple man who was very pious, "I envy your piety, which is greater than mine. I am a leader, whether I want to be or not. Everyone looks toward me. If I, Heaven forbid, do anything wrong, they will immediately say, 'The *Chozeh* did as follows.' You, on the other hand, work in the shadows. You can act whichever way you want, and yet you are pious. It is thus clear that you are a truly pious person."

⋅⋖ *I Don't Believe It*

He would also say: "If a king tells me that I am truly pious, I won't believe him. Even if Hashem Himself would tell it to me, I wouldn't believe Him, for even if a person is perfectly righteous, he has no idea how he will be a minute later."

᜕§ Two Pockets

R' Simchah Bunim of Pshischa would say: "A person should always have two pockets in his clothing. In one pocket he should have a slip of paper upon which is written: 'For me was the world created' (*Sanhedrin* 38a). In the other one it should be written: 'I am but dust and ashes' (*Bereishis* 18:27)."

᜕§ Where Hashem Really Is

R' Asher of Stolin would say: "Men think that Hashem's place is in Heaven, in the highest of the heights, but they are wrong. Hashem is on the earth below, at the lowest point of the earth. Every single man can reach Him. The least worthy person can reach Him. Every second wasted in not doing so is a pity."

᜕§ You Believe What You Want

R' Chaim of Sanz said: "I don't understand it. If a person says he is feeling sick, he is not believed; if a person says he is poor, he is not believed; but if a person says he is a sinner, everyone believes him."

᜕§ The Torah Is Not Heavy

When a new Torah scroll was dedicated, R' Moshe David of Chortkow took the Torah scroll and danced with it for a long time. It was an extraordinarily heavy scroll.

"Rebbe," someone asked, "isn't it too heavy for you?"

"No," R' Moshe David answered with a smile, "if one *keeps* the Torah, it is never too heavy for him."

᜕§ How to Gain Fear of Heaven

A chasid came to R' Avremele of Stretin, and begged, "Rebbe, please help me acquire *yiras shamayim* (fear of Heaven)."

"I have no advice on how to acquire that," answered R' Avremele, "but I can tell you how to acquire love of Heaven."

"That's even better, Rebbe," the man said, "because love of Heaven is even greater than fear of Heaven."

"The way to acquire love of Heaven," R' Avremele counseled him, "is by loving your fellow Jew."

ᴈ Starting at Home

When R' Mordechai Eliashberg was the *Rav* of Boisk, a plague struck the town. The Jews proclaimed fast days and spent much time praying and reciting *Tehillim*. There were some among them who thought that they should see whether the plague had been brought about by improper actions of members of the town, but R' Mordechai refused to allow them to hold such an investigation.

"If you wish to investigate," he told them, "investigate your own actions, but not those of others."

ᴈ I Just Can't

When R' Yechiel Michel, the author of the *Aruch Ha-Shulchan*, was the *Rav* of Novarodok, he had a neighbor who was a *maskil* — a freethinker. Yet this man would constantly come to R' Yechiel Michel and spend time with him.

R' Yechiel Michel was asked, "Rebbe, how can you allow a man such as this, who transgresses all the Torah, to visit you?"

"Perhaps," said R' Yechiel Michel, "I should hate him, but I simply am unable to."

ᴈ The Middle Road

R' Meir Hildesheimer, the head of the Agudah, was once verbally attacked by a man, who told him, "I have complaints against the Agudah. You are too extreme. Whenever you adopt a course, it is to the right, and you are never willing to move even a fraction to the center. In our times, a person has to be willing to compromise a little, to walk in the center."

"Let's go outside," said R' Meir, "and look at what happens on the street. On the right side, people are walking. On the left side, there are people walking as well. But the middle of the road is reserved for horses. Sometimes, the people in the center are there because they don't have any strong principles."

⋖ A Plot of the Yetzer Hara

When R' Shmelke was invited to Nikolsburg to become *rav*, he saw clean-shaven young men, wearing glasses and carrying walking canes, as was the fashion.

"See the plot of the *yetzer hara*," exclaimed R' Shmelke. "In earlier days, when a Jew turned fifty and needed glasses, he remembered that we are mortal, and repented his sins. When he became old and his beard turned white, he would think of his deeds, and would repent his sins. When he became older, he would need a cane, and that would make him prepare himself for the Day of Judgment. What did the *yetzer hara* do? He introduced a custom that *young* men should shave, that they should wear glasses, and that they should carry walking canes."

⋖ The Distance Between Truth and Falsehood

R' Chaim of Sanz would say: "If a person tells you, 'I saw,' believe him, whereas if he tells you, 'I heard,' don't believe him. I learned this from two non-Jews.

"Once I heard two non-Jews talking to one another. 'Tell me, my friend,' the one said to the other, 'what is the distance between truth and falsehood?'

"'I don't know,' answered the other.

"'I do know,' said his friend. 'It is the distance between one's eye and one's ear.'

"It was then," R' Chaim said, "that I learned that if a person tells you, 'I saw,' believe him, but if he tells you, 'I heard,' don't believe him."

◄§ Before and After

Once, R' Yisachar Ber of Belz took his son with him to the *mikveh*. The water was very cold, and when the child put his foot in, he cried out, "Oy! Oy!" After they had immersed themselves and had come out of the *mikveh*, the boy felt much better, and exclaimed, "Ah! Ah!"

"My son," said R' Yisachar Ber, "see the difference between a *mitzvah* and a sin. With a *mitzvah*, one starts with 'Oy! Oy!,' but in the end it is 'Ah! Ah!' With a sin, on the other hand, it is first 'Ah! Ah!,' but then it is 'Oy! Oy!'"'

◄§ How to Study Musar

R' Simchah Zisel of Kelm visited a yeshivah at the time of the day set aside to study *musar*. He saw that a number of the young men were leisurely reading through *Mesilas Yesharim*, one of the major *musar* works. He went over to them and asked, "Is this the way to deal with your mortal enemy — the *yetzer hara*?"

Humility

✎§ *Who Is Chasing Whom?*

R' Chaim of Brisk was asked: "We are taught by our Sages that honor runs away from one who pursues it, while honor pursues one who runs away from it. In both instances there is a distance between the man and honor. How are the two cases different?"

"When a person runs away from honor and honor pursues him, it is the man who is in front and honor is in the rear," said R' Chaim. "On the other hand, when one pursues honor and honor runs away from him, honor is in front, while the man is in the rear."

✎§ *Pretenders*

A chasid once came to R' David'l of Talna and told him, "Rebbe, our Sages tell us that honor runs away from one who pursues it, while honor pursues one who runs away from it. I know from my own experience that as much as I run away from honor, it never pursues me."

"The reason," said R' David'l, "is that honor runs away from one who *pretends* to run away from it."

◄§ The Difference Comes Later

The *Chafetz Chaim* would say: "Our Sages tell us that honor runs away from one who pursues it, while honor pursues one who runs away from it. But then there is no difference between the two men. Neither receives honor, one because it runs away from him and the other because he runs away from it.

"That, though, is only true during the man's life. After his death he no longer runs away or pursues honor. Then, the man who always ran away from honor is finally overtaken by the honor which had pursued him, and people honor him after his death. On the other hand, honor constantly ran away from the one who pursued honor in his life. Now, after his death, too, it is distant from him."

◄§ Looking Back

"Rebbe, our Sages tell us that honor pursues one who runs away from it. All my life I have been running away from honor, yet honor has never pursued me."

"Your trouble," said the sage, "is that you constantly looked behind to see if honor was indeed pursuing you."

◄§ What Reason Does It Have to Be High?

Once, R' Avraham, known as the *Malach* (the Angel), spent a considerable amount of time looking out his window at a high mountain outside.

"Rebbe," one of his friends asked him, "why are you looking so intently at that mountain?"

"I am amazed," said R' Avraham, "that a section of mere earth can raise itself so high."

⌘ Cauterization

Once, R' Mordechai Dov of Hornostipol had a terrible sore on his back. A doctor was brought in, and decided that the sore had to be cauterized. Anesthesia was not available.

The doctor heated an iron until it was red-hot and plunged it into the sore. R' Mordechai Dov did not utter a sound. Again, the doctor heated the iron and plunged it into the sore. Again, not a sound from R' Mordechai Dov.

At this, the doctor jumped up and said: "He isn't a man! He must be a devil!"

"Tell the doctor," R' Mordechai Dov said, "that I am only human. However, people tell me all their troubles, and their pain and hurt burns me much more than any hot iron can. It is they who have taught me how to endure pain."

⌘ He'll See Me as I Truly Am

When R' Yisrael Salanter lived in Frankfurt, he would often enlist Baron Rothschild's aid for worthy causes. R' Yisrael never went to see the baron, but would always write him letters.

Once, however, when he was asked to have the baron participate and donate to a cause, R' Yisrael refused to use his influence.

"I'm sorry, but I can't help you," he told those who had turned to him. "To enlist the baron's help on this, I would have to see him personally."

"And why could you not do that?" he was asked.

"The baron considers me to be a Torah scholar and a man of good deeds. If, however, he meets me in person, he will no longer think so and he will not be willing to help me further."

▸§ This Suits Me Best

R' Hirsh Michel of Yerushalayim was extremely poor. His jacket was old and threadbare, with patches on its patches. His friends wished to buy him a new suit, but he refused to accept charity.

"I am grateful to my jacket," he said, "because it instills humility far more so than all the *musar* works that have been written about the subject."

▸§ This too Is Lashon Hara

The *Chafetz Chaim* was taking a walk outside Radin, when a horse and wagon drove up and the driver asked him, "Excuse me, do you know where the *Chafetz Chaim* lives?"

"Why are you looking for him?" asked the *Chafetz Chaim*.

"I would like a blessing from him," replied the man.

"You are wasting your time," said the *Chafetz Chaim*. "He is nothing special. He is a common man."

When the man heard how the *Chafetz Chaim* had been demeaned, he became furious and slapped the *Chafetz Chaim's* face.

When the man finally arrived in the city and came to the *Chafetz Chaim's* home, he saw whom he had slapped — and fainted.

When he came to, the *Chafetz Chaim* told him, "I want you to know that I deserved that punishment. I also learned a lesson from it; one is not even permitted to talk *lashon hara* about himself."

▸§ A Small World

R' Noach of Kobrin would say: "Why is a human being referred to as 'a small world'? Because if he regards himself as small, he is a world, whereas if he regards himself as a world, he is small."

◄§ Titles Can Teach

R' Zvi Ashkenazi, the *Chacham Zvi*, would on occasion take out the different letters which he had received from people throughout the world, and reread the various titles and praises about himself contained in these letters.

"Rebbe," he was asked, "why do you do this?"

"When I read these," replied R' Zvi, "I realize how people regard me, and I resolve to be careful not to sin out of respect for the writers."

◄§ No Action Is Necessary

R' Pinchas of Koretz said: "All sins require some type of physical action — a movement of the hand or the foot, an opening of the lips — except for pride. A person can lie in bed without moving a muscle, and say to himself, 'I am great.' "

◄§ "Why Am I Being Punished?"

When R' Dov Ber, the *Maggid* of Mezritch, began to be known throughout the Jewish world, he prayed: "Lord of the universe! Tell me for what sin I am being punished with this terrible punishment."

◄§ "What I Could Have Become"

R' Akiva Eiger received a question from a rabbi. As was customary, the rabbi began by addressing him with flowery titles. R' Akiva Eiger read the opening to the letter a number of times.

"Rebbe," one of his students asked, "why did you read the opening so many times?"

"The rabbi wrote about what I could have become, and as I read the words I realized how far from them I really am," said R' Akiva Eiger.

～⁵ The Perfect Guest

R' Yaakov of Lissa, the author of *Chavas Da'as*, had come to Nikolsburg. R' Mordechai Benet, the local *rav* who was also a very great Torah scholar, came to visit him and they spent a delightful time talking in learning. R' Mordechai honored R' Yaakov by inviting him to give a discourse in the synagogue, to which he invited all the scholars of the town.

R' Yaakov began the lecture and showed his brilliance. At one point, R' Mordechai asked a question. R' Yaakov thought for a while and then stopped his talk, implying that the question was so solid that it had undermined his entire thesis.

When R' Mordechai went back home and checked the sources, he found that he had been wrong and that R' Yaakov had been right. He immediately ran to the inn where R' Yaakov was staying and said, "I realize that you were correct after all. Why then did you break off your talk rather than answer my question?"

"I knew," said R' Yaakov, "that I was correct, but I said to myself that it was preferable for me, a visitor, to be embarrassed than, Heaven forbid, to embarrass a rabbi in his own home town."

～⁵ No Excuse

R' Rafael of Barshad would say: "When I stand before the Court on High, I will be able to answer all accusations against me except that of pride.

"They will ask me, 'Did you learn Torah?'

"I will answer immediately, 'I was an ignoramus.'

"Then they will ask me: 'Did you spend a great deal of time praying and in afflicting your body?'

"I will answer: 'I was physically weak.'

"Again they will ask me: 'Did you give *tzedakah*?'

"I will answer them: 'I was a poor man.'

"'If you were an ignoramus, and weak and poor, then why

were you so proud?' they will say.

"And here I will have no answer."

◄§ Really Knowing a Person

R' Shimon of Yaroslav would say: "The closer people are to me, the better they know me. Those who are not of our town, and do not know me, refer to me as the *Tzaddik* R' Shimon. In my own town, where people know me, I am referred to as R' Shimon. My wife, who knows me better than anyone, calls me Shimon."

◄§ The Worst Kind of Pride

R' Menachem Mendel of Lubavich would say: "The worst kind of pride is pride of being a *yarei shamayim* (G-d-fearing)."

◄§ Two Levels of Humility

R' Shalom of Belz would say: "There are two types of humble people. If a person regards himself as nothing and the entire world as nothing, that is imperfect humility. If a person regards himself as nothing and the rest of the world as important, that is true humility."

◄§ True Humility

R' Yoshe Ber of Brisk was once in St. Petersburg, where he was invited to a gathering of Torah scholars, including R' Itzele Peterburger. They began discussing various topics, and R' Yoshe Ber mentioned a question that had been posed by his son, R' Chaim. The question was a profound one, as was to be expected, and all discussed it at length, each offering his own answer. R' Itzele, though, sat without saying a word.

After they had discussed the question, R' Yoshe Ber offered R' Chaim's answer, and again there was discussion. Some supported it; others tried to argue against it. Again R' Itzele sat in silence.

R' Yoshe Ber was surprised at R' Itzele's behavior, because he had the reputation of being an outstanding scholar. When he returned to the inn where he was staying, he asked that R' Itzele's work, *Pri Yitzchak*, be brought to him. There he found the same question that R' Chaim had asked and two answers, including the one given by R' Chaim. R' Yoshe Ber was astounded and remarked, "How great is R' Itzele's humility."

⫸ With People

⫷ The Escort

R' Yisrael Salanter was sitting in his *beis midrash* in Kovno late one night, when he heard two poor men talking. In those days, the poor who had no other place to sleep would sleep in the local *beis midrash*.

"Please come with me to the well," said one to the other, "I am very thirsty and I'm afraid to go alone."

"If you're thirsty," the other replied, "go by yourself."

"Please come with me," begged the first one. "I am very thirsty. I will even give you ten kopeks to come with me."

The other refused to budge.

R' Yisrael rose, went to the well and brought water for the thirsty man.

"What you did, my son," said R' Yisrael to the other, "was not proper. One must be merciful and feel the distress of another. If your friend, who is one of the poorest of the poor, was willing to pay you ten kopeks to go with him, it is clear that he was in very great misery."

◆§ One More "Guest"

In Kovno, as in many other cities, there was a special building known as the *hekdesh*, a community-owned building where the poor could sleep. But it had fallen into a terrible state of disrepair. It was damp, and the poor had to spend the night in filth. No one, though, seemed to care, for the community had many other demands on it. R' Yisrael Salanter found out about this. One night, he went to the *hekdesh*, lay down on the ground, and slept there that entire night.

In the morning, they saw that R' Yisrael had spent the night there, and a commotion arose in the city. The community leaders immediately began to repair the building.

◆§ Where Does This Water Come From?

When R' Yisrael Salanter was widowed, he lived in the home of R' Yaakov Karpas, one of the wealthiest men of Kovno and a special friend.

The family members came to realize that R' Yisrael washed his hands before the meals with the absolute minimum amount of water required by *halachah*, even though there was a large pail available. They found this surprising, because one should ideally use an abundance of water in washing. Finally, after having observed his behavior a number of times, R' Yaakov asked R' Yisrael at one of the meals, "Excuse me, Rebbe, I wish to understand the *halachah*. Why do you wash with so little water? Doesn't the *halachah* say that even though a person fulfills his obligation with a *revi'is* (about 4.5 fl. oz.), he should ideally use an abundant quantity of water?"

"I saw," said R' Yisrael, "that your maid carries the water quite a distance from the well, and your house is on the side of a hill. I noticed how she struggled to carry the water, and felt that it is improper for a person to carry out the *mitzvos* on the back of others."

◆§ This too Is Part of Halachah

R' Zundel of Salant was very insistent on having everything clean and in its proper place.

He had a young man from the yeshivah eating at his table on a regular basis, as was the custom. One day, the young man came for his daily meal, and R' Zundel's wife was not home. The table had been set and the meal was waiting for him. The young man washed, ate, recited the *birkas hamazon*, and rose to leave.

"My son," said R' Zundel, "you have not acted properly."

"Why, Rebbe?" asked the young man. "Didn't I wash properly? Didn't I recite the blessings properly?"

"One who acts properly," replied R' Zundel, "knows that just as a person should wash and recite the blessings, he should also clear the table, and especially when the woman of the house is not present."

◆§ Caring for Animals

R' Moshe Leib of Sasov was not only concerned for the welfare of humans, but for that of animals as well. When he would travel to various fairs, he would help every wagon driver who was having problems, unloading the wagon and reloading it, in order to make it easier for the horse which pulled the wagon.

Once, he was seen at a fair where sheep were being sold, going from stall to stall with a bucket and giving water to the animals that had been forgotten by their owners.

◆§ Learning from Others

R' Moshe Leib of Sasov would say, "I learned how to love my fellow Jew from two peasants.

"Once, I saw two peasants drinking in a saloon. One asked the other, 'Do you love me?'

" 'Yes,' answered the other.

" 'How can you say you love me,' asked the first, 'when you don't know what I need?'

"It was then I learned that a Jew does not truly love another Jew unless he knows what the other needs."

❧ "I Didn't Take It"

R' Abush, the Rav of Frankfurt, was a great Torah scholar and somewhat innocent in the ways of the world. It was his custom to go to the different homes and stores and seek money for the poor.

During *Elul*, he came to a wealthy man, a merchant from another city, to ask for a donation. The merchant did not realize he was the rabbi, and assumed he was just another beggar. Since he was busy working on his accounts, he shouted at R' Abush, "Get out of here! I don't have time!"

R' Abush didn't say a word, and left.

After he had left, the merchant looked about and couldn't find his walking cane. He said to himself, "I am sure that beggar must have stolen my cane." He ran after R' Abush, caught him, and began screaming at him, "Swindler! Thief! Give me back my cane. Did you steal it just because I didn't give you any money?"

"Heaven forbid," answered R' Abush. "I never touched your cane."

The merchant became very angry and began beating R' Abush. R' Abush did not say who he was, and accepted the beating in silence.

On *Shabbos Shuvah*, the visiting merchant went to the synagogue to hear the *derashah*. When he entered, he found the synagogue already packed, and the rabbi in the midst of his discourse. The merchant gradually pushed his way forward to hear better. When he saw the rabbi, he fainted. He was immediately carried out into the corridor and revived. And then he began sobbing uncontrollably. "Woe is to me! Woe is to me! I insulted and beat the rabbi," he said.

Those about him calmed him down and told him to go to the rabbi and beg his forgiveness. They were sure that a righteous man such as the rabbi would not bear him a grudge and would forgive him.

The merchant did as they had suggested. After R' Abush had finished his discourse and everyone pushed forward to compliment him, he, too, moved forward, so as to beg the rabbi to forgive him.

When R' Abush saw him, he assumed the merchant was still angry about the cane, so he stepped forward in an attempt to appease him, and exclaimed in front of the entire congregation; "I want to apologize for causing you grief, but I assure you that I did not take your cane."

◄§ Empathy

R' Baruch of Leipnik, author of *Baruch Ta'am*, was a great Torah scholar and very righteous. He loved every Jew as himself, rejoicing at his happiness and feeling distress at his misfortune.

Once, the bathhouse keeper in Leipnik became very ill, and R' Baruch went about in anguish. When he got home from the *beis midrash*, he found his daughter and the maid laughing together. Reprimanding them, he said, "How can you laugh when the bathhouse keeper is so ill?"

◄§ Relatively Speaking

The daughter of R' Chaim of Sanz asked her father for money to buy a new pair of shoes. There was a bride in town, and all the young girls would dance before her. It was for this that she wanted the shoes. R' Chaim, though, told her that her old shoes would have to do.

Some time later the daughter of a local *melamed* came in and told him of her distress. She wanted to dance before the bride, but she only had old shoes.

R' Chaim immediately gave her money to buy new shoes. In fact, he told her to buy the nicest shoes possible.

Those who were present at these two conversations were amazed.

"Rebbe," they asked, "why don't you treat your daughter as well as you treat other young women?"

"The *melamed's* daughter comes from an honest but poor family, and if she wears old shoes no one will show her any respect," said R' Chaim, "whereas my daughter will not have any such problem if she wears old shoes."

◆§ A Reason to Cry

R' Shlomo Zalman, the author of *Chemdas Shlomo*, was the Rav of Warsaw, and there were those who opposed him.

Once, as R' Shlomo Zalman was making his way through the market, a man publicly berated and insulted him. R' Shlomo Zalman silenced all those who expressed their anger, and immediately returned home.

When his wife entered, she saw him sobbing terribly.

"Why should you cry?" she said. "After all, that man was just a worthless, uneducated individual. You don't have to take it so hard."

"I am crying and praying for him," said R' Shlomo Zalman. "I don't want him to be punished by Heaven on my account."

◆§ What Is Fair?

When the poor of Slutzk would come to R' Yoshe Ber and tell him their troubles, he would find ways to help them.

Just before *Pesach*, a wagon driver came crying, "Rebbe, I'm in tremendous trouble! Throughout the winter I earned nothing because of the snow on the ground. Now, when I am finally able to find work and buy what I need for *Yom Tov*, my horse died."

R' Yoshe Ber, without a moment's delay, told him, "Go to my yard, take my cow to the market, and trade it for a horse."

The wagon driver immediately did as he had been told, and went away with the cow.

A little later, R' Yoshe Ber's wife went to milk the cow — but it had disappeared. She ran into the house shouting, "Yoshe Ber, someone stole our cow!"

"It wasn't stolen," said R' Yoshe Ber calmly.

"Well, where is it then?"

"If that man hasn't traded it yet," he said, "it's in his possession."

"That man? Traded? What are you talking about?"

R' Yoshe Ber told her the whole story; how he had given the cow to a poor wagon driver, whose horse had died and left him without a way to earn a living.

"What did you do?" said the *rebbitzen*, very upset. "We had but a single cow. Where will we get a drop of milk?"

"Think about it," said R' Yoshe Ber. "Is it fair for us to have both bread and milk, when that poor man would not even have bread to eat?"

◆§ How to Not Bear a Grudge

R' Yisrael Salanter was traveling by train from Kovno to Vilna. As was his custom, he traveled alone, and was dressed like a prosperous merchant. Not far from him sat a young man who had evidently just gotten married. As it was a smoking car, R' Yisrael took out a cigarette and smoked.

"Disgusting!" called out the young man in the direction of R' Yisrael. "What a stink there is from the cigarette smoke!"

"I'm sorry," said R' Yisrael mildly. "I didn't know that you can't stand smoke. I'll put out my cigarette," And as he spoke he extinguished the cigarette.

The other passengers looked at one another. "What audacity! Whoever cannot stand smoke should go to a non-smoking compartment," said one man, furiously.

A few minutes later, the angry voice of the young man again pierced the silence, "I can't stand sitting next to that man. The window is open and I'm freezing!"

"I'm sorry, sir," said R' Yisrael. "I wasn't the one who opened the window, but if you're uncomfortable I'll close it." And so he did.

Those in the railroad carriage were amazed at the forbearance of the old, impressive-looking man, who indulged the young man as if he were an only son.

When the train arrived in Vilna, the platform was packed with people who had come to welcome R' Yisrael. As soon as he got off the train, he was surrounded by the throng: "*Shalom Aleichem*, Rebbe! *Shalom Aleichem*, Rebbe!" could be heard from all sides.

The young man saw the reception and asked weakly, "Who is that?"

"Don't you know? That's R' Yisrael, R' Yisrael Salanter."

The young man felt sick and slunk away, but not before he had asked, "Do you know where he's staying?"

"With his son-in-law, R' Elye Lazar," he was told.

The young man went to the inn where he was to lodge. He tried to eat, but the food caught in his throat. He went to his room to lie down, but he couldn't find rest. That entire night he lay sleepless. What had he done?

Early in the morning, he arrived at the home where R' Yisrael was staying. R' Yisrael greeted him graciously, "Have a seat. How are you? Have you rested from the trip? What do you think of Vilna?"

The young man remained standing, and suddenly burst into tears. "Rebbe, forgive me . . . I didn't know . . ."

"Sit down and relax," R' Yisrael told him. He assured the young man that he had nothing against him, that a young man is liable to let his emotions get away from him, that we are only human, that a person learns from his mistakes.

The young man's eyes lit up. He drank in eagerly everything that R' Yisrael told him, and promised that from then on he would be considerate of everyone.

He got up to leave, and R' Yisrael stopped him. "Would you mind telling me why you came to Vilna? Do you have any relatives here?" he asked.

"I have no one here," answered the young man. "I came here to receive *kabbalah* — permission to act as a *shochet*."

"If that's so," said R' Yisrael, "I can help you. My son-in-law can give you *kabbalah*. Let's ask him right now."

R' Yisrael took the young man by the hand and entered R' Elye Lazar's study.

R' Elye Lazar tested the young man, and found that he was ignorant of the laws involved.

"I presume," said R' Yisrael, "that it must be because of the tiring journey. Why don't you rest up at your inn? Come back in a few days. I'm sure you will receive *kabbalah*."

Only with difficulty did the young man find the front door.

A few days passed, and the young man did not return. R' Yisrael went to the inn, found him, and asked, "Why haven't we seen you?"

"I am grateful to you, Rebbe," the young man replied. "You have caused me to open my eyes and see things as they are. Now I know my place and I will be going home."

"Don't rush," said R' Yisrael. "Stay in Vilna for a time, go over the laws, and you will surely receive *kabbalah*."

R' Yisrael arranged for an experienced *shochet* to teach the young man the laws, and while he was learning R' Yisrael paid all his expenses.

Soon the young man became a proficient *shochet*, and received *kabbalah* from a number of eminent rabbis. Finally, R' Yisrael arranged a position for him in a suitable town.

Before the young man left Vilna, he came to R' Yisrael to thank him for everything he had done for him. In the course of their conversation, he said, "Rebbe, excuse me if I ask you one question. Why did you do so much for me?"

"When you first came to me and asked for my forgiveness, I told you that I forgave you completely, and I bore you no grudge whatsoever," replied R' Yisrael. "And, indeed, I said that in all sincerity. However, a person cannot control his feelings, and I was afraid that deep down I might still bear you somewhat of a grudge. Now there is a general rule that by taking an action, one can undo one's thoughts. I therefore sought to do you a favor, so as to remove from my heart any possible grudge. It is part of man's nature that if he helps another, he grows to love the one he has helped."

⋖§ "Idle Talk"

R' Yisrael Salanter stood in the marketplace chatting with another man. The conversation went on for some time, and R' Yisrael kept telling the man jokes and otherwise amusing him. This seemed very strange to R' Yisrael's students, who knew how he valued every moment for Torah study. Later, one of them got up enough courage to ask him why he had done what he had done.

"Well," said R' Yisrael, "this man was very depressed, and joking helped me relieve his depression somewhat."

⋖§ Not Standing on One's Rights

R' Yisrael Salanter came to the synagogue on his father's *yahrzeit*. There was another man present, who had *yahrzeit* for his daughter, and who wanted to lead the service. Halachically, R' Yisrael's right took precedence. R' Yisrael saw that the other man was very upset, and he allowed him to lead the service.

"Excuse me, Rebbe," asked one of the bystanders, "why did you decide to allow the other man to lead the service? After all, you had the greater right, and the purpose of leading the prayer and reciting the *kaddish* are for the benefit of the departed."

"My helping a fellow Jew brings greater benefit to my father than my reciting the *kaddish* a hundred times," said R' Yisrael.

⋖§ I Should Thank You

R' Mendele of Slutzk was one of the great Torah scholars of his time. He was very much against serving as a rabbi and never took a position as one. He founded a yeshivah in Slutzk, in the *beis midrash* of the wealthy Isserlin, and it was there that he would study Torah and give Torah discourses to the twelve Torah scholars who were supported by Isserlin.

He and his students would drink tea each day at Isserlin's. He himself would serve the students, filling their cups for them.

Once, a representative from the Mir yeshivah came to Slutzk. He entered Isserlin's home, and saw a group of young men sitting around a table, and an old man serving them. He sat down with the young men and asked the old man to pour him some tea as well. He drank cup after cup, each time calling R' Mendele to refill it. All the young men looked at one another, but didn't say a word.

On the following Shabbos, the representative from the Mir yeshivah again found himself in Isserlin's home. It was Isserlin's custom on each *Shabbos* to give a large *kiddush* before the meal. When everyone was seated, Isserlin and R' Mendele would enter together. This *Shabbos*, as usual, they did so, and all greeted them with, "*Gut Shabbos, Rebbe, Gut Shabbos*."

"Who is that old man?" asked the representative from Mir.

"That's R' Mendele," they told him.

The man felt terrible. He had treated such a great Torah scholar as a servant. He ran over to R' Mendele and begged him, "Rebbe, please forgive me, I didn't know . . ."

"What did you do that I should forgive you?" asked R' Mendele.

"I didn't know who you were, Rebbe, and I had you pour my tea."

"I really can't understand what sin you committed," said R' Mendele. "You asked for a cup of tea and I gave you one. I should be grateful to you for having allowed me to fulfill the *mitzvah* of helping another."

⊌§ Keeping a Secret

R' Yitzchak Elchanan, the Rav of Kovno, was constantly involved in raising funds for worthy individuals and causes. Once, he went about collecting money for a man who had lost everything he owned. As that particular individual was well known in the community, they had agreed that R' Yitzchak Elchanan would not tell anyone whom he was collecting for.

R' Yitzchak Elchanan came to the home of a very wealthy man, who, he was sure, would give a sizable donation. The man received him graciously and asked why the rabbi had come.

"I am coming to you for a worthy cause," said R' Yitzchak Elchanan.

"For the community?" asked the man.

"No," replied R' Yitzchak Elchanan, "for an individual."

"Who is it?" asked the rich man curiously.

"I can't tell you," said R' Yitzchak Elchanan. "He is a well-known man who has lost everything, and we must help him."

"Rebbe, I will give you twenty-five rubles if you tell me who it is," the man told R' Yitzchak Elchanan. In those days, that was a princely sum.

R' Yitzchak Elchanan answered immediately, "I can't tell you."

"Rebbe, I will give you fifty," said the rich man.

Again the same answer.

Finally, the man said: "Rebbe, I promise I will not reveal the name to anyone under any circumstances. I will give you a hundred rubles if you tell me the name."

But R' Yitzchak Elchanan replied, "Do not bother to ask. Even if you gave me everything you owned, I would not tell you. A man's honor is worth more than all the money in the world."

When the rich man heard this, he told R' Yitzchak Elchanan the truth. He, too, was in a terrible financial state, and was losing money each day. For some time he had been planning to come to ask the rabbi for advice, but had been afraid that people would find out. Now that he saw how careful R' Yitzchak Elchanan was, he wanted to know if the rabbi could help him as well.

BETWEEN MAN AND HIS FELLOW MAN: *With People* / 133

⋅§ A Logical Analysis

During the anti-Jewish disturbances in Russia, a young man from Brisk was arrested. The young man's mother came crying to R' Chaim and begged him to try to appeal to the authorities to release her son. R' Chaim agreed to do so.

His relatives, though, tried to dissuade him from becoming involved, because he might himself get into trouble if he went to the authorities.

"Listen," said R' Chaim. "That it is a *mitzvah* to ransom captives is a definite fact — a *vadai*. It is a fact, too — a *vadai* — that the woman is in great distress. As far as my getting into trouble, that is a matter of doubt — a *safek*. And are we not told that a *safek* has no status when it stands against a *vadai*?"

⋅§ Foiling Their Plans

When the *Chafetz Chaim* was a young man, he studied in a small village named Amstivova. There was a poor unfortunate man there who made his meager living by drawing water from the local well and carrying the heavy buckets of water to various people. For some reason, the children of the village made this poor man the butt of all their jokes.

Once, in midwinter, the children came up with a new way to torment the man. Each night, on the way home from their learning, they would go to the town well and fill his buckets with water. The first one there the next morning was always the water carrier, and when he arrived he found that the water had hardened into ice. Each day he would have to spend time hacking the ice out of the bucket before he could begin to draw water.

When this became known to the *Chafetz Chaim*, he adopted a new practice. Late each night, after he had finished learning for the day, he would stop by and empty the water bucket back into the well.

◆§ To the Defense

R' Yaakov Berlin, the father of the *Netziv*, was a prosperous merchant.

Once, when he came back from a long business trip, R' Yaakov brought an expensive glass vase, such as could not be bought locally. His wife was overjoyed at the gift, and it became one of her prized possessions.

One day, as the maid was cleaning the vase, it slipped from her fingers and was shattered. R' Yaakov's wife began berating the maid angrily for her clumsiness, but R' Yaakov stopped her. "You can't shout at the maid," he said, "she is a Jew like you, and comes from the same distinguished line."

"But look at the damage she did," said his wife. "That vase cost a fortune."

"According to the *halachah*," R' Yaakov said, "you have the right to sue her in a *beis din*, but not to be angry at her."

"Well, if that's the case," exclaimed his wife, "I'll go right now," and as she finished speaking she seized her coat and told the maid to follow her to the *beis din*.

When R' Yaakov saw her leaving, he rose and donned his coat.

"You can stay home," said his wife. "I don't need your help. I know exactly what to say."

"You misunderstand me," said R' Yaakov. "I am not going to help you, but to help the maid, who does not know how to defend herself."

◆§ Who Comes First

When R' Avraham Aharonson was the Rav of Karutcha, there was a smallpox epidemic there, and many people died. Everyone rushed to be vaccinated. The rabbi was urged to be vaccinated as soon as possible, but he refused.

"First," he said, "you have to see to it that the maid is vaccinated."

"We're in the midst of an epidemic," he was told, "and each added minute without the vaccine is dangerous."

"That's exactly why I want the maid vaccinated first," said R' Avraham. "Her life takes precedence over mine, because she is younger than I."

∽ Ready for the Plucking

R' Dov Ber, the Maggid of Mezritch, was asked, "As it states, 'Truth springs out of the earth' (*Tehillim* 85:12). Why, then, aren't people always truthful?"

"People are too lazy to bend down and pick it up," he replied.

∽ On Credit

R' Moshe Leib of Sasov heard that a poor woman who lived at the edge of the forest, in a tumbledown shack, had become ill and had no wood for a fire to keep her warm. It was at the height of an intensely cold winter.

R' Moshe Leib put on a heavy coat similar to those used by the peasants, placed a fur hat on his head, tied a rope around his waist, stuck an ax in his belt, and left for the forest. To all the world, he looked like a typical non-Jewish peasant. The cold penetrated right through one's bones. The forest was deep in snow, but R' Moshe Leib trudged on.

Near the woman's shack, he chopped down some firewood, tied it with the rope, and put the bundle over his shoulder.

He came to the shack, knocked on the window, and shouted in Russian, "Jewess, I've got wood for you!"

The woman let out a sigh and said, "But I have no money to pay you."

"I'll give it to you on credit," he replied.

"But I'm sick and cannot make a fire."

"I'll take care of that," said R' Moshe Leib.

He entered the shack, took the bundle of firewood, and made a fire. Only when the shack was warm did he leave.

⊷§ Why Only for Him?

Once, the son of R' David of Lelov became very ill. They decreed a fast day, said *Tehillim*, and brought in specialists. Eventually, he passed the crisis point, and began to recover. When R' David saw this, he burst into tears.

"Rebbe," he was asked, "why the weeping? On the contrary, you should rejoice now that your son is recovering and out of danger."

"Woe, woe," sighed R' David, "when my son is sick, everyone does everything possible to help him recover; but if the son of a common man becomes ill, everyone ignores him."

⊷§ No Double Standards

R' Yaakov of Lissa took the money he had received as his wife's dowry and gave it to a wealthy man to invest for him. With the proceeds, he supported himself and learned Torah.

Some time later, the wealthy man went bankrupt. He paid R' Yaakov everything he owed him, for he realized that this was R' Yaakov's only source of support to keep him learning, and whatever remained was divided up among his creditors.

When R' Yaakov found out about this, he returned all the money to the *beis din* with instructions that it should be divided up evenly among all the creditors. As he put it, "It is not proper that I should receive everything owed me, while the other should lose."

⊷§ You Have to Investigate First

R' Menachem Mendel of Lubavich would say, "Anger is one of the worst sins, and is as bad as idolatry, as we are told in the *Zohar* on *Bereishis*. Thus, even if a person feels he has the obligation to be angry, he must first look through the Talmud and the different authorities to be sure that he may become angry, with the same thoroughness that one clarifies the complex laws concerning a woman abandoned by her husband."

◈ Waiting a Day

If anyone upset R' Meir of Gustinin, he made a point of not becoming angry. He would wait until the next day, go over to the man, and say, "Yesterday I was upset with you."

◈ Now Isn't the Time

When R' Yaakov Berlin, the father of the *Netziv*, married off his daughter to R' Yechiel Michel of Novarodok, he invested a sizable cash sum for her with one of the Slutzk notables, a very wealthy and trustworthy man, so that the income could be used by the young couple.

A short time later, rumors began circulating that the wealthy man had gone bankrupt. The family began badgering R' Yaakov to travel to Slutzk and see what the situation really was, and, if necessary, to salvage whatever could be salvaged. At first, R' Yaakov ignored them. After all, he said, if the man was still solvent, then the money was, no doubt, intact. If, on the other hand, the man had gone bankrupt, there was nothing that could be done.

Because his entire family was in such great distress, R' Yaakov finally consented to travel to Slutzk. When he returned, they asked, "What is the news from Slutzk?"

"The news is not good," replied R' Yaakov.

"Is the man solvent? What did he say? Did he pay part?"

"I never even saw him," answered R' Yaakov.

"What happened?" they said in amazement. "You went all the way to Slutzk and never even saw him?"

"As soon as I came to Slutzk," said R' Yaakov, "I began to ask about the man. Very reliable individuals told me that it is indeed true, that he had lost everything he owned. I therefore said to myself, 'What purpose is served in going to see him in his distress and to humiliate him further?' "

৵ The Snuff Box

R' Yoshe Ber of Brisk kept a snuff box on his desk. When anyone came to speak to him, he would open the snuff box, look inside, and then begin his conversation. One of his close friends was unable to restrain himself, and looked inside the snuff box. Engraved there he saw the Hebrew letters *shin, pei, vav, shin, mem, nun*. He had no idea what this stood for, and he asked R' Yoshe Ber, who replied, "They are the first letters of the verse, '*Shomer piv uleshono shomer mi'tzaros nafsho*' — 'Whoever guards his mouth and his tongue keeps his soul from troubles' (*Mishlei* 21:23)."

৵ An Interesting Observation

R' Zundel of Salant would say, "I have often seen that when a man passes a *shul*, someone in the *shul* knocks on the window and calls out, '*Kedushah, kedushah*. Come and join us.' However, never in my life have I ever seen someone in a house knock on the window and call out, '*Se'udah, se'udah* — a meal, a meal. Come and join us.'"

৵ Surely Telling the Truth

R' Yehoshua Leib of Brisk was once falsely accused of a serious crime, and was to be tried in court. He therefore hired a lawyer to defend him, but the lawyer, while Jewish, did not observe the *mitzvos*.

Once he and the lawyer had to travel together in the same carriage. R' Yehoshua Leib did not look at the lawyer during the entire ride. The lawyer realized this, and asked, "Rebbe, why do you not look at me?"

"One is forbidden to look at someone who is wicked," said R' Yehoshua Leib.

The lawyer was astounded, and said, "Now I am sure that the accusation against you is false. A man who does not conceal the truth, even when it might affect his fate, cannot possibly have committed such a crime."

ঙ Praying Early

R' Elye of Kartagina would always pray *ma'ariv* at the earliest possible moment. "It is improper to begin supper later than necessary and to keep the maid waiting," he said.

ঙ Putting Things in Perspective

When R' Chaim was the Rav of Brisk, there was a fire which destroyed the entire town. R' Chaim worked ceaselessly to collect money for those who had lost everything, so as to enable them to rebuild their homes and their lives.

"Rebbe," he was asked, "shouldn't you worry about yourself as well? Your home burned down too."

"The others," said R' Chaim, "are in great trouble. They were left with nothing. I, thank Hashem, am not lacking anything. The house which was burned was not mine, but belonged to the community. My occupation was also not affected. What did happen? My coat was burned. Had it been my weekday coat, that would have been a loss to me. But it was only my *Shabbos* coat. I am not missing a thing."

ঙ The Common Touch

R' Chaim of Brisk was once in the *beis midrash* engaged in earnest conversation with an obviously very simple man.

"Rebbe," someone asked him afterwards, "what could you possibly find in common with that man, who clearly knows nothing?"

"You forget," said R' Chaim, "that a person such as he also has problems that bother him, and that he needs someone to talk to about them."

✑ My Own Obligation

When R' Elye Chaim of Lodz was taking a walk, he saw a little child crying.

"My child," he asked, "why are you crying?"

"I've lost my mommy," blubbered the child.

R' Elye Chaim asked about, but no one knew to whom the child belonged. He therefore took the child by the hand and started off to his own home, to wait for the mother to be found.

"Rebbe," those around him said, "why don't you let one of us take care of the child? Why should you have to bother yourself?"

"Only a fool," replied R' Elye Chaim, "carries out half-measures. I want to fulfill the *mitzvah* in full."

He took the child home, where his wife cared for it until the mother was found.

✑ Wages Must Be Paid on Time

R' Meir Michel of Shat was ordered by his doctor to go for a walk outside the city each day. To get to where he could walk, he would hire a horseman and his carriage for two hours daily.

Once, soon after R' Meir Michel started out in the carriage, he felt sick, and was forced to return home. His son paid the driver for only one hour. At first the driver refused to accept this, arguing that he was entitled to two hours' pay, but in the end he accepted the pay for one hour and left.

That evening, R' Meir Michel thought about what had happened, and came to the conclusion that the driver had been correct and deserved to be paid for two hours. If he waited until the next morning, he would have violated the *halachah* that a person who is hired by the day must be paid before dawn of the next day.

And so R' Meir Michel sent his son in search of the driver in the middle of the night, to pay him for the extra hour.

✑ Not to Embarrass One (I)

Before the *Chafetz Chaim* published his *seforim*, he owned a small grocery store in Radin. As was often the case, there were a number of people who had bought on credit, but were in no rush to pay their debts.

The *Chafetz Chaim* did not pass the homes of those who owed him money, so that he should not meet and embarrass them.

✑ Not to Embarrass One (II)

Before he became famous, the *Chafetz Chaim* would travel from town to town selling his works. He would hire a driver to take him and a box of the books by horse and wagon from one town to the next. He would generally dress in plain clothes, and he appeared to be just another merchant.

Once, when he was traveling from one town to another, he got off the wagon to walk beside it for a time, so that he could stretch his legs. The driver decided to have what was his idea of fun, and raced away. The *Chafetz Chaim* was left stranded miles from his destination. He walked until he reached the town, located the wagon driver, paid him his wage, and retrieved his books. He immediately left the town without selling a single book, before the wagon driver found out who his passenger had been.

✑ The Chafetz Chaim's Cow

The *Chafetz Chaim*, like many other people in Radin, had his own cow. It was known by all as "the *Chafetz Chaim's* cow," because it had no horns.

The *Chafetz Chaim* had gone to much trouble to find such a cow, for he wanted to be sure that his cow would not be able to cause damage by goring anyone or anything.

~§ Speak No Evil

The *Chafetz Chaim* said: "It would be better for a person to be dumb, without the ability to speak his entire life, than to speak *lashon hara* for even a single hour."

~§ Pick It up

R' Sheftel, the *rosh yeshivah* of Slutzk, saw a man stoop down and pick up a printed page from the floor. He started to read it, but as soon as he realized that it was not from any of the holy works, he promptly threw it down again. R' Sheftel went and picked it up.

"Rebbe," said the man, "it's not from a holy book."

"That's exactly the point," said R' Sheftel. "I am picking it up so that someone else won't make the same mistake and bend down needlessly to pick it up."

~§ Slandering Hashem's Tefillin

When R' Levi Yitzchak of Berdichev would hear a Jew slandering another Jew, he would approach him and say, "My dear friend, aren't you afraid of slandering Hashem's *tefillin*, in which it is written, 'Who is like Your people, Israel'?"

~§ The Difference Between a Fool and a Wise Man

R' Bunim of Pshischa would say, "What is the difference between a fool and a wise man?

"A fool says what he knows, while a wise man knows what he says."

~§ That Is Not the Answer

Once, R' Chaim Shimon of Borisov was faced with a very difficult case. When he rendered his decision, the man who had lost, who was known for his quick temper, began pouring out all types of curses on his head, but the rabbi stood by and did not say a word.

The man finally left, and one of the rabbi's friends said to R' Chaim Shimon, "Rebbe, you let him get away with it just like that?"

"What should I have done?" asked R' Chaim Shimon.

"Rebbe, you should have treated him like he treated you, and thrown him out of the house."

"Right now, he is guilty as far as *halachah* is concerned, and I am innocent," said R' Chaim Shimon. "Had I thrown him out, he would have been innocent and I would have been guilty."

The Jew and His Neighbor

~§ You Be the Judge

R' Levi Yitzchak of Berdichev constantly sought to point out the merits of Israel to God.

Once, in the middle of the night, R' Levi Yitzchak said to his *shamash*, "Take a bottle of schnapps and come with me."

They came to the bathhouse, where the poorest of the poor would sleep. R' Levi Yitzchak told his attendant to pour a glass of schnapps. He then woke up one of the Jews sleeping there and said to him: "Do you want a drink? Here!"

The man rubbed his eyes, saw the glass of liquor before him, and said: "Yes, Rebbe, but I can't drink it until I've washed my hands."

And the same response came from the next one he awoke, and the next. No one was willing to drink without washing his hands first.

Finally, R' Levi Yitzchak woke the *Shabbos goy* (the gentile employed to assist Jews on *Shabbos*) who was sleeping there as well: "Ivan, would you like a drink?" he asked.

"Pour me one," exclaimed the man, and in a single gulp downed the whole glass of liquor.

R' Levi Yitzchak raised his eyes to heaven and said, "Lord of the universe! Look down from Heaven and see! Who is like Your nation, Israel, a holy and pure nation? A Jew will not touch food or drink until he has washed his hands and offered praise to You. Indeed, Your children are befitting before You, and You are befitting to them."

⇜ A Question of the Date

Baron Shimon Ze'ev Rothschild of Frankfurt was scrupulous in all details of Torah observance, and always endeavored to perform every *mitzvah* as handsomely as possible.

He once brought a *sofer* (a scribe) from Russia to write *mezuzos*, *tefillin* and the five *megillos*. When the *sofer* had finished, he came to Rothschild for his final payment.

"Have you received anything on account?" asked Rothschild.

"Yes I have," said the *sofer*, "and I have everything written down in my diary. Let me see," he continued, taking his diary out of his pocket. "In April I received such-and-such an amount, in May such-and-such ..."

"You go by the secular date and not by the weekly *parashiyos*?" exclaimed R' Shimon Ze'ev.

Rothschild paid the *sofer* what he owed him, and told him to take everything he had written with him.

⇜ The Day's Program

The *Chafetz Chaim* would say: "Fortunate is Israel, because we have a *Shulchan Aruch*. When a Jew gets up in the morning, he immediately has his day planned out for him, and he knows how to act at home and at work, in drinking and in eating. His entire life is arranged for him. The non-Jew, on the other hand, who has no *Shulchan Aruch*, must live with uncertainty his whole life. That is not a satisfactory way to live."

⋑ Do Clothes Make the Man?

A chasid came to R' David Moshe of Chernobyl. He was dressed in modern dress, and not the traditional chasidic garb. When R' David Moshe saw this, he asked him: "What made you change your clothing?"

"Rebbe," the man apologized, "I live among non-Jews who do not like Jews, and I was forced to change my clothes for the sake of peace."

"And now," R' David Moshe asked him, "that you dress like they do, have they begun to like you?"

⋑ The Packaging Is What Counts

R' Yechezkel of Kuzmir would say: "The Jewish people may be compared to a box full of glass dishes. If the dishes are packed well and tightly, one next to the other, the box can be moved about and none of the dishes will break. If the dishes are packed loosely, even the slightest jar is liable to break them.

"So too with Israel. If they live in friendship and peace and all make room for one another, they cannot be harmed. If there are arguments in their midst and each demands his own space, they cannot withstand the smallest disturbance."

⋑ Whose Law Is Better?

A government official once bragged to R' Yoshe Ber of Brisk: "Our laws are better than yours. Under our laws, both a judge receiving a bribe and the person giving the bribe are guilty, whereas under your laws, only the judge who takes a bribe is guilty."

"On the contrary," said R' Yoshe Ber, "our laws are better than yours. Under your laws, a judge isn't afraid of taking a bribe, knowing that the giver is equally guilty, and will therefore never turn him in. By our law, though, the judge is afraid that after he takes a bribe, the bribe giver may reveal their secret."

◄§ Fire and Water

R' Yaakov David of Slutsk would say: "The Jewish people are compared to fire, while the other nations are compared to water. If there is a partition between the fire and the water, such as a pot, then the fire can overcome the water and boil it. If there is no partition between them, the water overcomes the fire and puts it out."

◄§ A Giveaway

R' Shmuel Ostraha of Brody would gather together children from the neighborhood to test their Torah knowledge, and reward each one with a candy.

A freethinker wished to poke fun at R' Shmuel. He found a non-Jewish child in the area who knew Yiddish, and taught him a single *Mishnah* perfectly. He then sent the child along with the others one Friday.

As soon as the child began reciting his *Mishnah*, R' Shmuel stopped him, and the child left empty-handed.

"That child," explained R' Shmuel, "is not Jewish." They checked and found that he was correct. Everyone believed that R' Shmuel must have *ru'ach ha'kodesh* (Divine inspiration). "Not at all," said R' Shmuel. "The non-Jewish child remained motionless as he recited the text, whereas a Jewish child would rock back and forth."

◄§ Reviving the Dead

When the wife of R' Shalom of Belz died, the Rebbe wept uncontrollably.

"Rebbe," his chasidim asked, "so much mourning?"

"You don't understand," said R' Shalom. "I am crying before Hashem and asking Him to be merciful to His nation, Israel. And this is what I say: 'Lord of the universe! You know that if I could revive my wife from the dead, there would have been nothing in the world that could stop me. But I cannot do it. You, though, have cast Israel to the ground, the same Israel which You betrothed forever, and it must wander about in the darkness of exile. Yet, You have it in Your power to raise Israel up again, but You don't do so.'

In the
Community

The Rabbinate

✒ A Lesson in Humility

When R' Shmelke came to Nikolsburg to serve as its Rav, the whole city came out to welcome him. As soon as R' Shmelke got off the wagon in which he had come, he asked to be alone for a while and he retired to a room. The time stretched on, and everyone waited for the Rabbi to come out. Finally, someone, unable to restrain himself, crept up and put his ear to the door. He heard R' Shmelke speaking to himself: "Good morning, Rav of Nikolsburg! Good morning, Rebbe. Please take a seat, distinguished Rabbi."

The man couldn't believe what he had heard.

When at last R' Shmelke emerged, he went over to him and said, "Excuse me for being so forward, Rebbe, but I heard you say to yourself: 'Good morning, Rav of Nikolsburg! Good morning, Rebbe. Please take a seat, distinguished Rabbi.' Could you tell me what that was all about?"

"I saw a huge crowd of people coming to pay their respects," said R' Shmelke, "and I became afraid that I might become conceited. I therefore took some time off and paid my respects to myself. That sounded absolutely ludicrous. From now on, whenever anyone pays his respects to me, I will let it affect me as much as the respect I paid myself."

⊷§ The Wages of the Rabbinate

R' Moshe Kramer of Vilna owned a store in that city. His wife would mind the store, while he would sit and learn Torah. R' Moshe was a great Torah scholar, and the community eventually asked him to become the Rav of the city. R' Moshe finally consented, but made a single condition — under no circumstances was he to be paid. He would continue to be supported by his store.

Soon, R' Moshe began to sense that his family income was greater, and he asked his wife: "How do we suddenly have extra money? Are the community elders paying you anything behind my back?"

"Heaven forbid," she replied, "but ever since you became the *rav*, we have had many more customers than before, and that is why our income has grown."

R' Moshe took out a piece of paper and calculated how much the family needed per week, and he told his wife, "I want you to know that we need such and such an amount weekly for our expenses. As soon as you have earned that amount, even if it is still Sunday, you are to close the store for the rest of the week, and are not to reopen it until the following Sunday. The other storekeepers also need to earn a living."

⊷§ True Humility

The community of Vilna needed a Rabbi, and decided to invite R' Akiva Eiger, then the Rav of Posen, who was known as the greatest Torah scholar of the era, to fill this important position. The community sent two of its leaders to ask him to accept the position.

The two came to Posen and went to see the Rabbi.

"Where are you from?" he asked them.

"From Vilna, Rabbi," they answered.

"No doubt you are here on business."

"We have come to invite you to be the Rav of our city, and we think it would be a very great privilege for the city if you would accept the position," they told him.

When R' Akiva Eiger heard this, a shudder went through his body. "Heaven forbid," he replied. "Who am I that I should be the Rav of so great a city? I wish that I could be worthy of being a *shamash* in Vilna."

◆§ A Change of Occupation

R' Akiva Eiger hated the Rabbinate and in his old age wanted to leave it.

He once discovered that the bath attendant in a town near Posen, who used to rent the facilities from the community, had died. He thereupon wrote to his daughter in that town, asking her to see if she could manage to rent the bathhouse for him. "It is my desire," he wrote, "to support myself in my last days legally, by my own hard work, rather than from others."

◆§ The Rav: Servant or Master?

When R' Yehudah was the Rav of Lissa, there was a case where the head of the community refused to accept his authority. R' Yehudah warned him a number of times, but the man ignored him. Finally, R' Yehudah was forced to put him in *cherem* (under ban), which meant that no one in the town could have any dealings with him. When the man heard this, he ran to R' Yehudah and told him angrily, "Rabbi, is this the way you repay me for making you the Rav of Lissa?"

When R' Yehudah heard these words, he burst into tears and

said to his *shamash*, "Go and rent a wagon for me. I am leaving Lissa immediately."

◄§ It's All the Same

R' Naftali of Ropshitz, who was famous for his sense of humor, would say: "At first I thought I would not become a Rav, because a Rav must flatter the members of his community. Instead, I decided I would be a tailor. Then I saw that tailors, too, flatter their clients. I decided I would become a shoemaker. Again, I saw that shoemakers flatter those who buy their shoes. I decided to be a bathhouse attendant — and again, I saw that they, too, flatter their clients. If that is the case — I said to myself — why is it any worse to become a Rav? And thus I became a Rav."

◄§ An Auspicious Beginning

When R' Naftali became the Rav of Ropshitz, the first question that was asked of him was one where he realized he would have to rule that the matter was forbidden. He was loathe to begin with a negative ruling, and said, "Had the circumstances been as follows" — and here he spelled out the conditions that would be necessary — "it would have been permitted. Now that the circumstances are not such, you may draw your own conclusions as to what the *halachah* is."

◄§ Half a Truth

Once, when R' Eizel Charif of Slonim was rejoicing on *Simchas Torah,* he, humorously told those near him, "Please do not refer to me as the Rav of Slonim, but as the Rav of Warsaw."

When everyone asked him why, he replied: "If anyone refers to me as the Rav of Slonim, he is telling a complete lie, because I do not want Slonim and Slonim does not want me. On the other hand, as far as Warsaw is concerned, while

Warsaw doesn't want me, I want it. If you call me the Rav of Warsaw, it will only be half a lie."

~§ "Who Is the Real Rav of Slonim?"

Until he became a Rav of a community, R' Yossele of Slonim was supported by his father-in-law, R' Eizel Charif.

R' Eizel once asked him, "Yossi, tell me, who is the Rav of Slonim? When it comes to questions about kashrus, neither of us is asked, because such questions are directed to R' Feitel. When it comes to court cases, we are both members of the beis din. As far as wages, we are both supported by Slonim. So who then is the Rav of Slonim?"

"That's a good question indeed," said R' Yossele, smiling. "Well, how indeed can we tell?"

"Go out into the market," said R' Eizel, "and see who the people are complaining about. That's the one who is the Rav of Slonim!"

~§ Not Worthy of the Honor

R' Hirshele of Salant was one of the great Torah scholars of his generation. Throughout his life, he remained the Rav of the small town of Salant. A number of important communities invited him to become their Rav, but he declined all offers.

Once the leaders of Minsk came to him bearing a written invitation for him to become the town Rav. R' Hirshele did not want to accept, but the Minsk notables kept begging him to reconsider. They said that it would be a great honor for Minsk to have him as its Rav, and that he would be able to live more comfortably. Finally, R' Hirshele sent them to his wife, that they might have her opinion on the matter.

They came to the rebbitzen and showed her the invitation, which also specified the salary the Rav would be receiving — considerably above what R' Hirshele was earning. The rebbitzen, without hesitation, agreed. They came back to R'

Hirshele happily, and said, "The *rebbitzen* has agreed. Now it all depends on you, Rebbe."

"My wife, may she live, is worthy of being the *rebbitzen* of Minsk just as she is the *rebbitzen* of Salant," said R' Hirshele. He considered the matter very sensibly and agonized over it. Finally, this righteous and humble man reached his decision. I am not worthy of even being the Rav here, and am certainly not worthy of being the Rav of so illustrious a community as Minsk."

◆§ *Even This Is Bribery*

R' Daniel, author of *Chamudos Daniel*, was the Rav of Horodno. His wages were extremely low, and the family was forced to subsist on black bread and kasha throughout the week.

Once, while eating, he saw little beads of oil in the kasha.

"How is it that we have oil in the kasha today?" he asked his wife.

"Our neighbor was making chicken fat today, and gave me a little," she replied.

R' Daniel stopped eating immediately, recited the after-meal blessing, and asked his *shamash* to summon the community leaders to an emergency meeting.

After all were seated, R' Daniel arose and said, "I would like to inform you, gentlemen, that today my wife unknowingly took a bribe from the wife of a man whose case I am trying, and I am no longer worthy of being a Rav and *dayan*."

◆§ *No Advance Payments*

R' Eliyahu Chaim of Lomza accepted the invitation to become the Rav of Lodz. On the day he was expected to arrive in the city, all dressed in their *Shabbos* clothes and went to the train station to honor their new Rav and escort him to his new home. The train arrived, and a few passengers descended — but not R' Eliyahu Chaim. The station buzzed: Where was the

Rav? Could he have been hurt? But then he would have informed them of the delay. They finally decided that he must have changed his mind and remained in Lomza.

The next day, R' Eliyahu Chaim arrived in Lodz and made his way to the *beis midrash*. When the community leaders discovered that the new Rav was in town, all rushed to welcome him; they found him immersed in learning.

"Rebbe, why did you do this?" they asked. "Yesterday, we all went out to greet you. But today no one was present to welcome you."

"You all went out yesterday in my honor, although I had done absolutely nothing yet for the community," said R' Eliyahu Chaim. "Honor must be earned, and I don't like being paid in advance for something I have not done."

⋖§ The Loyal Shepherd

R' Meir Simchah, the *Or Same'ach*, was the Rav of Dvinsk for thirty-nine years. During World War I, when the enemy forces approached Dvinsk, the Jews all fled in every direction. Only the poor and the unfortunate, who had no means of escape, remained behind.

Some of the last remaining Jewish residents came to R' Meir Simchah and told him, "Rebbe, hurry and leave. The city is in imminent danger of falling."

"No!" replied R' Meir Simchah. "As long as there are nine other Jews who remain in the city, I will be the tenth."

⋖§ Different Rabbis

When R' Yaakov David of Slutsk was the Rav of Bobroisk, there were two other Rabbis in the town — R' Shemaryah Noach, who was the Rabbi of the chasidim, and another Rabbi, who had been appointed by the government without the people's approval and knew almost nothing. The government appointee, though, dressed and acted like a chasid.

R' Yaakov David used to say: "There are three Rabbis in

Bobroisk: a Rabbi with a *shtreimel*, a Rabbi without a *shtreimel*, and a *shtreimel* without a Rabbi."

◄§ A Reason to Stay

When R' Yaakov David was the Rav of Slutsk, he was very dissatisfied with his community, for he felt the people did not show the proper respect for his position. Often they even tormented him.

"Rebbe," the community leaders asked him, "if you aren't happy with Slutsk, why don't you take a position in another town?"

"We are told that there are seven levels of *gehinnom*," said R' Yaakov David. "Why are so many needed? The answer must be that eventually the wicked become accustomed to a particular level of *gehinnom*, and the punishment loses some of its force. At that point, they are shifted to another level of *gehinnom*, and there they have a new series of punishments which they must endure.

"And this also applies to me. Slutzk is a *gehinnom* for me, but I am used to it and its torments. If I move to another town, though, I will have a new *gehinnom* with its new torments."

◄§ Theft From the Community

R' Arele, the Rav of Wilkomir, was a great Torah scholar and an exceptionally pious person. For sixty years he remained the Rav of Wilkomir, and throughout that time he barely eked out a living from the small salary he was paid.

When he became old, the community wished to increase his salary, but he refused to hear of it.

"I am earning enough to survive," he told the community leaders, "and for me to take money in order to bequeath it to my children is theft of community funds."

◆§ Residing Versus Living

R' Yechiel Michel of Novarodok would say, "Why is it that Rabbis customarily write in their letters, *ha-choneh poh* — 'who encamps here' (i.e., in this particular town) rather than *ha-yoshev poh* — 'who lives here'? This teaches us that every Rav only resides in a place temporarily, and it is customary for a Rav to move from one community to another."

◆§ Rabbinic Authority

All his life, the *Chafetz Chaim* hated the Rabbinate. Even when he was a young man and was barely able to subsist, he refused to hear of any appointment as a *rav*.

Once, the leaders of his town, Radin, begged him to become the town Rav. After all, they told him, why should the community have to go searching for a Rav when he already lived there?

After much deliberation, the *Chafetz Chaim* agreed to their proposal, but made a clear condition — that every single Jew in the town would agree to obey him.

A short time later, there was a dispute between two of the Jews in the town, and they came to the Rav for a decision. After hearing both sides, the *Chafetz Chaim* ruled in favor of one of the parties. The one who had lost, though, refused to accept the verdict.

That day, the *Chafetz Chaim* called together the community leaders and resigned from his position. And until his dying day he remained an untitled Jew.

◆§ Rabbinical Responsibility

R' Meir, the Rav of Slutzk, was a great Torah scholar and an extremely pious man. He was the Rav of Slutzk for a number of years, during which he founded a yeshivah in the town which produced numerous Torah scholars. Those were the times when the enlightenment and various movements were making inroads on the community and Torah life was under sharp attack. When his own granddaughter enrolled in a non-Jewish public school, R' Meir resigned from his post. "If I was unable to educate my own family properly, I have no right to be in charge of an entire Jewish community," he said.

◆§ Making Jews

R' Zvi, son of R' Yitzchak Elchanan, was invited to come to the United States and take the position of Chief Rav of New York. R' Zvi, though, refused the offer. His friends asked him why he was not interested in going overseas. After all, the United States was a spiritual desert at the time, and there was so much that could be done.

"I am able to be a Rabbi of Jews," R' Zvi explained, "but I am unable to be a Rabbi who makes Jews."

◆§ If There Were Only Fifteen Like You

When R' Chaim Leib was the Rav of Smargon, a very wealthy man lived in the town. The man was very miserly, and gave very little to charity.

Once, this rich man was sitting with the Rav and discussing various matters. The conversation turned to the different religious functionaries and what they earned.

"Rebbe," the man asked R' Chaim Leib, "how do you do financially?"

"Well, if there were fifteen such as you," R' Chaim Leib answered, "I would have no financial problems at all."

"Pardon me, Rabbi," the man responded, "I know I may not be of the big givers, but the times are hard. I have many expenses, and people always exaggerate how much others own."

"You've misunderstood me," R' Chaim Leib told him. "I really meant what I said. If there were fifteen such as you in Smargon, I would have no financial problems at all. The problem is that there are two hundred such as you."

◄§ Who Is to Do the Moving?

When R' Yaakov Frommer was the Rav of Cleveland, he had many opponents among the *baalei batim*. These people did everything possible to force him to leave the city.

Once, R' Yaakov arose to speak and made the following statement: "I would like to tell all of you that I am the Rav of Cleveland, and Cleveland is my community. If you wish to live in the city and be members of the community, you are welcome to stay here. And if not, you have the right to move away from the city. I am not stopping you."

◄§ The Difference

R' Chaim Ozer of Vilna would say: "Both *baalei batim* and Rabbis are commanded to keep the provisions of the Torah. The difference is that *baalei batim* are *shomrei chinam* — unpaid keepers — while Rabbis are *shomrei sachar* — paid keepers."

◄§ But What About the Future?

When R' Yosef, author of *Mishnas Chachamim*, was the Rav of Zamushtsh, there was a local regulation that every butcher had to give the Rav a pound of meat each week. There was one butcher, though, who ignored the regulation and gave the Rav nothing. "The Rav is a wealthy man, and doesn't need it," he said to himself. When R' Yosef discovered this, he called in the butcher and ordered him to bring in a pound of meat each week. To be sure that this was done, he would even check with his wife each week.

Once, his wife said to him, "Why are you so insistent on this? *Baruch Hashem* we don't need the meat."

"I really am not insistent on receiving the meat for my sake," the Rav explained to his wife. "I am afraid that the person who follows me in this position may be poor, and if the butchers grow accustomed to not giving the Rav his due, they will be stealing from a poor Rav who may follow me."

✎§ Rabbis Suit Their Generations

When R' Naftali was invited by the town of Ropshitz to be its Rav, he said: "We are told that Hashem showed Adam every generation and its leaders, every generation and its wise men (*Sanhedrin* 38). This seems strange. Why did Hashem feel it necessary to show Adam not only the leaders, but also the people of the generation?

"Had Hashem shown Adam that Naftali was acting as a Rav of a congregation, Adam would have fainted away. However, Hashem first showed Adam the generation. And for a generation such as this, even Naftali can be a Rav and leader."

✎§ Better off than Moses

R' Eizel Charif was once sitting and talking with the leaders of his town. As they discussed various matters, they got to talk about the pay the Rav received.

"You know," said R' Eizel, "I am better off than Moshe."

"What do you mean by that?" they asked.

"When Korach and his people wanted to remove Moshe from his position," said R' Eizel, "we are told that Moshe was upset, as it states, 'And Moshe heard and fell upon his face' (*Bamidbar* 16:4). After all, it was not so easy to lose the position of the leader of all of Israel. For me, on the other hand, if you remove me from my position, I will not be at all sad, because it is very easy to find a job in the Rabbinate that doesn't pay a salary."

✎§ Matzah and Maror

When R' Eizel was the Rav of Slonim, another man was appointed by the Russian government to be the official Rav of the town. This man was an ignoramus, and no one paid him any attention. Such was the fate of government-appointed Rabbis.

The government Rabbi once met R' Eizel and said to him, "I don't understand it. We both serve as Rabbis in the same town, yet everyone honors you and everyone ignores me."

"On *Pesach*," said R' Eizel, "we are required to eat both *matzah* and *maror* — the bitter herb. If we do not eat one of them, we have not fulfilled our obligation. Yet there is a difference between the two. The *matzah* that we use is prepared carefully, weeks and weeks before the festival. We make sure and doubly sure that no water ever touches the flour before it is baked. When we finally bring the *matzah* home, we take scrupulous care of it, keeping it in a safe place. As far as the *maror* is concerned, though, we don't do anything about it until the very last minute. Then, on the day of the *seder*, we grind up the horseradish one, two, three — and we have *maror*. The reason for this is that we do not eat the *maror* because we like it; after all, it is really bitter. We nevertheless force ourselves to partake of the *maror* because it is a positive commandment, a decree by the King."

"I am like the *matzah*; you, my dear sir, are the *maror*."

◆§ Doing Without a Rabbi

After the *Malbim's* departure, the community of Mohilew remained without a Rav for a number of years. Thus, when R' Yoshe Ber left Slutzk, the leaders of Mohilew came to him and invited him to be their Rav. R' Yoshe Ber turned them down outright.

"Why don't you accept our offer, Rebbe?" they asked. "Is being the Rav of Mohilew beneath you?"

"Heaven forbid," answered R' Yoshe Ber. "Mohilew is a marvelous town, an important town, and what greater honor can a Rav have than to occupy the position once held by the *Malbim*? But let me give you a parable. If a person needs to marry a widow, he should look for a woman who was widowed recently. Such a woman feels that she cannot survive without a husband. After all, who will support her? Who will make *kiddush* and *havdalah* for her? We can rest assured that such a woman will appreciate being remarried. On the other hand, if a woman has been a widow for a number of years, she already knows that she can survive without a husband. Thus she will not be as appreciative of her second husband.

"So, too, if a community has just lost its Rabbi, it believes that it cannot do without one. Who will make halachic decisions? Who will give the sermons? Such a community will appreciate having a new Rabbi. However, Mohilew has been without a Rabbi for years. It has no doubt reached the conclusion that a community can survive quite satisfactorily without a Rabbi."

⋅ঌ Changing Occupations

A young man who was a tremendous Torah scholar did not derive his living from his Torah knowledge, but owned a factory which produced soda water.

This man, and a number of others, were once in the company of R' Chaim of Brisk and spoke in learning. In the course of their discussion, the young man presented a number of brilliant insights in Torah. "What a pity," said one of the others present, "that this young man isn't the Rav of a large city."

"I disagree," said R' Chaim. "I too, would leave the Rabbinate if I had a factory."

⋅ঌ A Simple Test

R' Yosef Shaul Natanson of Lvov would not give a man *semichah* (ordination) unless he knew all the laws, and especially those dealing with the blessings to be recited over different foods, and which blessing takes precedence over which. As part of the test, he would have a tray bearing various foods placed before the candidate and would see if the young man knew which food should be chosen first.

Once, a young man came to him to ask for *semichah*. As usual, R' Yosef Shaul had the tray of foods brought out. The young man was not sure what to take first, so he excused himself for a few moments and reviewed the laws. Given the choices on the plate, he reasoned, this food should be first, followed by that, etc. When he returned a few minutes later, the plate of food had been replaced by another one, and again he had no idea what blessing to recite first.

R' Yosef Shaul did not give him *semichah*.

⋄§ A Difference in Salaries

When R' Chaim was the Rav of Brisk, he received a poor salary, while his brother, Avraham Baruch, the Rav of Smolensk, received a fine wage.

Once, R' Chaim was asked: "Rebbe, why is it that you do not receive as much as your brother in Smolensk receives?"

"We know that the basic necessities of life, such as bread and basic clothing, are cheap," replied R' Chaim, "while luxury items, such as meat and jewelry, are expensive. Now, in Smolensk, where many people are not so observant, the Rabbinate is a luxury, and that is why it is so expensive. In Brisk, though, where all are observant, all are learned and God-fearing, the Rabbinate is a necessity, and that is why it is so cheap."

⋄§ Too Large or Too Difficult

R' Chaim, *Maggid* of Shtzutzin, was a tremendous Torah scholar and very wealthy. Eventually, the people of his town invited him to become their Rav, and he accepted, with the understanding that he would not be paid for his work.

Once, two men came to him for a ruling, in a case involving more than four hundred rubles. Now the regulation of the region was that any case involving four hundred rubles or more had to be sent to the regional Rav, and could not be dealt with by the local Rav. R' Chaim, though, refused to accept that provision and handled the case himself. The regional Rav, from Tiktin, thereupon summoned R' Chaim and asked, "Why,

Rabbi, did you break the regional regulation by dealing with a case involving more than four hundred rubles?"

"I'd like to thank you," responded R' Chaim, "for having answered a question which had been bothering me. All my life I could not understand why Moshe did not accept Yisro's advice as it was, but amended it. Yisro told Moshe to delegate some of the work: 'Every *large* matter they shall bring to you' (*Shemos* 18:22), while Moshe changed his statement and we read, 'and every *difficult* matter they brought to Moshe' (v. 26). Now you have come and supplied me with the answer. Yisro, who had been the priest of Midian, thought in terms of the money involved. Thus, he thought: Anything small, namely which did not involve a large sum of money, should be dealt with by the other judges, while every case involving large sums of money should be dealt with by Moshe. Moshe, however, was not concerned with the amount involved, but with the nature of the case. He therefore decreed that where the case was a simple one, even if it involved a large sum of money, the other judges could handle it. However, if it was a complicated matter, and even if it involved a small sum, it was to be brought to Moshe.

"It appears," said R' Chaim, "that you rule like Yisro, while I hold with the opinion of Moshe."

◆§ Even After Death

When R' Samson Raphael Hirsch was the Rav of Frankfurt, he was paid in advance every three months. In his will, he left instructions that his family should refund to the community the pay for the period between his death and the end of that quarter.

◆§ True Humility

R' Akiva Eiger and R' Yaakov of Lissa had arrived in Warsaw for a large gathering of Rabbis. The Jews came out to meet two of the greatest Torah sages of the generation. As a token of their esteem, they had sent a magnificent carriage pulled by noble horses. As soon as the carriage entered the city, the horses were unharnessed and the people themselves enthusiastically drew the carriage.

When R' Akiva Eiger realized what had happened, he thought to himself, "Surely this must be in honor of R' Yaakov." He felt it only proper that he, too, should honor the great sage, so he left the carriage and began walking alongside it. In the crush, no one realized who he was.

R' Yaakov, too, thought to himself, "Surely this must be in honor of R' Akiva." He, too, left the carriage and walked alongside it.

Thus the crowd pulled the carriage for some distance before they realized that it was empty.

๏ Why He Got Shlishi

On *Shabbos*, R' Akiva Eiger and R' Yaakov of Lissa went to pray in the same *shul*. The *gabbai* of the *shul* was in a terrible quandary. To whom should he give *shlishi*, the most esteemed *aliyah*? After much thought, he decided to give *shlishi* to R' Akiva Eiger and *shishi* to R' Yaakov of Lissa.

When the two Rabbis returned to their inn after the prayers, R' Yaakov sensed that R' Akiva was very disturbed. He realized that R' Akiva was upset because he had been given greater honor than himself. In order to make R' Akiva feel better, R' Yaakov said, "Do not think that you were given *shlishi* because you were considered the greater Torah scholar. It was because you are the Rabbi of Posen, which is far larger than Lissa."

Only then did R' Akiva Eiger feel better.

๏ Who Should Come to Whom

Once, R' Meir Michel of Shat visited Neuheim, near Frankfurt, in the summer. When Baron Shimon Ze'ev Rothschild of Frankfurt, who had great respect for Rabbis, heard that he was in Neuheim, he invited R' Meir Michel to come and see him.

R' Meir Michel refused, and said, "Were I a merchant, I would go to Rothschild. However, as I am a Rabbi, if Rothschild wishes to see me he should come to me."

◄§ Double Thanks

Once, R' Aryeh, the author of *Lev Aryeh*, was in Tarnopol and visited the local Rabbi, R' Yosef. As they talked, R' Yosef said to R' Aryeh, "Our Sages tell us that one who gives a gift to another must inform him of it. I would therefore like to tell you that I tried to have the community of such-and-such take you as its Rabbi. However, they did not listen to me, and my good intentions remained only that."

"Then I owe you a double debt of gratitude," said R' Aryeh.

"Why is that?" asked R' Yosef. "After all, the community did not accept my recommendation."

"Had the community accepted me, it would have meant that in Heaven they wanted me to be the Rav there," answered R' Aryeh. "Heaven could have arranged the matter in many ways. Your recommendation would have only been one means. Now that the community turned me down, it is clear that in Heaven they did not want me to have that position, and you were not Heaven's messenger. What you did was purely out of your desire to help me. Therefore I am doubly grateful."

◄§ The Rabbi Who Was Concerned About His Wages

R' Meir Leibush, the *Malbim*, was appointed the Rabbi of Bucharest. The first *Shabbos* he was there, he took a walk and saw that Jewish stores were open and were conducting business. That afternoon, the city notables came to visit their new Rabbi. The *Malbim* said to them, "Gentlemen, I am afraid I may be forced to resign and leave the city."

"Why?" asked the leaders, taken aback.

"I am afraid," said the *Malbim*, "that I will not receive my wages."

"Rebbe," they protested, "why should you be worried about that? Have we ever failed to pay our Rabbi what he agreed to?"

"When you appointed me Rabbi of the city, you offered me a fine salary," said the *Malbim*. "I therefore said to myself: This is obviously a well-off community, which can afford to pay so fine a salary. Now that I see that your people are so poor that they cannot survive by working only six days a week and are forced to work even on *Shabbos*, how can you possibly have the money to pay me?"

◂§ Foiled!

A group of leaders of a community came to R' Yitzchak Elchanan of Kovno to ask his help. They were dissatisfied with their Rabbi, and wished to consult with him on how to terminate his contract. R' Yitzchak Elchanan received them graciously, and before hearing a word of their request, told his wife, "Would you mind serving refreshments? We have important guests of this-and-this town, whose Rabbi is a great Torah scholar and very righteous in all his ways."

And he kept heaping praise on the Rabbi.

The community leaders were unable to get a word in, and left without having asked R' Yitzchak Elchanan anything.

◂§ An Increase

Once, R' Hillel Lichtenstein of Kolomia summoned the leaders of the community and told them, "I want an increase, and if I do not get it, I will leave."

The committee leaders decided to have a meeting about the issue. At the meeting, R' Hillel told them, "Gentlemen, what I want is an increase in *Shabbos* observance. The storekeepers and craftsmen must begin *Shabbos* earlier, while there is still daylight. If not, I will leave."

☙ Who Should Be a Rabbi?

One of R' Yisrael Salanter's disciples told him, "Rebbe, I am in very serious financial trouble, because I don't have a job."

"Why not become a Rabbi?" asked R' Yisrael.

"Rebbe, I am afraid that I might give an incorrect ruling," said the disciple.

"Who then should become a Rabbi?" said R' Yisrael. "One who is not afraid of ruling incorrectly?"

☙ Why Are There Those Who Scorn Torah?

R' Shalom Rabinowitz of Vilna, the author of She'ilas Shalom, would say, "Why did Hashem allow for people who are arrogant and scorn Rabbis and who make life miserable for them in every generation?

"So that those who study Torah should do so for its own sake."

☙ Not the Rabbinate of Frankfurt

Baron Shimon Ze'ev Rothschild of Frankfurt was a religious man, who had a very high regard for R' Akiva Lehrn of Amsterdam. The baron was very interested in having R' Akiva become the Rabbi of Frankfurt, but he refused.

"Why not?" asked R' Shimon Ze'ev.

"The Kohen Gadol (the High Priest) must be greater than his brothers in wealth and possessions, so that he should not be dependent on anyone," said R' Akiva. "Anyone, however, who becomes the Rabbi of Frankfurt, no matter how wealthy he is, cannot possibly be totally independent."

◆§ What a Bribe Looks Like

Once, two men were to appear before R' Heshel for a *din Torah*. One of the men came the day before he was to appear in court, and asked R' Heshel to help him. As he spoke he laid a hundred rubles on the table. R. Heshel took the money and told the man to come back the next day.

That evening, R' Heshel asked that a big dinner be served, and he called together his sons and sons-in-law. During the meal, R' Heshel took out the hundred rubles and began counting them in front of everyone. All looked on expectantly, hoping to receive some of the money.

After R' Heshel had counted the money a few times, he put it into his pocket and said, "Know, my children, that the money that you see is a bribe, and bribery is forbidden by the Torah.

I wanted to show you what a bribe looks like, so that you will know what to avoid."

The next day, R' Heshel returned the hundred rubles to the man and warned him that one is forbidden to either give or receive a bribe.

⊷§ A Rabbi's Get-Well Remedy

R' Shmelke of Nikolsburg once came to Cracow. While he was there, a poor woman came to him weeping, holding her infant child in her arms.

"Rebbe," she said through her tears, "this is my only child, and he is very ill."

R' Shmelke took a cloth, wrapped something in it, and gave it to the woman, with instructions to hand the cloth to the town Rabbi.

The woman went to the Rabbi, R' Yitzchak Landau, and gave him the cloth.

When the Rabbi unwrapped it, he did not find any note. All that was inside was a gold coin. He did not understand what R' Shmelke meant. Then it dawned on him that there was a famous children's doctor, a professor of the university, in the city, who charged a gold coin for consultations. Obviously, the woman could not afford to pay for this doctor. Handing the coin to her, he told her, "Take this and go to the specialist."

⊷§ How to Tell a Liar

Two men came to R' Yaakov of Lissa. One had found a gold coin, and the other claimed it had fallen from his pocket. R' Yaakov felt that the man who claimed to have dropped it was not telling the truth. He ordered the two men out of his room, into two adjacent rooms, in preparation for hearing the case.

As soon as the men had left, R' Yaakov moved close to the room where the man who claimed to have lost the coin was waiting, and began speaking to himself, "Had the man who claims to have lost it stated that there is a hole in the coin, that would be clear proof that it is his, because a hole in a coin is considered to be valid proof," he said.

A little later, he called the man in for questioning. As soon as the man entered, he burst out, "Rebbe, you know that I never saw the coin that was found, but I can prove to you it was mine. The coin had a hole in it."

"If that is so," said R' Yaakov, "you must be mistaken. This cannot be your coin, because it does not have any hole in it."

◄§ A Test

Once two women came to R' Hirshele Orenstein with a dispute. Both had hung out their underclothing to dry, and someone had stolen one of the washes. Each claimed that the other's laundry had been stolen. For the desperately poor people of the time, such a loss was a major tragedy.

R' Hirshele ordered that the remaining wash be brought to him. He then had the two women leave temporarily, and asked his wife to add some of her own laundry to the pile. He then called one of the women back and asked her, "Do you recognize your laundry?" She began sorting the clothes. "This is mine, this isn't. . ." she said.

R' Hirshele then ordered that the clothes be mixed up again, and called the other woman in. "Do you recognize your wash?" he asked her. She began going through the pile: "This is mine, and this, and this . . . all are mine," she said.

"Are you sure that all are yours?" asked the Rabbi. "Yes," she said decisively, "everything here is mine."

"You are a liar," R' Hirshele told her, "and the laundry belongs to the other woman."

◄§ Catching a Thief

R' Dov Ber Meizlish, the Rav of Warsaw, was not only a great Torah scholar, but also wise in matters of everyday life.

A man once came to him panic-stricken and cried out through tears, "Rebbe, help me! I'm in terrible trouble!"

"Sit down, my son," R' Dov Ber said to him, "and tell me what the problem is."

"I am from out of town, and came here to do business. I arrived on Friday, carrying five thousand rubles with me. I was afraid to stay at the local inn, because I didn't know the people there, so I made my way to the house of a friend, a famous Warsaw merchant. Before it became dark, before candle-lighting time, I gave him the five thousand rubles for safekeeping until after *Shabbos*. On Sunday morning I asked for my money back, because I had to buy merchandise. But he denied everything! I kept demanding, but he was adamant; he claimed he had no idea what I was talking about. What am I to do, Rebbe? It isn't even my money. My life is ruined!"

"Do not worry," R' Dov Ber said to him. "You will get your money back. I will summon that man, and I want you to remain in the next room. You are to wait for me until you hear me raise my voice, and then you are to come out."

R' Dov Ber sent for the merchant, saying that he needed to consult with him on a matter of public concern. The man came. The Rav began discussing matters with him, like a friend, but suddenly he raised his voice. At that moment the out-of-town man came out of the other room, and screamed, "He's the one, Rebbe. Make him give me back my money!"

"Do you know this man?" R' Dov Ber asked the Warsaw merchant.

"Yes, Rebbe, I know him. He spent *Shabbos* with me, and now he has accused me of having five thousand rubles of his. He must have become insane."

The other man, though, was persistent: "You and no one else took the money from me on Friday afternoon, and you counted it in front of me. How can a Jew do a thing like that?"

"It appears to me," said R' Dov Ber to the Warsaw merchant, "that you're not going to be able to get rid of this pest so easily. Give him something, so that he will leave off."

"You're right, Rebbe," the merchant said. "I'll give him twenty-five rubles."

"What? You'll give me twenty-five rubles of my five thousand? What should I do with them? Buy a rope to hang myself?"

"Offer him a little more," suggested the Rav.

"Fine, Rebbe," the Warsaw merchant said. "I'm willing to give him fifty rubles."

The other merchant, though, continued shouting and weeping, for unless the money was returned, it meant that his life was over, he said.

"Well, it seems that you've really hit a major nuisance who won't leave you alone. I suggest you offer him a hundred rubles."

"I'll go along with that, Rebbe. I'll give him a hundred rubles, and let that be the end of the matter."

But the other merchant insisted on receiving every last ruble which was due him.

"What more do you want?' shouted R' Dov Ber, pretending to be angry. "I think a hundred rubles is a fine bit of charity."

"I don't want any charity," said the man amid tears, "I want my money back."

"Let's try just once more," said R' Dov Ber to the Warsaw merchant. "Give him five hundred rubles."

"All right! Five hundred, if he leaves me alone, once and for all."

R' Dov Ber stood up, turned to the Warsaw merchant, and raised his voice:

"You are a thief! Return the stolen money! Now I am sure that you have his money! I know that you're not one of the most generous men, and on occasion I have approached you for ten rubles for some charitable cause and you turned me down. Suddenly you have turned into the soul of generosity, and are willing to give five hundred rubles to someone to whom you owe nothing. I will not let you leave here until the money is returned. If you refuse to return the money, I will bring in the police, and they will find the money in your home."

The Warsaw merchant became very fearful, and confessed.

A few minutes later, the money was back in its owner's hands.

ᴇ§ Respect When It Is Due

At the time that R' Ze'ev, author of *Maros Ha'Tzovos*, was the Rav in Bialystok, there were two extremely wealthy Jews who were known throughout Poland and Lithuania, Zimmel Epstein and Koppel Halperin. They were partners, and controlled many large businesses. Besides their other ventures, they were contractors to the government, paving roads and building bridges. They employed hundreds of Jews and were also very generous men, giving freely to every charitable cause. R' Ze'ev knew them, and treated them with the greatest respect.

One day, after *shacharis*, as R' Ze'ev sat in *tallis* and *tefillin* studying Torah, his *shamash* saw a magnificent coach halt at the door. The two famous rich men descended. The *shamash* ran to R' Ze'ev and said: "Rebbe, Reb Zimmel Epstein and Reb Koppel Halperin have arrived."

"Ask them why they have come," R' Ze'ev ordered the *shamash*.

The *shamash* left, and soon returned with the answer: "They have come to have you rule on a dispute between them."

"Bring them in," commanded R' Ze'ev, and he pulled his *tallis* over his eyes.

When the two wealthy men entered, R' Ze'ev did not greet them. He did not even look at them, and called out from beneath the *tallis*, "Zimmel and Koppel, who is the plaintiff and who is the defendant?"

Both of them were completely taken aback. They had never expected such a cold reception. The Rabbi was referring to them by their first names only, without even the courteous "Reb."

"I'm the plaintiff," Zimmel barely whispered.

"State your case," said R' Ze'ev.

Zimmel was almost struck dumb, but he finally managed to give his side of the dispute.

"Koppel, what do you have to say to these claims?" R' Ze'ev asked the defendant.

After hearing both sides, R' Ze'ev ordered his *shamash* to have the two leave, and he began to discuss the case with the *dayan* who sat with him. After they had clarified the matter and reached their verdict, R' Ze'ev asked his *shamash* to bring the two back in.

"According to the Torah law, the decision is as follows," R' Ze'ev stated, and then read off the verdict. "Zimmel, do you accept this?"

"Yes, Rebbe," answered Zimmel.

"Koppel, do you accept this?"

"Yes, Rebbe," answered Koppel.

R' Ze'ev removed the *tallis* from his eyes and greeted the two men. "*Shalom aleichem*, Reb Zimmel, *Shalom aleichem*, Reb Koppel."

R' Ze'ev then ordered his *shamash* to bring refreshments for his honored guests.

Such was the extent to which the Rav remained impartial in judging a case.

֍ ֍ ֍

When the two wealthy men left R' Ze'ev, they wanted to pay him for his troubles, as was customary, but R' Ze'ev refused to take any money.

"I have no need for money," he said. "Thanks to Hashem, I have a salary. What I receive from the town is enough for my food and other needs. Accumulating money is simply foolish, because the more money one has, the more he has to worry about."

↬ The Position Makes the Man

When R' Moshe Yitz'l left Smargon, his position as Rav of the town was filled by R' Leibele Shapira, who would later become the Rav of Kovno.

Some time later, R' Moshe Yitz'l appeared in court before R' Leibele. R' Moshe Yitz'l began displaying his great Torah learning, bringing proof after proof to bolster his case. Finally, R' Leibele stood up and said to him, "Once, you were R' Moshe Yitz'l, the Rav of Smargon, and I was Leib Shapira. Now I am R' Leib, the Rav of Smargon, and you are Moshe Yitz'l, a man who has come before me. One who appears in court should only state his case and accept the verdict."

⊷§ Do Not Fear

When R' Leibele of Kovno was the Rav of Smargon, a violent man, David'l the tax collector, lived there. Because of his wealth, he had been appointed as the community leader, and he ran the community in a high-handed manner, instilling fear in everyone.

Once, David'l appeared in court before R' Leibele. It was a very complicated case, with a lot of money involved. David'l was clearly in the wrong, but some of the townsfolk came to R' Leibele and asked him to be moderate in his verdict and seek to make it more palatable to David'l. After all, he was a violent man, and he might harm him if the verdict was too severe.

"The Torah tells us," said R' Leibele, " 'You shall not fear any man.' The 'you' refers to judges. Which person do you think the Torah is talking about? Do you think it refers to Moshe Baruch the *melamed*, who cannot harm a fly? Obviously, the Torah must be speaking about someone like David'l, of whom we are told, 'You shall not fear.' "

R' Leibele immediately went and told David'l that he was required to pay.

⊷§ One Does Not Charge for the Truth

A famous *shadchan* (matchmaker), Raphael, lived in Kovno while R' Leibele was its Rabbi.

He once tried to arrange a marriage between the son of a prominent family in Kovno and the daughter of a wealthy family in a distant city. If the marriage would come about, he would earn a sizable fee. In the manner of *shadchanim*, Raphael praised the attributes of the young man; he was learned and wise, a true Torah scholar. As the father of the prospective bride did not know the groom and had no way of checking these claims, he asked the *shadchan* to have R' Leibele send a letter to him, attesting to the groom's learning. Here, Raphael was in a bind, because he knew R' Leibele would never write that a person was learned, unless he was a truly great Torah scholar. But Raphael thought of a way to solve his problem. He approached R' Leibele's son, one of the *dayanim* in Kovno, and asked him for a letter about the groom's learning. That would satisfy the bride's father, no doubt. Raphael also casually hinted that R' Leibele's son would not lose by writing such a letter. The son, who was convinced that the groom was indeed a learned young man, gave him the letter.

The match was arranged and the wedding took place. Raphael received his fee, and gave twenty-five rubles to R' Leibele's son. He, however, thought that it was too small a sum. He deserved more, he said, because without him there would not have been a wedding. As they were arguing, R' Leibele entered and asked them, "What is your argument about?"

"We have a dispute between us," said Raphael, "and I would like you to decide who of us is right."

"If I am acceptable to both of you," said R' Leibele, "I am willing to hear both sides." He sat down at the table and both men stated their cases.

When R' Leibele had heard them out, he rebuked his son. "Moshe Shmuel, what have you done?" he asked his son. "If the groom is indeed a Torah scholar, then you should have been willing to write that without being paid, and if he is not a Torah scholar, you lied for the sake of money."

R' Leibele then called the leaders of Kovno together and said: "My son is not worthy of being a *dayan*. He must be removed from that position."

Fairness to Both Sides

Two wealthy merchants came to R' Binyamin Diskin for a ruling on a complicated case. There were five thousand rubles involved, and they entrusted this sum to him until the conclusion of the case.

A few days later, one of the merchants approached R' Binyamin and begged, "Rebbe, I am in urgent need of two thousand rubles to pay a note that has come due. Please do me a favor and lend me the money from the amount we left with you. In a few days, I'll return the sum to you."

R' Binyamin did not answer him.

"Don't you trust me, Rebbe?" the man asked.

"Heaven forbid!" R' Binyamin answered. "Of course I trust you, but the other merchant already asked me to lend him four thousand rubles of the money in my safekeeping."

"Rebbe," said the man angrily, "How could you lend him the money without my being present or knowing about it?"

"Don't worry," said R' Binyamin. "I only said that he *asked* for the money. I acted according to the law and did not give him a single ruble."

"Until You Return to the Earth"

Two men who disagreed about who owned a tract of land came to R' Lippele, the author of the *Oneg Yom Tov*. Each said it belonged to him. Both were adamant, and R' Lippele was unable to have them reach a compromise. R' Lippele then went to see the piece of land involved.

When they arrived there, they again quarreled. Each repeated his version and his claim, and they almost came to blows. Finally, R' Lippele lay down and put his ear to the ground.

"What are you doing, Rebbe?" they both asked in amazement.

"One of you says, 'The land is mine,' while the other says,

'The land is mine,' " said R' Lippele. "I decided to hear what the earth itself says. It says, 'Both of you belong to me.'"

◆§ Jewish Compassion

R' Pinchas Michael, the Rav of Antipolia, applied his logical mind both to Torah learning and day-to-day life.

A Jew once came to him and told him his troubles: "Rebbe, I work in the forest. My employer, who owns the forest, is a very difficult man, and wants to fire me and leave me without any income. If he does fire me, I will have to go begging in order to support my family. Give me your advice. What can I do?"

"Tell me," said R' Pinchas Michael, "does your family live with you in the forest?"

"No," said the man, "I live alone. How can I bring my family there, if I don't know what will happen tomorrow?"

"Well, if you want my advice, I suggest you move your wife and family with you into the forest," said R' Pinchas Michael.

"Rebbe, you don't know my employer," said the man in fear. "He has a violent temper, and when he sees that I have brought my wife and children, he will become furious and throw me out on the spot."

"Don't be afraid," said R' Pinchas Michael. "Take my advice and may Hashem help you."

The man followed R' Pinchas Michael's advice and settled his wife and family with him in the forest. But he remained terrified that his employer would find out.

When his employer visited the forest and found the man's family living with him, he became very angry. He screamed at him for having had the audacity to move his family in with him without permission. A few days later, though, he changed his mind and agreed to the new arrangement. Furthermore, he decided to increase the man's salary, and when it came time for the man's daughter to marry, he paid for the wedding. Then, when the forest had been depleted, he moved the man to another of his forests.

Some time later, the man came to R' Pinchas Michael and thanked him for his good advice.

"To me," said R' Pinchas Michael, "it was obvious. I know that your employer is a good Jew, and, no matter how hardbitten he is, will not take away a job from another Jew who has a wife and children to support. Jews are merciful children of merciful parents."

◈ You Shall Not Take a Bribe

A butcher once sent R' Yoshe Ber a cow as a gift.

A short time later, the man came to R' Yoshe Ber and asked him to forbid the importing of meat from animals that had been slaughtered elsewhere. R' Yoshe Ber did not answer him, but called in his wife and said to her, "Return the cow to this man immediately, and pay him for the milk which we obtained from it."

◈ A Widow's Tears

A widow came to R' Avremele of Sochachow for a ruling on a particular matter. As she outlined the story of her woes, she burst into tears.

R' Avremele told her, "I am not fit to judge your case. Tears are also a form of bribery."

◈ Fear of Error

R' Meir Michel, the Rav of a community, was afraid to decide halachic questions, because he feared that he might forbid that which is permitted or permit that which is forbidden. Once he was seen running after a man whose chicken he had declared *treif*, begging him to accept the cost of the chicken.

Eventually, he left the Rabbinate, so that he would not have to give any rulings.

ᴥᴈ A Fair Decision

Two men came to R' Moshe Yitz'l of Ponovezh. They had both bought plots in the cemetery, and each wanted the better of the two. After they had argued back and forth for some time, R' Moshe Yitz'l rendered his verdict: "Whoever dies first gets the better plot."

Never again did they argue the issue.

ᴥᴈ A Time to Rule

Throughout the years that he was the Rav of Brisk, R' Chaim did not rule on questions of *halachah*. His *beis din* would make all the rulings.

Once, when R' Chaim came back from the market, he saw a maid leaving the *beis din*, carrying a slaughtered chicken. "Show me the chicken," he said.

R' Chaim examined the chicken and found no reason to question its *kashrus*. Everything was in order. He then took the chicken, entered the *beis din*, and asked, "How did you rule on this chicken?"

"It's kosher beyond any doubt," they answered.

"Go home," R' Chaim told the maid, "and bring me the other chicken."

The maid left and returned with another chicken. They found that it was, indeed, not kosher.

Everyone was amazed. How did R' Chaim know there was another chicken? He must have *ru'ach hakodesh*!

"No," said R' Chaim. "One does not ask questions about something which is obviously kosher. I therefore realized that two chickens must have been slaughtered, and when the maid was sent to the *beis din*, she must have taken the wrong chicken."

✺ Watered Milk

R' Elye Meir of Lodz was told that all the milkmen in the town were diluting their milk with water. R' Elye Meir decided to do something about this, and called together all the milkmen.

"Gentlemen," he said, "I have a case concerning meat mixed with milk, one that involves a great deal of money. However, I think I can find a way to rule that it is permitted if the milk is not pure milk."

"Rebbe," they all burst out, "everyone knows that the milk is diluted with water."

"Every single one of you sells diluted milk?"

"Every single one of us."

"Are you sure?" R' Elye Meir persisted.

"Rebbe," they answered, "we ourselves add the water to the milk."

"If that is so," said R' Elye Meir, "I hereby warn you that from now on, you are only to sell pure milk, without a single drop of water added. If anyone is caught selling diluted milk, I will forbid everyone to use his milk."

✺ Finding a Solution

A very poor woman asked R' Elye Meir to rule whether or not a chicken was kosher. R' Elye Meir searched and searched, but could not find a way to permit the chicken to be eaten. Taking a ruble from his pocket, he gave it to the woman along with the chicken, and ruled, "It's *treif*."

✺ The Fifth Shulchan Aruch

A young man who was a true Torah scholar once came to R' Zalman of Mariampol to be tested for *semichah*. R' Zalman tested him at length, and found that the young man was really fit to receive *semichah*.

"Do you know the fifth *Shulchan Aruch*?" R' Zalman asked him.

The young man did not know what to answer, because the *Shulchan Aruch* only has four parts.

"Rebbe," he finally blurted out, "I've never heard of it."

"There is indeed a fifth part," said R' Zalman smilingly, "and its first line reads, 'One must always be a decent human being.'"

◆§ At Least One Commandment

A man came to R' Shmuel Salant. "Rebbe," he said, "my sons now live in America, and don't keep *Shabbos* or any other commandments. They want to support me. Am I allowed to take their money?"

"Your sons," answered R' Shmuel, "wish to keep only one commandment, that of honoring their parents, and you wish to deprive them of that as well?"

◆§ A Business Deal

A merchant came to R' Chaim Elazar, the Rav of Kalish. "Rebbe," he said, "I have the possibility of making a tremendous amount of money on a business deal, but it requires one small act of deception, the way all business deals do. Can I go through with it?"

"You know," said R' Chaim Elazar, "that the Ten Commandments were written on both sides of the tablets (*Shemos* 32:15). That teaches you that no matter how you turn them, they still read, 'You shall not steal.'"

◆§ Promise Enough

A woman once came weeping bitterly to R' Meir Simchah of Dvinsk. "Rebbe, help me!" she cried. "My husband is deathly ill, and the doctors have decided he only has three days to live!"

R' Meir Simchah replied, "Is that what you are crying about? Your husband was told he has three more days to live. Do *I* have a guarantee that I will live until tomorrow?"

ৰ্ওই "Don't Lick the Bones"

The *Chafetz Chaim* was very concerned about the welfare of young Jewish men who were drafted into the Russian army. He wished to ensure that they would remain Jews. That is why he wrote his *Machaneh Yisrael*.

Once, a group of young men who had been drafted came to him to say farewell. "My children," he said, "if I tell you not to eat *treif* food where there is nothing else around, very few of you will be able to resist the temptation. I only have one request of you: When you eat non-kosher meat, don't lick the bones — don't go out of your way to enjoy the meat."

ৰ্ওই *Annulling the Threshold*

When R' Yosef Nobel was the Rav of a town in Hungary, an argument broke out between two brothers. The older one finally swore that he would never again allow the younger one to cross his threshold. There were many people who tried to make peace between them, but were unsuccessful; the older brother refused to be mollified.

One day, as he was home, he heard chopping outside his house. He opened the door and saw a laborer demolishing the threshold, as the Rabbi stood by supervising the work.

"From now on," said the Rabbi with a smile, "your vow is null and void, and your brother can enter your house."

ৰ্ওই *A Simple Man's Blessing*

A man came to R' Yosef Shaul Natanson of Lvov for a blessing. R' Yosef Shaul blessed him with long life, a decent living, riches and respect, and concluded with the words of the *Gemara*, "The blessing of a simple man should not be insignificant to you" (*Megillah* 15a).

"What do you mean?" the man asked. "Rebbe, you are one of the leading Torah scholars of our generation. Do you consider yourself a simple man? I'm astonished."

"When a Torah scholar blesses a man," said R' Yosef Shaul, "what does he wish him? That he should have a love of Torah and that he should fear Heaven. What is the blessing of an ordinary man? A decent living, wealth and respect. Thus, what I gave you is the blessing of a simple man."

⊰§ One Way or Another

A woman came to R' Eizel Charif and complained: "Rebbe, my husband left me. He refuses to support me and won't divorce me."

R' Eizel summoned the man and tried to bring about a reconciliation between the two, but the man would have none of it.

"I hate her, and cannot stand living with her," was his response.

"Well, if that's the case," said R' Eizel, "give her a divorce."

"I'm willing to," said the husband, "provided she pays me a hundred rubles." In those days, that was a large sum.

"A hundred rubles?" cried the woman. "Where can I get a hundred rubles? I'm a poor woman, without a kopek to my name."

"Well, if that is so," said the hard-hearted husband, "she'll just have to do without a divorce."

R' Eizel tried to argue with the man, but he would not budge; without the hundred rubles there would be no divorce.

Finally, R' Eizel rose, went over to his bookcase, and took out *Maseches Kiddushin*. He opened to the very first *Mishnah*, and told the husband, "See what it says: 'She acquires herself (i.e., goes free) in (one of) two ways . . . by divorce or through the death of the husband.' Now you can choose by which of the two your wife will acquire her freedom."

The man was shaken, and gave his wife a divorce.

◄§ Nobody Knows — Except the Rebbe

R' Menachem Mendel of Lubavich, the *Tzemach Tzedek*, was known for his ability to reunite husbands who had abandoned their wives and their families. If a woman came to complain: "Rebbe, my husband ran off, and I don't know where he is," R' Menachem Mendel would say, "Go to this-and-this town, and you will find your husband."

She would go and find her husband living there.

Everyone considered the Rebbe to be a miracle worker, and one who was able to foretell the future.

His son, R' Leib of Kopust, once asked R' Menachem Mendel, "Father, do you really have the gift of prophecy?"

"Not in the least," answered R' Menachem Mendel. "There is a very simple explanation. Why does a husband abandon his wife? Normally because the two cannot get along together. When the husband cannot take any more, he decides to go to a place where nobody knows him. Before he leaves, though, he comes to consult with me as to where to go. I then advise him to go to a specific town. Later, when the wife comes to ask me where her husband is, I tell her exactly what I know."

◄§ Strike While the Iron Is Hot

R' Shmuel Salant was sitting with his *beis din* in the Churvah synagogue in Yerushalayim when a man walked into the synagogue. R' Shmuel invited him over and told him to sit down. He then told his *shamash* to summon the *dayanim* and the *sofer* — the scribe — in order to write a *get*.

"Rebbe," the man said, as if in all innocence, "for whom?"

"Don't talk any more than necessary," R' Shmuel ordered him. "Tell me your name and that of your wife, and do as we tell you to."

R' Shmuel then proceeded to have the divorce document taken care of in all its details.

When the man had gone, the *dayanim* asked R' Shmuel,

"Why did you decide to do what you did?"

"You see," explained R' Shmuel, "some time ago I read an advertisement by a woman whose husband had abandoned her, and the advertisement carried a photograph of the husband. As soon as he came in I recognized him. I therefore decided that I had to do everything possible to free the poor woman from her plight."

⋖§ The Expanding Hour

A man asked R' Yisrael Salanter, "Rebbe, I only have one free hour a day. What should I do with it? Should I learn *musar* or study Torah?"

"Go and learn *musar* for an hour," R' Yisrael told him, "and then you'll realize you have enough time to study Torah for a few more hours."

⋖§ Priorities

One of his chasidim once came to R' Meir Yechiel of Ostrovtze, and complained, "Rebbe, I am so busy trying to earn a living that I don't have time to bring my children up with the ways of the Torah."

"Tell me," said R' Meir Yechiel, "have you ever seen a small fish inside a large fish?" You will never find the tail of the small fish facing in the same direction as the tail of the large fish. On the contrary, the head of the small fish will be facing the tail of the large fish. This indicates that the large fish did not swim to catch the small one, but the small one swam in by itself.

"From this we learn that a person should not spend his time trying to earn a living, but should wait for his living to come to him."

⋖§ Missing the Grace After Meals

R' Yaakov Zeliner, a distinguished resident of Yerushalayim, came to R' Shmuel Salant at midnight, with a problem.

"Rebbe," he said, "as I was lying in bed, I realized that I hadn't recited the after-the-meal blessing after finishing my supper. What must I do?"

"Don't worry," R' Shmuel told him, "you don't have to recite it because you never ate supper."

R' Yaakov was astounded. He was sure that had eaten supper and had forgotten to recite the blessing. However, out of respect for R' Shmuel he said nothing, and went home.

As he entered his home, he went to the kitchen and saw his supper on the table, uneaten.

The next day he approached R' Shmuel and said, "Rebbe, I'm really sorry for having bothered you last night. You were right. I found my supper untouched on my table. You must have *ru'ach hakodesh* — Divine inspiration — to have known that I had not eaten."

"Nothing of the kind," said R' Shmuel. "I assumed that a God fearing person such as you would not forget to recite the blessing after meals, and if you did not, it is proof that you hadn't eaten."

◄§ *The Letter of the Law*

A woman came weeping hysterically to R' Elya Chaim of Lodz. "Rebbe," she managed to get out between tears, "I'm lost!"

"Please tell me what's involved," R' Elya Chaim said, as he tried to calm her down.

"Rebbe, I'm not from Lodz," she said, "but a merchant from Bialystok. I came here to buy merchandise for my store, and brought ten thousand rubles with me. I went to my wholesaler, and I was able to make a very good deal. However, when I wished to pay, I found that my pocket was empty. Ten thousand rubles! How can I go home? How can I continue living?"

"Try to calm down," R' Elya Chaim told her. "Lodz is a Jewish city, and its people are honest. If the person who found the money was a Jew, I am sure that he will perform the *mitzvah* of returning a lost article to its owner. Go home and leave me your address. If I hear any news I'll will contact you immediately." The woman left and traveled back to Bialystok.

A short time later, one of the Jewish porters who worked in the market came to R' Elya Chaim and said, "Rebbe, I want to speak to you in private."

R' Elya Chaim brought him into his private quarters and the man began: "Rebbe, I found the ten thousand rubles that woman lost, and I want to know what the law is. I'm not interested in what's fair or what is over and above the law. I am a poor porter, with a wife and children to support. If the law requires me to return the money, I will do so immediately. However, if doing so is beyond the letter of the law, I cannot return it. I have also heard from Rabbis that if the woman gave up hope of having the money returned, it belongs to me."

"Tell me your name," R' Elya Chaim said, "and where I can find you. In a few days I'll have an answer for you."

"That's not necessary," the porter said, "Each day you'll find me in the Great Synagogue between *minchah* and *ma'ariv*."

R' Elya Chaim then sent the question to R' Yitzchak Elchanan Spektor of Kovno. R' Yitzchak Elchanan replied, quoting the *Yerushalmi*, that a woman does not have the ability to give up hope on a lost object, because whatever she acquires belongs to her husband.

R' Elya Chaim then sent a telegram to Bialystok, and the woman returned to Lodz. That same day, between *minchah* and *ma'ariv*, R' Elya Chaim sent a messenger to the Great Synagogue for the porter. When the man entered, he took the money out of his pocket and placed it before R' Elya Chaim. After the woman had counted the money, the porter got up to go.

"Wait," said the woman. She took three thousand rubles from the packet and offered it to him.

"No, thank you," said the porter. "Had I wanted other people's money, I would have kept the entire sum."

✑ A Mistake

When R' Elya Chaim was the Rabbi in Lodz, one of the local Jews came in to him in great distress. "Rebbe," he said, "I'm in tremendous trouble, because I was an honest man."

"Tell me about it," said R' Elya Chaim.

"A few days ago," the man began, "as I was walking in the market, I found a bundle of money. I came home and counted it, and found that it contained one thousand rubles. The next day, I read that the local noble had lost a sum of money, and that the finder would receive a hundred rubles as a reward for finding it. I immediately went to the noble and returned his money. He was overjoyed. He took the money and counted it. When he finished counting, he suddenly became extremely angry. 'Thief! All Jews are thieves!' he screamed. 'There were two thousand rubles in the bundle, and you only returned a thousand!' I realized what he was up to; he didn't want to pay the hundred ruble reward.

"I became terrified. I was being falsely accused.

" 'Your excellency,' I said, pleadingly, 'I am an honest person. You yourself see that I returned the money you lost. I am willing to forgo the reward money.'

"However, he would not give in. 'You stole a thousand rubles from me!' he said.

"In short, he brought the police, and now I am to stand trial in a few days. What am I to do, Rebbe? How can I possibly hope to win a case against him, when he is the ruler of our area?"

"Do you have a lawyer?" asked R' Elya Chaim.

"Yes," he answered.

"Well, go and bring him to me," R' Elya Chaim instructed him.

The lawyer came to R' Elya Chaim. They talked for some time, and R' Elya Chaim told him how to conduct the case in court.

On the day of the trial, the noble declared, "I lost two

thousand rubles and this Jew found the money I had lost and only returned a thousand rubles."

The Jew protested that he had only found a thousand rubles.

The lawyer then stepped in and asked the noble, "Are you willing to swear that you lost two thousand rubles?"

"Yes," said the noble, and he promptly swore to that effect.

The lawyer then addressed the judges, "Your honors, you now have a sworn statement by the noble that the money which was found was not his. The finder is an honest man. If he had been dishonest, he would not have returned anything. If he found only a thousand rubles, that is clear proof that this money must have been lost by someone else, and not by the noble."

The Jew won the case and kept the thousand rubles.

◄§ Speaking Out One's Fill

Two men once came to R' Avraham Yitzchak of Karlitch for his decision in a dispute between them. For hours they both spoke, each bringing up all the possible points in his favor. Finally, after they had said everything they wished to say, R' Avraham Yitzchak retired to decide the case. In a short while, he summoned them back and rendered his verdict, one which they both accepted immediately. They left, friends once more.

After they had gone, one of his friends asked R' Avraham Yitzchak, "Rebbe, if you could decide the verdict in so short a time, why did you allow them to go on and on?"

"Had I cut them off before each had his full say," replied R' Avraham Yitzchak, "neither of them would have been satisfied. Both would have felt that an injustice had been done. After I gave them all that time to say everything they had to say, they felt that justice was done, and they accepted the verdict gladly."

◄§ The Rumor Is Bad Enough

When R' Avraham Shmuel Binyamin Spitzer was the Rav in Hamburg, a number of people came to him to complain that the local *shochet* had been seen eating shrimp in a non-kosher restaurant.

R' Avraham Shmuel Binyamin sent for the *shochet* and rebuked him, saying, "I am not happy about the rumor that I hear that you ate shrimp in a non-kosher restaurant."

"It's a complete lie!" said the *shochet*, excitedly.

"Don't be so agitated. I said *rumor*, not *fact*," said R' Avraham Shmuel. "But even such a rumor indicates a fault."

⊷§ You Are Both Right

Two men, a father and son, came to R' Yehudah (known by the acronym as *Yesod*) of Vilna. They were both extremely poor, and had a single coat between them.

"I am old, and cannot take the cold weather. It is only proper that I should have the use of the coat," said the father.

"I have to go out every day to earn a living to support both of us, and it is only fitting that I should use the coat," said the son.

After *Yesod* had heard both sides, he said, "Come back tomorrow, and I'll give you my decision."

That same day, *Yesod* ordered a second coat to be made. When the two returned the next day, he said to them, "You are both right. Here is another coat. Now you can both enjoy the warmth."

⊷§ Rabbinic Authority

R' Leibele of Kovno was very firm in his dealings with his community, and insisted that everyone accept his decisions.

Once, a number of horse dealers came to him to complain about a merchant, who was considered to be one of the leading members of the community. They said that he was not paying them what he owed them. R' Leibele sent his *shamash* to summon the merchant, but the man refused to come. R' Leibele then took his letter of appointment as Rav of Kovno and went to see the merchant. When the man saw R' Leibele at his door, he asked fearfully, "Rebbe, what brings you to my home?"

"I have come," said R' Leibele, "to return my letter of appointment to the leaders of Kovno. A Rabbi whose congregants do not listen to him does not deserve to remain in the community."

The man's face turned all colors. In the end he managed to placate R' Leibele and promised to obey him in the future.

⋟ Taking a Divorced Woman

A man with a riding whip came to R' Abele of Posvil and asked, "Rebbe, may a *kohen* take a divorced woman?"

The Rabbi looked at him and said, "Yes, he may."

Everyone present was astounded. The Torah itself forbids a *kohen* to marry a divorcee.

"This man, who is a *kohen*, is a coachman," said R' Abele. "He drives people in his coach from one place to another, and he is unlearned. Somewhere, he had heard that a *kohen* may not *take* a divorced woman. He thus came to ask me whether it is permitted for him to take a divorced woman in his coach."

⋟ A Relative Question

A chasid once complained to R' Moshe Zvi of Sveran, "Rebbe, I am unable to recite the entire book of *Tehillim* without a break."

"And I," said R' Moshe Zvi, "am not able to recite a single verse of *Tehillim* without a break."

⋟ The Fortune-Teller

A man who claimed to be a fortune-teller came to R' David Budnik of Novarodok and offered to tell him his fortune for a fee.

"Away with you, fellow," R' David told the man. "If you could foretell the future, you would have known that you're wasting your time with me."

☙ Correcting a Wrong

Two men came to R' Uri of Bohaslav for his ruling on a dispute. After hearing the evidence, R' Uri gave his verdict. The one who had lost the case paid the other, and both men left.

The next day, R' Uri checked the sources again, and found that he had made a mistake. He thereupon went to the man who had lost the case and said to him, "I want you to know I was in error, and caused you to pay money that you were not obligated to pay. Here is my coat. Go and sell it, and take what you lost out of the proceeds."

R' Uri then put down the coat and ran away before the man could say a word.

☙ The Long-Range View

A chasid came to R' Yisrael of Ruzhin and complained, "Rebbe, I am suffering tremendous pain, and I cannot bear it."

"Let me tell you a story," said R' Yisrael.

"A man died and came for judgment before the Heavenly Court. They placed all his *mitzvos* on one balance pan and all his sins in the other, and the sins outweighed the *mitzvos*. One of the angels came to his defense and said, 'This man suffered all kinds of suffering. It is only proper that his suffering be added to his *mitzvos*.'

"They placed all his suffering on the pan of his *mitzvos*, and still they did not quite outweigh the sins. He was sentenced to *gehinnom*.

"As they were leading him away, he cried out, 'Hashem, You had the power to do anything. Couldn't You have made me suffer just a little more?' "

☙ Fasting Is Not the Answer

R' Yechezkel of Kuzmir was not in favor of those who took upon themselves fast days and other afflictions.

Once a man who was known to be a sinner came to him and told him: "Rebbe, I regret all my sins, and I want to do *teshuvah*. I would like you to give me a list of fasts and other afflictions so that I can atone for my sins."

"That is not the way," said R' Yechezkel. "You have already lost your soul by your deeds. Now you want to lose your body by your afflictions. *Teshuvah* only requires prayer, giving *tzedakah* and good deeds."

✦§ Bring Me a Signature

A certain man came to R' Naftali Amsterdam, and asked him to sign a *heter me'ah rabbanim* (a document), which when signed by a hundred Rabbis would allow him to marry another woman even though he had not divorced his first wife. (This is applied only in the most extreme cases, where the Rabbis feel the husband is in the right, but where the wife will not — or cannot — accept a divorce.)

As the man discussed the case with R' Naftali, he began to belittle his wife, and described how impossible it was to live with her.

"While you're about gathering the hundred signatures that will permit you to remarry, I'd like you to bring me the signature of even a single Rav who permits you to speak poorly about your wife," R' Naftali told him.

Maggidim

◦§ *Hitting the Target*

The *Maggid* of Dubno was known for always using parables to illustrate his points. Once the Gaon of Vilna said to him, "How is it that you always find a parable to fit every point that you wish to make?"

"Let me answer your question with a parable," said the *Maggid*:

There was once a duke who had an only son, whom he loved dearly. He employed the finest teachers, so that his son would learn the different sciences and foreign languages. When his son grew up, he sent him to faraway lands, so that he might learn from the wise men in those lands. After having spent some time abroad, the son returned, a truly educated man.

The duke now made a large banquet to celebrate his son's return, and invited all his friends. At the banquet, the young man amazed everyone with his brilliance.

After the dinner, the duke and his guests went out to the forest to hunt. In the forest, the duke's son displayed great ability with the bow. He consistently hit his target. Everyone was astounded at his marksmanship.

As they were returning, they passed through a small village. There, they saw a fence on which were painted a number of targets, and in each bull's-eye, dead center, there was an arrow. Who was the marvelous archer? They asked around in the village, and found that he was a local farmer. The farmer was summoned. "How do you always manage to hit the bull's-eye?" he was asked.

"It's really very simple," said the farmer. "I shoot an arrow and then paint a target around it."

"I, too," concluded the *Maggid,* "find the parable first, and then find the point which it will illustrate."

⋙ How Dare You?

The Baal Shem Tov was once in Alik for a *Shabbos*. The local community leader was gracious enough to lodge him for the day. A *maggid,* an itinerant preacher, spoke before the *minchah* prayer on *Erev Shabbos*. Everyone, including the Baal Shem Tov, was in attendance.

In his talk, he castigated the people for their sins — for not studying Torah, for not praying with the proper intention, and the like — as was the custom of *maggidim* at the time.

While he was yet speaking, the Baal Shem Tov rose, called the community leader, and both left the synagogue. With them gone, everyone else followed suit, one by one. The *maggid* was forced to cut his speech short.

The next day, the *maggid* came to greet the Baal Shem Tov and asked, "Why were you so angry at what I said?"

"How dare you speak evil of the Jewish people?" said the Baal Shem Tov, with tears in his voice. "A Jew is forced to work the whole day to try to eke out a living, and then, just before sunset, he realizes he hasn't prayed. He runs into the synagogue and prays *minchah* in a rush. He doesn't concentrate on the words, yet his prayer makes a mighty impact in the Heavens."

⋑§ Who Was the Target?

A *maggid* came to R' Meir'l of Titkin and asked permission to speak in the synagogue. R' Meir'l gave him permission, and he himself went to hear the lecture.

The *maggid's* speech was a fiery one, calling on the people to repent of their sins, both those between man and God and those between man and his fellow man. R' Meir'l burst into tears.

After the speech, R' Meir'l called the *maggid* aside and said to him, "I am very appreciative to you for having called attention to my sins. But why did you have to do it in public? Could you not have done so in private?"

"Rebbe," said the *maggid* trembling, "I was not talking to you, Heaven forbid! I was talking to the congregation."

"The entire congregation is holy," said R' Meir'l, "and you could not have been speaking of them. You must have been referring to me, for I am full of sins."

⋑§ Not Even a Spark

A freethinker said to R' Yaakov, the *Maggid* of Dubno, "Rebbe, they say you are a master at getting people to repent through your powers of persuasion. Try to bring me back to the proper path."

"Let me give you a parable," said the *Maggid*:

A blacksmith came to the big city and saw a bellows for the first time. He bought a pair and brought it home. "Here is a tool," he told his wife, "which will make the fire in your fireplace burn more brightly."

The next day, his wife came to him and complained, "This tool which you brought from the market just doesn't work. I've tried and tried, and nothing happened."

"Foolish woman," said the blacksmith to his wife, "it only

works if there is a glowing ember which can flare up. However, if there is no glowing ember, nothing can cause a fire."

"I have the power," the *Maggid* concluded, "to excite a man and bring him to repent if there is still a spark present. With you, though, there is no longer a Jewish spark, so nothing I say will make a difference."

~§ The Message Came Through

R' Meir of Lublin once came to a city to raise money for his yeshivah, *Yeshivas Chachmei Lublin*. He spoke in the *shul* about the importance of supporting those who learn Torah, and aroused the congregation to donate generously.

After he had finished his speech, R' Meir saw a child standing in the crowded *shul*. "My child," R' Meir asked him, "did you understand my speech?"

"No," answered the child truthfully, "I didn't. I only understood one thing: that one must give money."

"If you caught that," said R' Meir with a smile, "you understood my speech better than many of your elders."

~§ If the Hat Fits. . .

R' Moshe Yitzchak, the *Maggid* of Kelm, would call upon everyone to mend his ways, especially with regard to those *mitzvos* which are often ignored. Some of those in his audience felt that he had insulted them personally, as if he had been speaking to them specifically.

To this he had a standard reply. "Gentlemen," he would tell them, "I am like a hatter. When he makes hats, he makes them in different sizes, but he doesn't make a hat of a specific size for a particular individual. If a customer comes, he tries on hats until he finds one which fits. The hatter then sells it to him, and tells him that he should wear it well.

"I also prepare my material with different types of men in mind; I do not prepare it for any particular individual. If my words do fit a specific person, let him take them up."

✑ The Same Prescription

R' Zvi Dainov, the *Maggid* of Slutzk, would give a speech in one place, and repeat it elsewhere.

He was asked, "Rebbe, why do you keep repeating the same speech?"

"The doctor does the same thing," answered R' Zvi. "He writes a prescription for one patient, and writes the same exact prescription for another suffering from the same disease."

✑ Knowing What Not to Say

R' Koppel Reich of Budapest was known as one of the foremost speakers in the Jewish world.

Once, his son was visiting him, and saw R' Koppel preparing a speech.

"Father," he asked, "do you still have to prepare before you give a speech?"

"My son," answered R' Koppel, "I don't have to prepare what I will say, but I do have to prepare what I will *not* say."

✑ One Day Before You Die

R' Leib Mochiach was known by this name because he would rebuke (*mochiach*) people and urge them to repent.

Once, R' Yaakov Yosef, author of the *Toldos*, said to him, "We know that Moshe only rebuked the Jews just before he died. Why then do you rebuke them every day?"

"We are told," answered R' Leib, "that we must 'repent one day before we die,' and as a person can die any day, he must consider each day as the day before he will die. If I am one day away from death each day, I have the right to rebuke them every day."

⊸§ Three Gifts

R' Yechezkel Benet once addressed an audience of people who were not particularly careful in their observance of the mitzvos.

"My friends," he told them, "when the Beis Hamikdash existed, each person would give the kohen three parts of the animal he brought as a sacrifice: the zero'a (the arm), the lecha'ayim (the cheek), and the keivah (the stomach). I, too, want to ask these three gifts of you: the zero'a — that you put on tefillin on your arm and head daily; the lecha'ayim — that you should not shave your cheek with a razor; and the keivah — that you should not eat non-kosher food (and have it enter your stomach)."

In the Chassidic Courts

~§ What Did Hashem Do?

A man who had been a sinner all his life came to R' Naftali of Ropshitz. He had repented, and now wished to turn over a new leaf. He then listed all the sins he had committed, each worse than the previous one.

"Tell me," asked R' Naftali, "what awful thing did Hashem do to you that you sinned so terribly against Him?"

~§ Clear Sight

A man once came to R' Naftali of Ropshitz to ask how he could repent for his sins. As the man was embarrassed to admit that he himself had committed the sins, he pretended that a friend had sent him to ask how one should repent. He gave a long, detailed list of the sins. After R' Naftali had heard the entire list, he smiled and said, "Your friend is a fool. He could have come by himself and claimed that he was coming on behalf of a friend."

⋖§ No Better than a Horse

A young chasid once came to R' Yisrael of Ruzhin and asked to receive *semichah* — ordination. R' Yisrael stood at the window, and looked out at the snow-covered courtyard.

The young man stood next to him and told R' Yisrael about how he afflicted his body. He drank nothing but water; he had nails in his shoes so that he should suffer pain when he walked; each day, even in the coldest weather, he rolled in the snow; and he had the *shamash* give him thirty-nine lashes.

Just then, a horse entered into the courtyard, drank water from the pail lying there, and rolled in the snow.

"See," said R' Yisrael to the young man, "that creature, too, only drinks water, has nails in its shoes, rolls in the snow, and certainly receives more than thirty-nine lashes daily — and it is still no more than a horse."

⋖§ Is It Worth Bothering Hashem?

A merchant, who earned his living by buying lumber, lashing it into rafts and floating the rafts down the river to Danzig for sale, approached R' Mordechai of Lechovich and told him his woes.

"Rebbe," he said, "I sent my rafts down the river, and suffered a great loss."

"My son," said R' Mordechai, "We are told that when a person is in distress, the *Shechinah* itself says, 'My head ails Me, My arm ails Me' (*Sanhedrin* 46). Hashem, as it were, suffers when an individual suffers. Let me ask you then: Is it worth making the *Shechinah* suffer over a few bits of wood?"

~§ You Have to Know What to Ask For

A chasid once came to R' Menachem Mendel of Kotzk to ask him for a blessing so that he would earn a decent living.

"Pray to Hashem," said R' Menachem Mendel," "and He will give you what you ask."

"Rebbe," said the chasid, "I don't know how to pray."

"Well then," said R' Menachem Mendel, "the first thing you should ask for, is the ability to pray."

~§ Tainted

When R' Menachem Mendel of Kotzk studied under R' Bunim of Pshischa, he was extremely poor, and was dressed in rags and tatters.

Once Tamar'l, a wealthy woman who supported many great Rabbis, came to Pshischa. R' Feivel of Gritza told R' Mendel, "You see how you are dressed. Why don't you appear before Tamar'l so that she will give you money for new clothes?"

R' Mendel looked at him with utter scorn. "What? Money? Feh!" he said.

When R' Feivel told the story in later years, he would add, "For months after that incident, whenever I saw money, I would feel nauseous and ready to throw up."

~§ An Obvious Deduction

A very wealthy chasid came to visit R' Menachem Mendel of Kotzk. The next day, the man was told that his warehouses had caught fire, and that everything he owned was going up in flames. The chasid fainted, and immediately after he was revived he fainted again.

When R' Menachem Mendel saw him, he said, "You have nothing to worry about. Your warehouses were not burned. Send a telegram to your home and ask them to tell you what happened."

The man did as advised. A few hours later, he received a telegram from his home that the fire had been in his neighbor's warehouse, while his warehouses had been spared.

All the chasidim were overwhelmed. A miracle! The Rebbe could tell what was happening in another town!

"No!" said R' Menachem Mendel. "There was no miracle or any ability on my part to tell what occurs elsewhere. Hashem does not submit a man to a test unless he can withstand that test. When I saw the man had almost died of the shock, I knew that the fire had not consumed his goods."

✥ A Tzaddik in Peltz

R' Menachem Mendel of Kotzk used the Yiddish expression, "a *tzaddik in peltz*" — a *tzaddik* in a fur coat — to refer to a person who did not help others. He explained this as follows:

"If one sits in a cold house in the middle of the winter, there are two ways he can become warm. He can either light a fire or put on a heavy fur coat. One who lights a fire thinks about others as well, because when a fire is burning it gives heat to everyone in its vicinity. On the other hand, one who puts on a fur coat only worries about himself. As far as he is concerned, everyone else can freeze, provided he feels warm."

✥ What Is Preferable?

Once a chasid came to R' Yisrael of Ruzhin and said, "Rebbe, I am in great pain, and my pain makes it impossible for me to pray or study Torah."

"How do you know," said R' Yisrael, "that Hashem prefers your prayer and study over your acceptance of pain?"

✥ Don't Get Involved

Sanz and Sadigora chasidim were opposed to each other. There were many others who became involved in this dispute, favoring one side or the other.

The chasidim of R' Meir'l of Dzhikov also wished to take sides, but their Rebbe forbade them to. "Let me tell you a story," said R' Meir'l to his chasidim:

The lion, king of the beasts, could not find any food for three days and three nights. Because he had not eaten for so long, he developed bad breath. As he saw he was about to die, he let out a roar and summoned his servants. Immediately, a horse ran over. "I want you to smell my breath," said the lion, "and tell me if there is a bad odor from my mouth."

The horse did as told, and said, "You are right, your majesty. There is a bad odor."

"You have rebelled against me," exclaimed the lion, "and you are sentenced to death."

The lion immediately killed the horse and ate him.

Three days later, the lion was again starving. He again let out a roar, and this time a wolf appeared.

"I want you to smell my breath," said the lion, "and tell me if there is a bad odor from my mouth."

The wolf said to himself: "I will be cleverer than the horse." He smelled the lion's breath, and said, "Your majesty, there is no bad odor."

"You are a liar," said the lion, "and to lie is to rebel against me. You are sentenced to death."

The lion thereupon killed the wolf and ate him.

Three days later, the lion was again famished, so he let out a roar. This time, a fox came running. "I want you to smell my breath," said the lion, "and tell me if there is a bad odor from my mouth."

"Your majesty," replied the fox, "I have a cold and am unable to smell anything."

"I want you all to have colds and not smell anything," concluded R' Meir'l.

◂§ Kissing the One Who Humiliated Him

R' Bunim of Pshischa once came to his Rebbe, R' Yaakov Yitzchak, the *Yehudi HaKadosh*, in a state of depression.

"Bunim," the Rebbe asked, "why are you so depressed?"

"Someone humiliated me today," said R' Bunim.

"Who had the gall to do that?" asked R' Yaakov Yitzchak.

R' Bunim remained silent.

R' Yaakov Yitzchak, though, was insistent. "Who was it, and what did you do?"

"I got up," replied R' Bunim, "and kissed him."

"Really?" said the *Yehudi* in amazement.

"Today I studied the volume entitled *Shevet Musar*, and it filled me with shame," said R' Bunim. "I realized that I had never in my life served Hashem the way one should. I became filled with remorse and humiliation. I therefore kissed the volume before putting it away."

✥ Go to the Specialist

Once a chasid who was ill came to R' Mordechai of Neschiz. The man had gone to many doctors, but none of them had cured him.

"Rebbe," groaned the man. "I have seen many doctors, but was not cured."

"Go," said R' Mordechai, "to the specialist of Hanipol, and you will soon be cured."

The man went to the village of Hanipol and asked, "Who is the specialist?"

"How can an isolated village such as ours have a specialist? We don't even have a doctor!" said the villagers.

The chasid came back to R' Mordechai and said, "Rebbe, I think you made a mistake. There isn't even a doctor in Hanipol."

"And what do the people of Hanipol do when they are sick?" asked R' Mordechai.

"They rely on Hashem."

"That is the specialist I sent you to," said R' Mordechai. "You, too, should rely on the One Who heals all flesh."

≈§ What's in a Name?

A woman once came to R' Meir of Premishlan and said, "Rebbe, my daughter has just given birth to a son, and we would like to name him Meir after you."

"You certainly may do so," said R' Meir, "but you should know that many thieves also have the same name."

≈§ Look at Yourself

A chasid once came to R' Yitzchak Meir, the son of R' Avraham Heshel of Apta. R' Yitzchak Meir greeted him, and the man stood staring.

"Why," asked R' Yitzchak Meir, "are you staring at me?"

"Rebbe," replied the man, "we are told that looking at a *tzaddik* (a righteous man) is a *segulah* for becoming God-fearing."

"We are also told," said R' Yitzchak Meir, "that all Jews are *tzaddikim*. Thus, you too are a *tzaddik*. If you look deeply into yourself, that too is a *segulah* for becoming God-fearing."

Chazzanim

⇜ Fighting One's Own Battles

A man came to R' Moshe Sofer, the *Chasam Sofer*, and spilled out his tale of woe.

"Rebbe, my whole life I led the prayers on the *Yamim Nora'im* without asking for any payment. Now, however, I've lost all my money and will have to ask for pay. Please do me a favor and put in a good word for me with the community leaders, and ask them to pay me."

R' Moshe promised to do so, but the man was still not reassured.

"Rebbe," he said, "I'm afraid that they'll refuse. Whenever I volunteered my services they praised me to the heavens. Now that I'm asking to be paid I'm afraid that they'll find fault with me."

"Listen to me," said R' Moshe. "You are a *chazan*, and you certainly know that there are prayers where the *chazan* and congregation pronounce alternate verses. I suggest that you say what you have to say; that you would like to be paid. Now the congregation may say that you aren't fit for the position. But why do *you* have to be the one who says what the congregation is supposed to say?"

◆§ Only One Thing Missing

R' Shabsai Kohen, the *Shach*, was a leader of the Jewish community of Vilna.

Once, the city needed to hire a *chazan* for the Great Synagogue. The *Shach* was very interested in having it hire R' Moshe Rivkes, author of *Be'er HaGolah*, because he was a great Torah scholar and was in need of a livelihood.

"Rebbe," argued the others, "R' Moshe does not have a good voice."

"We are told," said the *Shach*, "that for a man to serve as the *chazan*, he must have a family and no means of support; be one whose house is empty; whose youth was free of sin; who is acceptable to the people, who has a good voice, and who knows how to learn Torah (see *Ta'anis* 16a). Now, R' Moshe has all the attributes which our Sages mentioned that are necessary for a *chazan*, except for one. What is so terrible? Where can one find a *chazan* that has all the other attributes?"

Community Leadership

◆§ Too High a Price

The local noble seized R' Meir of Rothenburg and demanded an exorbitant ransom for his release. All the community heads gathered together to see what they could do, for R' Meir was the greatest Torah authority of his generation. When R' Meir heard of this, he ordered them not to raise the money, because the payment of so great a sum would invite further extortion in the future. R' Meir remained in captivity until the day of his death. Years later, a wealthy Jew ransomed the body, so that it was given a proper burial. The man had a single request: When he died, he wished to be buried next to R' Meir. His wish was granted.

Cutting out His Tongue

R' Shmuel Hanagid was once walking with the King of Spain, when a man in the crowd began cursing R' Shmuel. The king became extremely angry. "Have that man's tongue cut out," he told R' Shmuel.

R' Shmuel discovered that the man was a penniless poet. He thereupon sent him a generous gift, and from then on supported the man on an ongoing basis. The poet eventually became a friend and admirer of R' Shmuel.

Some time later, R' Shmuel was again walking with the king, when they passed the same poet. This time, he recited poems in honor of the king and R' Shmuel.

"Is this dog still barking?" said the king in amazement. "Didn't I order you to have his tongue cut out?"

"Your majesty," replied R' Shmuel, "I did exactly as you commanded me. I cut out his evil tongue and replaced it with a good one."

Reimbursement of Expenses

During the pogroms in Russia, many Jewish families fled to the big cities. Thousands of people sought refuge in Brody. In most cases they were destitute, having left everything they had behind. They were in terrible straits, and their cry of distress was heard by Jews throughout the world. Samuel Montagu, an extremely wealthy man, came all the way from London to assess the situation and to find a way for the refugees in Brody to move elsewhere. R' Shmuel Mohilever, too, came to Brody from Russia, in spite of the tremendous dangers involved.

As R' Shmuel was about to leave Brody, Samuel Montagu came to see him off. As they were about to part, Montagu gave R' Shmuel a fifty-pound note, but R' Shmuel refused to accept it.

"But you've spent so much of your own money coming here," Montagu told him, "and this will cover your expenses."

"And who," asked R' Shmuel, "is paying for the expenses you have incurred? The same God will pay me."

◄§ One's True Wealth

R' Shmuel Hanagid, one of the great Jewish leaders of Spain, was highly respected by the Spanish king. R' Shmuel was an exemplary man in every way: wise and learned, a philosopher and poet, and, above all, a man of truth, who was not interested in the accumulation of wealth. The king greatly appreciated R' Shmuel, and eventually appointed him as his minister of finance.

The other ministers were jealous of him. After all, why should a Jew be given such a lofty position? They therefore spread rumors that R' Shmuel was stealing money from the royal treasury. The king ignored these tales, because he knew R' Shmuel, and knew how honest he was. However, to prove R' Shmuel's innocence to the other ministers, he asked him to bring him a complete list of his assets.

R' Shmuel immediately did as told, and brought the king his accounting books. When the king examined it, though, he found that it only represented a tenth of R' Shmuel's means.

"Tell me," said the king angrily, "is that all you own? I myself gave you much more than this."

"My lord the king," answered R' Shmuel, "you ordered me to bring you a list of my assets. I did as you asked, and here it is. This is what I have spent on charity. These are my assets, because they cannot be taken away from me. All the rest of my possessions are not truly mine."

◄§ A Poor Memory

During R' Itzele Volozhiner's days, the Russian government, in an attempt to force the Jews to assimilate, decided to decree that they had to cut off their *peyos*, wear only short jackets (the standard-length jacket that is generally worn today), and send their children to secular schools. Before the decree was executed, the government summoned Rabbis from all over Russia to meet with the minister of education, Ovarov, so as to have them persuade their flocks to accept the new decree without argument. The chief spokesman for the Jews was R' Itzele, acknowledged as the greatest Torah scholar of his day, who was also on good terms with various government officials. One of those who was instrumental in arranging this conference was Dr. Lilienthal, a *maskil*, a man of secular learning, who served as the mediator between the government and the Jews.

Between sessions at the conference, Ovarov would sit and talk to R' Itzele. R' Itzele was dressed in the manner of Rabbis of that time, with a big *tallis katan* with long *tzitzis* over his shirt.

Once, Ovarov asked R' Itzele: "Why, honored Rabbi, do you wear such a large *tallis katan* with such long *tzitzis*? Can't a person be a religious Jew with a smaller garment and shorter *tzitzis*? Look at Dr. Lilienthal, who is also a religious man and a Rabbi. His *tzitzis* are not worn outside his shirt."

"Your excellency," R' Itzele answered, "the Torah gave us the commandment of *tzitzis* to remind us to observe all the commandments given to us by God. The Bible states this: 'You shall see it, and remember.' Now, not everyone is blessed with the same memory. Dr. Lilienthal is a learned man, with an excellent mind and a remarkable memory. All he needs is short *tzitzis*. I, however, am but a simple Rabbi, one of the old generation, and as one gets older, one's memory is affected. I need a large *tallis katan* and long *tzitzis* that can be seen easily, to remember God's commandments and observe them."

✺§ Another Encounter

At various meetings of Rabbis with government officials in St. Petersburg, R' Itzele was the major speaker for the Jews, and his speeches were highly admired by the Russian officials present. Once, Ovarov said to him, "You know, Rabbi, had you used your mind for secular studies rather than for studying Torah, you could have been a minister in the government."

"And you, your excellency," replied R' Itzele, "had you used your mind for studying Torah rather than for secular studies, could have been a Rabbi."

◂§ A People's Cry

Once, Maria Theresa, the queen of Austria, decreed that the Jews of Bohemia had to leave the state. The Jews then sent R' Zalman Karov, the *dayan* of Prague, to the minister of the interior, in order to ask that the decree be rescinded.

When R' Zalman came to the minister and began begging the minister to show compassion and repeal the law, he was in such anguish that he began wailing aloud.

"Why are you wailing?" asked the minister.

"It is not *I* that am wailing," said R' Zalman. "It is the cries of tens of thousands of Jews which come forth from my throat."

◂§ A True Saint

When R' Akiva Eiger was the Rabbi in Posen, he was very much involved in working within the community, seeking to do everything possible for the poor and the ill. Each day, after giving a discourse in his yeshivah, he would visit the sick people in the town, ask them how they were feeling, and, if they were poor, he would see to their food and medical needs.

When a cholera epidemic broke out in Posen, no house was untouched. Each sick person was a danger to others, for the disease is highly infectious. Each day the disease spread more widely, and people died in great numbers, but nothing stopped R' Akiva. Each day and night he continued to make his rounds, doing whatever he could to help, and persuade others to lend a helping hand. Indeed, it was through his efforts that many were saved from death.

When word of this reached the authorities, they decided to send R' Akiva Eiger a letter of appreciation for everything he had done. It was delivered by one of the government ministers.

When the minister arrived, R' Akiva Eiger greeted him with

utmost courtesy, and ushered him into his study. There the minister saw a small box with stamps in it, some whole and some torn in half.

"Rebbe," the minister said, "what is the meaning of these stamps?"

"Whenever I send a letter by a messenger rather than by mail," replied R' Akiva, "I buy a stamp and tear it up, so that the government should not lose money."

The minister was astounded. When he returned to his colleagues, he told them how saintly a man R' Akiva Eiger was.

◂§ Who Has More Troops?

The *maskilim* in Lvov once wished to set up a Rabbinical seminary in the city, and the local governor agreed to allow this.

R' Shalom of Belz came to the governor, and told him point-blank that under no circumstances would he permit such a thing.

"And what gives you the idea that you can do anything about it?" asked the governor angrily.

"Sir," answered R' Shalom, "You have 80 policemen who obey you and follow your orders. I, though, have 30,000 chasidim, who are willing to go through fire and water if I tell them to."

◂§ Who Were Their Teachers?

During the disturbances in Russia, forty young Jews were seized in Vilna for having been involved in revolutionary acts. The next day, the local governor summoned the leaders of the Jewish community, including R' Yekele Barit.

The governor angrily berated the Jews. "You Jews are nothing but a bunch of nihilists!" he said.

All the Jewish leaders were gripped by fear, and could not open their mouths. Finally, R' Yekele Barit got up and asked, "Do you think *we* are nihilists?"

"If not you, then certainly your children, whom you raised and educated," replied the governor.

"Your excellency," answered R' Yekele, "it is not we that raised these young men, but you. As long as we were the ones raising our children in the yeshivos, our children were not nihilists. It was when *you* decided to raise our children in *your* schools that they became heretics and revolutionaries."

⤳ *The Right Gate*

R' Yonasan of Prague was a good friend of the king, and the king loved to talk to him and hear his wisdom.

The king once set out for war, but before doing so, he said to R' Yonasan: "I know that you are very wise. Could you tell me through which of the two gates of the city I will return?"

"Your majesty," said R' Yonasan, "I can't tell you now, because whatever I tell you, you will do the opposite, and I will have lied. Let me give you a counterproposal. I will write my answer on a piece of paper and fold it up. Both you and I will put our seals on the folded paper. When you return, you will then order the seals to be broken and the paper to be read."

"Granted," said the king.

When the king returned from the war and came to the city's gates, he thought to himself: "I will trick the Rabbi, and will not enter through either gate." Instead, he ordered that the wall be breached and a new gate constructed, and it was through this new gate that he entered the city.

The king came to his palace, and summoned R' Yonasan, and in front of all the court nobles he ordered the seal to be broken and the contents of the paper to be read aloud. On the paper was written a quote from the *Gemara*: "A king may breach a wall to make a path for himself" (*Bava Basra* 100b).

⤳ *What Counts*

R' Shmuel Fraind, the Rabbi of Prague, once appeared before the city governor and complained about the city councilors whose regulations were aimed at harming the Jews.

"Rebbe," asked the governor, "why do you think that your head is greater than the ten heads of the city councilors?"

"Your excellency," replied R' Shmuel, "if everything depended on numbers, why did you mention ten *heads* rather than twenty *feet*?"

⋙ Clean Hands

When R' Yehoshua Tzeitels lived in Shklov, he was on close terms with the governor, a man known far and wide for accepting bribes.

Once, R' Yehoshua was at home, writing his *chiddushim*, when messengers came from the governor and ordered him to appear at his residence immediately. They were in such a rush that they did not give him time to wash his hands, and his fingers were still stained from the ink he had been using.

R' Yehoshua came to the governor and extended his hand. The governor, noticing the ink-stained fingers, was furious. "Your hands are filthy!" he said.

R' Yehoshua held his hands with the palms upward, and replied, "Your excellency, *here* they are clean."

⋙ You've Seen All There Is to See

When R' Yoshe Ber of Brisk was the head of the yeshivah in Volozhin, he used to travel to Vilna for various meetings with Rabbis and public figures. His son, Chaim, was still a child, and like other children, begged, "Father, I want to go with you. I want to go to Vilna, the big city, and see what the world is like."

R' Yoshe Ber consented.

Along the way they passed the village of Ivnitz and stopped there. The leaders of the community came to R' Yoshe Ber with a request. It seemed that that day there was to be a public meeting of the community. Would he agree to attend? R' Yoshe Ber agreed.

As R' Yoshe Ber, accompanied by his son Chaim, entered

the hall, they were met by a tremendous din. There were shouts and counter-shouts. The more boorish came to the fore to press their points. In the end it was the more forceful group which won.

After the meeting, R' Yoshe Ber said to his son, "Chaim, you can go back to Volozhin and I will travel on to Vilna."

"But why, Father?" wondered the young Chaim. "You told me you'd take me to Vilna."

"Yes, I did," said R' Yoshe Ber. "You wanted to see what the world was like, and you've already had your wish granted. What you saw in Ivnitz is what you'll find in Vilna and in the rest of the world. The boors are the ones who press forward and those who are the more forceful are the ones who win."

◆§ Putting Vilna to Shame

When R' Menachem Krakowski was the Rav of Vilna, the leaders of the community held a meeting to decide on salaries. Their decision was to increase the salaries of all the lesser Rabbinic court judges, but not of the major ones.

When he was asked why, R' Menachem explained the action. "The leaders were perfectly right," he said. "We're afraid that the minor judges might be enticed away from Vilna, and then we'll find that, because they're not top caliber, they've given Vilna a bad name. The major court judges, on the other hand, will never give Vilna a bad name if they leave here, and therefore, we do not have to raise their salaries."

◆§ A Raise in Salary

When R' Shmuel Mohilewer was the Rav of Bialystok, his income was never sufficient, because he spent a tremendous amount of money on charity and on his work for *Eretz Yisrael*.

The leaders of the community once assembled and decided to offer R' Shmuel a salary raise. When they told him their decision, he only asked one question: "And the *dayanim* — the judges of the religious court?"

"No, Rabbi," they told him, "we just don't have enough in the treasury."

"If that is the case," said R' Shmuel, "I don't want any addition to my salary."

⊷§ An Old Regulation

The Vilna Gaon had an agreement with the leaders of the Vilna community that he was not to be summoned from his learning unless there was a discussion about a new regulation.

The leaders of the community once wished to pass a regulation that would only allow the poor of Vilna to beg in the city, and would exclude the poor of other areas from doing so. The leaders thus convened a meeting and invited the Gaon.

After the Gaon had heard the proposed regulation, he told the leaders, "Didn't I say that I was only to be called when you are discussing a new regulation?"

"Yes, Rebbe," they replied, "this is a new regulation."

"Nothing of the sort," said the Gaon. "It's an old regulation passed by the Council of Four Lands." (The Council of Four Lands was a quasi-governmental organization which controlled the major aspects of Jewish life in Poland and Lithuania, until late in the 18th century.)

"The Council of Four Lands, Rabbi?" they asked. "We've gone through all the minutes of the Council and find no mention of such a regulation."

"You misunderstood me," said the Gaon. "I was referring to the four lands of Sodom, Gomorrah, Admah and Tzevoim. They too enacted regulations forbidding the poor to beg."

⊷§ Price Gouging

When R' Yechezkel Faivel was the Rabbi of Vilna, the fishermen in town got together and decided to raise the price of fish. Most of the residents were unable to afford fish for *Shabbos*. R' Yechezkel Faivel summoned the fishermen and warned them that unless they lowered the price, he would forbid anyone to buy fish. The fishermen ignored his warnings. R' Yechezkel Faivel then sent a note to be read in all the synagogues in the city: No Jew is permitted to use fish, either for *Shabbos* or for the rest of the week.

A week passed, and another. Not a single Jew broke the Rabbi's ban. The fishermen lost a sizable amount of money.

Finally, the fishermen gave in and requested a meeting with R' Yechezkel Faivel, and they begged and pleaded that he revoke his ruling. R' Yechezkel Faivel did not give in.

As they left downcast, R' Yechezkel Faivel said, "I want you to know that the prohibition against using fish applies to you as well. You and your families may not eat fish either."

⊸§ A Forceful Decision

Yudel Apatov was one of the richest Jews in Vilna and a community leader. He was an ignorant man who had attained great wealth, and had no compunctions about whom he might hurt in order to further his own fortune. He was widely feared by the Jews, because he had the ear of the local district governor. At Yudel's command, the police were quite willing to give a beating to anyone whom he named. He himself was also quite capable of thrashing anyone who stood in his way.

Once Apatov decided that he wanted to receive the liquor concession for the district, a concession which was held by the community council, with the profits going to the communal fund. He thereupon paid the required deposit to register his right to bid.

When this became known, there was a great tumult in the community. He was trying to deprive the community of income. However, once Apatov had decided he wanted something, who was to stop him?

On the day that the bids were to be accepted, the Rav of the city called together all the community leaders for a meeting, including, of course, Apatov. At the meeting, they tried to persuade Apatov to withdraw his bid, but he stood by his own view; he was allowed to do what he wanted, he said, and no one would stop him. During the entire time, he kept looking at his watch, to be sure he arrived in time to bid for the concession. Finally, he got up to leave, and made his way to the door, only to find it locked.

"Who," he asked, "locked the door?"

"I, Reb Yudel," answered the Rav. "I have the key, and the door will not be unlocked until the time for the bidding has passed."

Apatov clenched his teeth, but there was nothing he could do. He didn't say a word, but sat down quietly. He lost his deposit, and did not receive the concession.

◄§ Do It Yourself!

The community leaders did not like the shamash of R' Yoshe Ber's beis din. They held a meeting and voted to discharge him. They then asked the Rabbi to tell the shamash of their decision. R' Yoshe Ber, though, refused to do so.

"Why don't you want to tell him, Rebbe?" they asked. "After all, you are the head of the beis din, and he is your shamash."

"You all know the story of Avraham's sacrifice of Yitzchak," said R' Yoshe Ber. "We are told that when Hashem asked Avraham to sacrifice his son, He Himself told Avraham to do so, and did not send an emissary in His place. Thus, the Torah says, 'Please take your son, your only one.' On the other hand, when Hashem told Avraham not to slaughter Yitzchak, He sent an angel to carry out that task, as it states, 'An angel called to Avraham.' This seems strange. Why didn't Hashem tell Avraham through a messenger to sacrifice his son? The reason why He didn't do so was that He knew that each angel would say, 'If You want to get rid of a Jew, do it Yourself.'"

◄§ Limiting the Rabbi's Speech

When R' Menasheh of Iliya was the Rabbi of Smargon, the leaders of the community would kidnap Jewish children and hand them over to the Czarist authorities for service in the army, in order to meet the quota that the authorities had placed on the town. R' Menasheh convened the entire community and castigated the leaders publicly for their conduct. He finally exclaimed, "One who can kidnap a Jewish child and hand him over to the authorities is not worthy of being called a Jew."

After his speech, the community leaders went to R' Menasheh's study and told him, "Rebbe, you have no right to discuss such topics in public."

"If that is so," said R' Menasheh, "I cannot be your Rav." And on the spot he resigned.

◆§ Don't Threaten Me

R' Yossele, the Rav of Tarnapol (author of *Minchas Chinuch*), once had a disagreement with the community leaders. They implied that he had better accept their view or be forced out of his position.

"Are you trying to threaten me?" said R' Yossele. "I can do without you. I can always find a job which will furnish me with enough potatoes to exist."

◆§ Not to Stand by Idly

R' Elya of Lida was visiting Horodno when he heard that a number of young boys who had been kidnapped to serve in the Russian army were being held in the community offices, before being sent to Siberia. R' Elya took a spade in his hand, went to the synagogue square, and cried out aloud, "Jews! Why are you silent? Let us go and rescue our brothers!"

The people saw R' Elya with a spade in his hand. Each picked up some type of implement that could be used as a weapon — an ax, an iron bar, and the like. They besieged the community hall and then smashed down the doors and rescued all the children.

Immediately afterwards, R' Elya had all the Jews gather in the synagogue, and explained to them the seriousness of the situation, making them swear that they would do everything in their power to prevent future kidnapings.

⊷§ Sending Away the Mother

When R' Yekele of Boisk was the Rav in Zhagar, the community leaders would kidnap Jewish children and hand them over to the authorities.

Once, on a *Shabbos* morning, a woman pushed her way into the men's section and cried out bitterly, "Fellow Jews! They took my only son!"

Immediately, the community head got up and cried out to the *shamash*, "Why are you just standing there? Throw her out!" And the *shamash* followed his orders.

R' Yekele went up to the *aron kodesh*, took a scroll, and burst into tears. "Our Torah tells us," he said, 'You shall send forth the mother and take the young for yourself' (*Devarim* 22:7). I am already eighty years old, and I have never yet seen anyone perform this commandment. Now the community head has performed it: He has sent away the mother and taken her son for himself. May Hashem give him the reward he deserves for his actions."

Everyone ran from the synagogue. They tore down the doors of the building where the children were being kept, and released all who had been imprisoned there.

Books and Authors

In One Small Book

When R' Shneur Zalman of Liadi published his *Tanya*, it was hailed by all the chasidic leaders of the generation for its profundity.

When the book reached R' Levi Yitzchak of Berdichev, he studied it from beginning to end, and said, "What a great work by R' Shneur Zalman. He has managed to enclose Hashem, Who is infinite, in the pages of this one small book."

A Shared Road

R' Yoshe Ber was told, "Rebbe, I was surprised to see that in your *Beis HaLevi* there are ideas which appear in other works as well."

"That is not surprising," answered R' Yoshe Ber. "If a person goes on the paved highway, he will find others using that same road as well. On the other hand, if a person takes a path which is faulty and out of the way, he will not find anyone else on it."

≈§ Books Are Like Children

The Netziv of Volozhin would say: "Books are like children. Just as it is more difficult to let a child out of one's home than it is to raise the child, it is harder to publish a book than to write it."

≈§ No Grounds for Being Upset

When R' Yaakov Yosef published his Toldos Yaakov Yosef, he traveled from town to town selling it. As the book was very expensive, he found few clients.

He arrived in Berdichev, took a place in the inn, and waited for customers, but none came. He was upset.

R' Ze'ev of Zhitomir was in Berdichev at the time, and visited him. He found R' Yaakov Yosef troubled.

"What is it that ails you?" he asked.

"I came here," said R' Yaakov Yosef, "to sell my book, which gives the Torah of the Baal Shem Tov, and no one is interested in buying it."

"Hashem Himself tried to 'sell' His Torah to the different nations of the world," said R' Ze'ev, "and they were not interested." (The Sages tell us that before Hashem offered the Torah to Israel He offered it to all the other nations, and they turned it down.)

≈§ A Powerful Work

When R' Baruch of Leipnik, the author of Baruch Ta'am, received a copy of the Noda BiYehudah, he was so taken by the work that he disappeared from his home for a day and a night, and did not eat, drink or sleep. His family had no idea where he had disappeared to.

The next morning he came down from the attic where he had been and told his family the reason for his disappearance.

~§ Dipping the Pen

R' Issac'l of Zidichov said: "When I write my book, I dip my pen once in ink and once in the blood of my heart."

~§ Poverty Is Good for an Author

R' Menachem Mendel of Lubavich would say, "Poverty is good for an author." When asked to explain his remark, he would go on: "I mean that literally. If an author cannot afford to print his book, he must leave it unprinted. Meanwhile, he checks and rechecks what he wrote, correcting this point and that one. However, an author who is wealthy can publish a book which has not been properly checked."

~§ Only for Myself

The *Chazon Ish* was asked, "Rebbe, why are your works written in such difficult language, which can be understood only by one well versed in Torah?"

"The truth is," answered the *Chazon Ish*, "that I only printed my works for myself. Even I myself find my handwriting difficult to read, and I therefore decided to print my books. However, as one cannot print only a single copy, I printed a number of additional copies."

~§ Why Not to Publish

R' Zerach Diskin of Horodno, the brother of R' Yehoshua Leib of Brisk, was a great Torah scholar, but his works were never published. All he left behind were notes written in the margins of his *sefarim*.

"Rebbe," he was asked, "why don't you publish your Torah thoughts in a book?"

"It is enough," answered R' Zerach, "that I know how ignorant I am. Do you want the whole world to know that too?"

∽§ Another Reason Not to Publish

R' Azriel Hildesheimer was always involved in communal affairs, and never had the time nor the desire to publish his works.

"Rebbe, why don't you act like the other Rabbis, and publish your thoughts in a book?" he was asked

"Those ideas worth publishing have already been published by others before me," answered R' Azriel. "As to those that are not worthy of being published, I do not want them quoted in my name."

∽§ And Another Reason

R' Heshel, the greatest Torah scholar of his generation, left no manuscripts or books. There was a story behind this.

Once, R' Heshel became engrossed in a topic. He looked at the explanation of the *Maharsha* and found what the latter had written seemed to be wrong. "Is this he who is called the one who lights up one's eyes in *halachah*?" he exclaimed.

Some time later, R' Heshel met a young man and they began "talking in learning." This particular *Maharsha* came up. R' Heshel showed the young man the text and his problems with it.

"Rebbe," said the young man humbly, "could it be that what the *Maharsha* meant was as follows?" and here he gave a detailed explanation.

R' Heshel's eyes lit up and he said, "The *Maharsha* is true and his Torah is true."

At that instant R' Heshel decided never to publish any work, because he himself had erred in understanding the written word.

✑ Why the Quality Has Deteriorated

R' Chaim of Lukishok, the author of the *Mekor Chaim*, would say: "Why is it that the earlier generations had so large a number of great Torah scholars but so few books, while the later generations have far fewer giants of Torah but many more books?

"In the past, there were very few printers, and these were all located in large cities. If an author wished to publish his book, he would have to make his way to the big city. Along the way, at every stop, he would show his work to the local Rabbi who would go over it and show him the flaws. He would then take out some sections and rewrite others. By the time he got to the printer, his book would have undergone numerous revisions. Nowadays, there are printers in every city, and a Torah scholar who wishes to publish a work stays at home and has the local printer put out whatever he has written down."

✑ More Care Is Needed

When R' Avraham Danzig wrote his *Chayei Adam*, he made sure to keep the language as simple and clear as possible, so that everyone might be able to use it, even the unlearned.

Once, he was traveling and spent a *Shabbos* at an inn in a little village, where the innkeeper had a reputation of being God-fearing. On *Shabbos*, R' Avraham saw the innkeeper do something which is forbidden on *Shabbos* by Torah law. He was astounded. "That is desecration of *Shabbos*!" he exclaimed.

"Don't worry, sir," the innkeeper replied, "I, too, know the law. I have the *Chayei Adam*, and it states that what I did is permitted." He brought the *Chayei Adam* and showed it to the visitor.

R' Avraham explained his mistake, and showed him what he had misunderstood, but the incident left him troubled.

"I am afraid that I have not been careful enough in my choice of words and did not write my book in as simple a form as is possible," he said.

◄§ Having Enough Strength

R' Avraham Yitzchak Kook, who wrote a large number of works, would say, "It is not that I have the strength to write, but I don't have the strength not to write."

◄§ It's His Stubbornness that Counts

R' Chaim Ozer Grodzenski of Vilna tried very hard not to give *haskamos* (approbations) to *sefarim*.

Once an author came to him and asked for a *haskamah*. R' Chaim Ozer turned him down.

"But, Rebbe," the man protested, "I saw that you did give a *haskamah* to this-and-this work."

"You are wrong," said R' Chaim Ozer. "That was not a *haskamah* to his work, but to his stubbornness."

◄§ Leaving out the Unnecessary

R' Avraham Yeshayahu Karelitz, the *Chazon Ish*, printed all his works anonymously. When he was asked why, he replied, "I find it very difficult to write. Thus, I only write those things which are essential, but leave out that which is not essential. My name is not essential."

Out of
the Mouths
of Babes

ᵈᵇ Where the Family Tree Begins

When R' Dov Ber of Mezritch was eight years old, there was a fire in his town, in which his home was consumed. His mother was inconsolable.

"Why are you crying so much?" asked the child. "Should one cry because a house burns down?"

"No, my son," she replied, "I am not crying for the house, but for the document bearing our family tree which was in it, and which went back to R' Yochanan HaSandlar."

"Don't worry, mother," replied the child. "I will be the start of a new family tree."

ᵈᵇ Better That the Marriage Not Take Place

When R' Akiva Eiger was a young child, he had a reputation as an *ilui*, a genius. He was so advanced at an early age, that it was often he who taught his teachers, rather than they who taught him.

When he was fifteen, various marriage proposals were made. R' Yitzchak of Lissa, a great Torah scholar and a very wealthy man, was interested in having his daughter marry the young genius. The two sides agreed to meet in a village near Lissa, where they would iron out the details of the proposed wedding.

R' Yaakov came from Lissa along with two other scholars, in order to test the young man's knowledge. These two discussed various topics, asking questions and answering them, all the while displaying their knowledge. R' Akiva, though, sat silent, not uttering a word. The three men from Lissa were amazed. Was this the young man with the reputation of a genius?

Finally, his father called R' Akiva into another room and asked, "Akiva, why didn't you open your mouth and say something? Didn't you understand what they were discussing?"

"Father," R' Akiva told him, "I am only able to tell you the truth. The one who asked the question overlooked the fact that the same question appears in this tractate on this-and-this page, whereas the other one completely misunderstood the entire topic. I did not want to speak, so as not to correct them. It is better for me to forgo the wedding rather than humiliate a fellow Jew."

◄§ Always Look Upward

When R' Menachem Mendel of Lubavich, the *Tzemach Tzedek*, was a young child, his grandfather, the *Baal HaTanya*, saw him and his little friends playing a game. They had placed a plank against a wall, so that it sloped upward. The object of the game was to see who could get to the top of the plank without falling down. All the other boys managed, at best, to get half way before falling down, while Mendel got all the way to the top.

Later, his grandfather asked, "Mendel, how is it that you succeeded where the others failed?"

"It was easy," replied the child. "The others kept looking down as they climbed the plank. As soon as they realized how high they were, they became dizzy and fell down. I, however, looked only upward to the heavens. I saw how low I was, and therefore kept going higher and higher until I reached the top."

◦§ A Counter-Offer

When R' Yitzchak Meir of Gur was a young child, a man once said, "Yitzchak Meir, I will give you a gold coin if you can tell me where Hashem is."

"And I," said R' Yitzchak Meir, "will give you two gold coins if you can tell me where He is not."

◦§ A Second Test

R' Avremele of Sochachew was known as a genius, and even as a youngster received many offers of marriage.

When he was eleven years old, R' Chaim of Sanz wished to have him marry his daughter. R' Avremele's father, R' Nachum Ze'ev of Biala, brought him to R' Chaim in order to have R' Chaim test him. R' Chaim spoke to him at length, and found him a true Torah scholar — a new vessel holding old wine.

Before the parents got down to writing the *Tena'im* (the contract indicating a commitment to go through with the marriage at a later date), R' Chaim wished to test Avremele a second time, but Avremele refused.

"If you insist that I need to be tested again," he said, "then you, too, must be tested."

"Avremele," his father said angrily, "what are you talking about?"

Avremele explained. "The prospective father-in-law tests the prospective son-in-law because our Sages tell us that one should not marry his daughter off to an unlearned man," he said. "But, since our Sages also tell us that one should not marry the daughter of an unlearned man, the prospective son-in-law should really test the prospective father-in-law. We son-in-law should really test the prospective father-in-law. We dispense with this test, and rely on the test that the prospective father-in-law was given before he married. If, however, R' Chaim feels that one test is not enough for me, then he too must be tested a second time."

◆§ *The Long Road Is Often the Shortest*

When R' Chaim of Brisk was a small child, his father, R' Yoshe Ber, sent him to summon the head of the community. The child entered the community head's home, approached the man, and said, "The Rav of Slutzk would like you to come and see him now."

"Chaim'ke," asked the man, "why did you refer to him as the Rav of Slutzk? Wouldn't it have been simpler to say 'my father'?"

"Had I referred to him as 'my father,' you would have asked who my father is, and I would have replied, 'The Rav of Slutzk,' " said Chaim. "I therefore bypassed that question and referred to him as 'the Rav of Slutzk.' "

◆§ *Loving One's Neighbor as Oneself*

When the Gaon of Vilna was a very young child, he went out to play with his little friends. They were playing on a seesaw and he left and came home.

"Eliyahu," his father asked him, "why didn't you play with your friends?"

"Father," he replied, "it states in the Torah, 'You shall love your neighbor as yourself.' How can I go up on the seesaw when it means I cause my friend to go down?"

Aphorisms

R' Pinchas of Koretz would say:
For thirteen years I trained my tongue not to tell lies and for
the next thirteen years I trained it to tell the truth.

❀ ❀ ❀

It is better for a person to die than to lie.
I have conquered anger and now have it in my pocket, where
I can take it out whenever I need it.

❀ ❀ ❀

R' Aaron of Karlin would say:
I wish I was able to love the righteous of Israel the way
Hashem loves its sinners.

❀ ❀ ❀

R' Yaakov Yitzchak, the *Chozeh* of Lublin, would say:
I prefer the wicked man who knows he is wicked to the righteous man who knows that he is righteous.
An insincere peace is better than a sincere quarrel.

❁ ❁ ❁

R' Yitzchak of Worka would say:
I am never more alone than when I am with other people.

❁ ❁ ❁

R' Mendel of Kotzk would say:
Do you know where Hashem's place is?
Hashem is wherever you let Him in.
Every human trait needs to be expressed deliberately, except for modesty. If one is deliberately modest, that is not modesty.
The advantage of taking a new path is that it has not been ruined by others.
There isn't a thing in the world for which one cannot find an imitation or copy. The only exception to this is the truth, because there is no such a thing as an imitation of the truth.
To say "I shall" shows a bad trait. To say "I wish" shows vacillation. To say "I am" shows a good trait.

❁ ❁ ❁

R' Yitzchak Meir of Gur would say:
There are only two who know whether a man is truly God-fearing: Hashem and the man's wife.
The weaker the generation, the greater the Torah leaders it needs. To what may this be compared? To sickness. The sicker the patient, the greater the doctor he requires.

❁ ❁ ❁

R' Noah of Lechovich would say:
One *cannot* fool Hashem, and one *may not* fool his fellow man.

❁ ❁ ❁

R' Moshe of Kobrin opposed those who would mortify themselves by fasting often. He would say:
It is better for a person to refrain from lying than to refrain from eating.

❧ ❧ ❧

R' Dov Ber, the *Maggid* of Mezritch, would say:
Sometimes a man must search through the ashes in order to find a single spark.

❧ ❧ ❧

R' Nachman of Breslov would say:
Tears open the gates (of Heaven); song breaks down its walls.

❧ ❧ ❧

R' Moshe Leib of Sassov, who was against additional fasts besides those decreed by the Sages, would say:
It is better for a person to have a *ta'anis* (fast) from speech (where one deliberately refrains from talking for a period of time) than to have a *ta'anis* from food and drink.
Any man who does not have some time free for himself is not a man.

❧ ❧ ❧

R' Moshele of Rozbadov would say:
Whoever is not afraid of thunder and lightning is either completely righteous or else completely evil.

❧ ❧ ❧

R' Yechiel Michel, author of the *Aruch HaShulchan*, would say:
The best philosophy text is *Bava Kama*.

❧ ❧ ❧

R' Aaron of Karlin would say:

Everything can be taken away from me, except for God in my heart.

We are commanded to give every person the benefit of the doubt — and, all the more so, must we give God that same benefit.

❧ ❧ ❧

R' Simchah Bunim of Pshischa would say:
Throughout my entire life I have been learning how to die.

No Jew, no matter how flippant, really denies the existence of God. As soon as he feels really sick, he cries out, *"Shema!"*

❧ ❧ ❧

R' Baruch of Mezhibozh would say:
Some people are afraid of swallowing an ant, but are not afraid of swallowing a man alive.

❧ ❧ ❧

R' Naftali of Ropshitz would say:
By the letter of the law, one is not permitted to cheat another. Going beyond the letter of the law, one may not cheat himself.

❧ ❧ ❧

R' Asher of Stolin would say:
Every man takes pity upon himself. The time has come for us to take pity on God.

Whoever becomes the head of any group must continue to maintain contact with those beneath him, because a head has need of feet.

❧ ❧ ❧

R' Chaim of Sanz would say:
One who lifts even his little finger without planning to do so is not a person.

❧ ❧ ❧

R' Yisrael of Salant would say:

Not everything that one thinks should be said, and not everything which is said should be written, and not everything which is written should be printed.

The easiest thing to do is to write; the hardest is to erase.

Not everyone who goes about bare-headed is a non-Jew, but a non-Jew goes about bare-headed.

Who fears Heaven? One who is worried about his own soul and his fellow's body.

❀ ❀ ❀

R' Yisrael, the *Maggid* of Kozhnitz, would say:

If all the Jews would make peace among themselves and link hands, the hands would reach all the way up to God's Throne of Glory.

❀ ❀ ❀

R' David of Lelov would say:

As long as I feel that I love my son more than another Jew, I have not attained the level of love of one's fellow Jew.

❀ ❀ ❀

R' Meir of Premishlan would say:

A human being was given two eyes so that he should see the goodness of his fellow with one eye and his own blemishes with the other.

❀ ❀ ❀

R' Levi Yitzchak of Berdichev would say:

Had the Torah not mentioned pride, I would never have believed that such a trait can exist. Man is but dust and ashes, and what can he be proud of?

❀ ❀ ❀

The *Chafetz Chaim* would say:

A common proverb says that every fool believes that he is wise, and I say that every wise man thinks he is a fool.

One who is haughty is not a sinner, but a fool.

❃ ❃ ❃

R' Elyakim Getzl of Bialystok would say:
One is forbidden to speak *about* a fellow Jew; it is a *mitzvah* to speak *to* a fellow Jew.

❃ ❃ ❃

R' Yisrael of Ruzhin would say:
One who criticizes another commits a sin, because at that time he is unable to criticize himself.

❃ ❃ ❃

R' Yitzchak Elchanan would say:
If there is something you wish to do tomorrow, see to it that it was done by yesterday.

❃ ❃ ❃

R' Nasan Zvi of Slobodka would say:
The Torah is not too small for the greatest of the great, nor too great for the smallest of the small.

❃ ❃ ❃

R' Chaim of Brisk would say:
The true *gaon* (Torah genius) is not the one who always offers good Torah explanations, but the one who never offers bad ones.

❃ ❃ ❃

R' Eliyahu of Vilna would say:
Had Hashem commanded us merely to study the Torah and not to know it, I would have spent my entire life studying one Mishnah.

❃ ❃ ❃

R' Yosef Shlomo of Kandia would say:
Before I teach others what I know, I must teach myself what I don't know.

Holy Days

Shabbos

❧ In Exile

R' Baruch of Medzhibozh lived a life of luxury, while his brother, R' Moshe Chaim Ephraim of Sudilkov, was poor and lived a life of want.

Once, R' Baruch came to visit his brother for *Shabbos*. R' Moshe Chaim Ephraim had his wife prepare a fine Sabbath for his brother, far above what he could afford.

After the Friday night services the host and his guest came home. Everything was set for *Shabbos*. Upon a tablecloth of coarse fabric, there were two small *challah* rolls, a bottle of raisin wine, a *kiddush* cup which was made of simple glass, and two small candles in earthenware candle holders.

After they had pronounced the *kiddush* and sat down to eat, R' Baruch asked his brother, "Ephraim, how can you stand living with this poverty?"

"Why?" asked his brother, "Do I lack for anything?"

"In my house," said R' Baruch, "I have a meal with good wine and the best meat, with a golden cup for *kiddush* and silver candlesticks."

"How did you acquire all those things?" asked his brother.

"What do you mean, 'how'?" asked R' Baruch. "I travel all over helping people to worship Hashem properly, and as a result they all give me presents."

"See the difference between us," said R' Ephraim. "Your gold and silver are in your house, while you yourself are in exile. I, however, find that my gold and silver are in exile, but I myself am at home."

⊷§ At One's Fingertips

Once, R' Zalmele, brother of R' Chaim of Volozhin, was at the home of one of the leading Rabbis of Vilna, when a man came with a question concerning someone whose life was in danger. Were they permitted to do certain tasks for the sick person even though it was *Shabbos*? The Rabbi was not sure, and took out a volume of the *Shulchan Aruch*.

As soon as he saw this, R' Zalmele called out, "It is permitted!"

Those who were present were astonished. It was against all the rules for a Rabbi to answer a question posed to another Rabbi.

After the man had left, R' Zalmele said, "I hope you did not take offense at my action, but it is essential that a Rav should have at his fingertips all the laws that deal with a person whose life is in danger, because we are talking about human life."

⊷§ Only the Best

R' Leib, brother of R' Meir of Premishlan, used to be very careful about preparing for *Shabbos* properly. On Fridays he would go out to the market and this is what he would do:

He would go to the flour merchant and say:
"Give Leib the best of flour for *Shabbos*."
Then he would go to the oil merchant and say:
"Give Leib the best of oils for *Shabbos*."
And so he would go from stall to stall to buy his *Shabbos* needs.

✣ Preparing for Shabbos

R' Meir of Premishlan did not eat fish from Wednesday to *Shabbos*, in order to be able to appreciate it properly on *Shabbos*.

✣ Who Will Buy Fruit?

Once, just as R' Chaim of Sanz was getting ready for *Shabbos*, the door opened and an elderly woman came in, carrying a basket of fruit. She was in great distress.

"Rebbe, I'm a poor old woman," she said, "and I barely make a living by selling fruit in the market. Today is Friday, and most of the day is gone, yet I haven't sold any fruit at all today. I don't have a penny for my *Shabbos* needs."

R' Chaim put on his *Shabbos* coat and told the woman, "Come with me." He went to the market, set down the basket of fruit, and started calling out, "Fruit for *Shabbos*! Brother Jews, fruit for *Shabbos*!"

Everyone came to see why the Rav was busy selling fruit, and within a few minutes the basket was sold.

R' Chaim gave the woman the money and told her, "This is all yours. Go and prepare for *Shabbos*."

✣ Much Greater Benefit

A Rabbi once spent *Shabbos* with R' Chaim of Sanz, and was amazed to see that he used an exquisite gold goblet for *kiddush*. He knew that R' Chaim was not a wealthy man, and was certainly not able to afford such an expensive cup.

As they were sitting at the table, he asked R' Chaim, "Rebbe, how is it that you have such a fine goblet?"

"A rich man," R' Chaim told him, "left me the goblet in his will, provided that I make *kiddush* in his memory."

Some time later the same Rabbi was at R' Chaim's for *Shabbos*, but this time he saw that the goblet was no longer there.

"Rebbe," he asked, "what happened to the beautiful goblet?"

"Well, a poor man was in serious financial trouble, and I gave it to him so that he could support himself," answered R' Chaim.

"But how could you do that?" he asked. "Didn't you promise to make *kiddush* in memory of the rich man?"

"I'm sure that the dead man would agree with what I did," said R' Chaim. "After all, he wished me to make *kiddush* in his memory so that the merit of the good deed would benefit his soul. I am sure that keeping a Jew alive will be of much greater benefit to his soul."

◆§ Looking for Workers

Every Friday morning, R' Leibele of Vilna, the son of R' Ber, would stand at his doorway. Whenever he would see anyone who seemed in distress because he did not have money for his *Shabbos* needs, R' Leibele would stop him and say, "Please help me with my work."

The whole morning the person would help R' Leibele. At noon R' Leibele would pay the "worker" well, and urge him to go out and prepare properly for *Shabbos*.

◆§ Only a Slight Change Is Necessary

One of the early freethinkers, who wished to poke fun at Jewish tradition, tauntingly asked R' Meir Leibush, the *Malbim*, "Rebbe, can you find a way in which I may smoke on *Shabbos*?"

"Certainly," said the *Malbim*, "just smoke in a different manner from the way you usually do."

"How?"

"Place the lit end in your mouth."

◄§ *Another Possibility*

A freethinker, out to provoke R' Elazar Moshe of Pinsk, asked the Rabbi a seemingly innocent question.

"Rebbe," he said, "is there any way that smoking is permitted on *Shabbos*?"

"Indeed there is," answered R' Elazar Moshe.

"And what is it?" asked the man.

"Have the action carried out by a non-Jew," replied R' Elazar Moshe with a smile.

◄§ *Teaching by Example*

One Friday night, R' Hillel, the son-in-law of R' Chaim of Volozhin, was seen striding through the market carrying a lantern, an action which is forbidden on *Shabbos*. Many were curious and followed him. He entered a house, stayed there some time, and came out without the lantern.

"Rebbe," they asked, "what happened?"

"Inside that house," explained R' Hillel, "is a man who is mortally ill, and since all the other members of the household are ignorant and refused to do anything for him which they thought might be a violation of *Shabbos*, I felt that I had to show them in practice that, when someone's life is in danger, it is a *mitzvah* to violate *Shabbos* for him."

◄§ *Compassion*

R' Nochumke of Horodno took pains to find a place for all the boys of his *yeshivah* to eat each day of the week, and especially so for *Shabbos* and Festivals.

One Friday night, as R' Nochumke was sitting at the table with his family, there was a knock at the door. A young boy came in, his eyes streaming with tears.

"What happened?" asked R' Nochumke.

"Rebbe," cried the young boy, "there is a huge dog standing near the house of the family where I am supposed to eat, and I'm afraid to go in."

R' Nochumke rose, took the youngster by the hand, and brought him to the home of his host.

While the boy was within, R' Nochumke waited outside.

After the young boy had finished his meal and had come out, R' Nochumke escorted him home. Only then did he return to his own *Shabbos* table.

⊷§ Build on What You Have

R' Yitzchak Elchanan would go for a walk through his town on *Shabbos* afternoons, accompanied by his *shamash*. As they were walking, they saw a man approaching them with a lit cigarette in his mouth. As soon as the man saw them, he hurriedly got rid of his cigarette and began to saunter along casually toward them. As he came abreast of the rabbi, he addressed him and said, "Good *Shabbos*, Rabbi."

"And to you too," said R' Yitzchak Elchanan with warmth.

After the man had passed, the *shamash* became furious and said, "A public sinner! How dare he? He deserves to be whipped!"

"Leave him be," said R' Yitzhak Elchanan. "We should do everything in our power to draw him closer to us. After all, he still has one tremendous attribute. He respects rabbis and is ashamed when meeting them. If we decided to alienate him from us, not only will he continue doing what he does now, but he will begin to deliberately flaunt all the laws."

⊷§ The Rabbi Who Defended Shabbos

When R' Elya Chaim was the Rav of Lodz, he made a point of defending the observance of *Shabbos*. He would say, "There will be no profaning of *Shabbos* in Lodz as long as I am its Rav."

And that was indeed the case. As long as he was the Rabbi in Lodz, not a single Jew opened his store on *Shabbos*.

Once, R' Elya Chaim heard that a man who lived on the outskirts of town kept his store open on *Shabbos*.

The next *Shabbos* morning, R' Elya Chaim sent word to his synagogue that they were not to wait for him. He walked to the store, and sat down outside it.

At nine o'clock the storekeeper came, keys in hand. There sat the Rabbi right opposite his front door. He waited. After all, the Rabbi was no doubt waiting to attend a *bris* or some other celebration. He would most likely leave soon.

An hour passed, and another, and then a third. The Rabbi continued to sit, and the store remained closed. Finally, the storekeeper realized what the Rabbi was doing. By this time, much of the day had already passed and the Rabbi hadn't eaten a thing. At last the storekeeper approached the Rabbi and said, "Rebbe, I give up. Go home and eat. I swear by my wife and children that from now on my store will remain closed on *Shabbos*."

◄§ Only a Display of Manhood

R' Meir Simchah of Dvinsk once went for a walk on *Shabbos* with his *shamash*. As they were walking, they passed a young man walking with a girl. The young man was flagrantly smoking a cigarette.

The *shamash* became very upset at this brazen act of defiance, but R' Meir Simchah was not.

"That young man is not an evil type or an apostate," said R' Meir Simchah. "He is only a pitiful young man who has been unsuccessful. He wants this young girl very much, but she shows little interest in him. He therefore has to show his manhood by smoking openly in the presence of the Rabbi."

◄§ A Fire on Shabbos!

R' Chaim Sonnenfeld was told on *Shabbos* that they were cooking in a particular house. Desecration of the *Shabbos* in

Jerusalem! He immediately ran to the house in question.

The people in the house quickly extinguished the fire when they saw R' Chaim coming. R' Chaim pushed open the door, and peered around. There was nothing to be seen.

"Rebbe," they said angrily, "that's no way to act! Barging in on people without knocking!"

"I'm sorry," said R' Chaim. "I was told that there was a fire here and I ran to save you. In such an emergency, one doesn't have time for the normal courtesies and niceties."

◄§ I Don't Smoke

R' Azriel Hildesheimer had to appear on *Shabbos* before Baron von Bismarck for some matter which was of concern to the Jewish community. Von Bismarck showed him great warmth and offered him a cigar. R' Azriel was a very heavy smoker, who had a cigarette between his lips almost continuously the other six days of the week.

"Thank you, your excellency," said R' Azriel, "but I don't smoke."

And from that time on until his death R' Azriel never smoked another cigarette.

◄§ Making Havdalah Immediately

R' Shlomo Kluger of Brody would always pray *ma'ariv* following the arrival of *Shabbos* as early as possible, and would make *havdalah* immediately with its departure.

"Rebbe," he was asked, "we know that the righteous extend *Shabbos* as long as possible. Why do you pray at the first possible moment when it enters, and usher it out as quickly as you can?"

"It is enough," responded R' Shlomo, "that we do not honor the *Shabbos* enough on *Shabbos* itself. Shall we then profane it before it arrives and after it has ended?"

◆§ The Shomer Shabbos Society

A man who was very active in community causes came to R' Chaim of Brisk and told him joyfully, "Rebbe, thanks to Hashem, we have been able to form a *Shomer Shabbos* society."

R' Chaim gave a great sigh. "Woe to us," he said, "that in our days the observing of *Shabbos* requires a society. Will we then live to see a '*Tefillin*-laying society'?"

◆§ Reciting Kiddush Aloud

R' Chaim'l of Zinkov would recite the *kiddush* on Friday night in a loud voice and with great emotion.

When he was once at a spa for his health on *Shabbos*, at which many non-believers were also staying, he recited the *kiddush* as always, loudly and with great intensity.

"Rebbe," some of his friends said to him, "you are not in your own home, and it is not polite to recite the *kiddush* so loudly."

"On the contrary," R' Chaim'l told them, "where those who deny the *Shabbos* are present, one must do everything possible to testify that the world was created by Hashem."

◆§ Do Not Lose Both Worlds

A man once came to R' Zvi Yaakov Oppenheim and asked him, "Rebbe, may I keep my business open on *Shabbos* and have a non-Jew run it?"

"It is forbidden," R' Zvi Yaakov told him.

"Rebbe," said the man, "why then does the rich man of the town employ non-Jews to work for him on *Shabbos*?"

"He is very wealthy and has this world. He has decided that he will do without the World to Come," said R' Zvi Yaakov. "You, however, are a poor man, and don't even have this world. Do you then want to lose the World to Come as well?"

⋑ The Malbim Cried

Each week, as *Shabbos* was about to end, the *Malbim* would lock himself in his room and burst into tears. This had a history.

When the *Malbim* was eighteen years old, he published his first work, *Artzos HaChaim*, which gained him a reputation throughout the world. He came to Pressburg and visited the *Chasam Sofer*, to ask for an approbation for his book. The *Chasam Sofer* began discussing Torah with him and was amazed. Here was a man, young in years, but with the understanding and knowledge in Torah of a venerable sage. He would not let him go, and spent hour after hour talking to him in learning.

On a *Shabbos* afternoon, when it was already becoming dark, the *Malbim* went to the synagogue. Those present were reciting *Tehillim*, as they waited for *ma'ariv*. Without realizing it, the *Malbim* sat down in the *Chasam Sofer's* chair and dozed off. When the *Chasam Sofer* entered the synagogue and saw that someone was sleeping in his chair, he sat down elsewhere. The *Malbim* woke, and realizing what had happened, he jumped up and ran over to apologize to the *Chasam Sofer*. The *Chasam Sofer* said to him, "You may stay in your place."

From that time on, the *Malbim* felt that he could no longer rise in learning, for he had been told to "stay in his place."

And that was why the *Malbim* would cry each week.

⋑ What a Marvelous Mitzvah

R' Shmuel Leib of Lenchna would say: "Come and see how great the *mitzvah* of *Shabbos* is. Every other *mitzvah* requires an action in order to observe it, while on *Shabbos* a Jew does not need to lift a finger to observe the *mitzvah*. Furthermore, the person does not leave the *mitzvah* for even a single instant until *Shabbos* is over."

⋑ The Value of One Shabbos

R' Baruch of Mezhibozh would say: "I am willing to give up ten Worlds to Come for one *Shabbos* in this world."

⋄§ A Conditional Observance

A Jewish farmer once came to R' Shalom of Belz to receive his blessing. R' Shalom asked, "Do you keep the Torah? Do you observe *Shabbos* properly?"

The farmer looked down at the ground and didn't answer. R' Shalom kept talking to him until he finally admitted that on *Shabbos* he would work in the fields, just as on weekdays. R' Shalom tried to show him the importance of *Shabbos* observance, and of the punishment of those who desecrated it. The farmer was deeply moved and said, "Rebbe, I undertake to repent and keep *Shabbos* properly throughout the year, except for the summer months. Then, there is a tremendous amount of work to be done, and it cannot be delayed for even a day."

"Let me tell you a story," R' Shalom told the farmer:

There was once a noble who made a big feast for the other nobles in the area. When they were all somewhat under the influence of alcohol, each of them began to tell about how marvelous his Jewish tax collector was.

The one who had made the feast then said, "My Jew is better than all the rest. Whatever I tell him to do he will do. I know, as I have tested him many times. Whatever I tell him, he does immediately."

"Even," asked one of the other nobles, "if you ask him to convert?"

"Yes," said the host, "even that."

He immediately summoned his Jewish tax collector. "Moshke," the noble asked him, "are you faithful to me?"

"Yes, your excellency," replied the Jew, "with all my heart and soul. I am willing to do whatever you order me to do."

"Well then," said the noble, "I want you to convert."

The Jew stood there stunned. He could think of no way out. The noble had ordered him and he had no choice. Finally, in a weak voice, he answered, "Yes.

The noble had him and his wife converted. Some time later, the noble summoned the new convert and said to him, "Moshke, from now on you have my permission to return to your own religion."

The man ran to tell the news to his wife: He had permission to return to Judaism.

"Woe is to us!" sighed the wife. "What will we do? It's almost *Pesach* and there is so much that a Jew has to do to prepare for the holiday. Please go and ask the noble not to allow us to return to Judaism until after *Pesach* is over."

The farmer understood the analogy.

◄§ Whom to Fear

A number of community leaders came to R' Avraham Shmuel Binyamin Sofer, the *Kesav Sofer*, and complained about the Reform Jews, some of whom had begun to observe Sunday rather than *Shabbos* as their holy day.

"My friends," the *Kesav Sofer* told them, "don't be afraid of those who deny *Shabbos*, but of those who accept *Shabbos* and desecrate it."

◄§ Missing Shalosh Se'udos

R' Yoshe Ber of Brisk was at an inn for *Shabbos*. When they were about to sit down to *shalosh se'udos*, they realized that they did not have the necessary two *challos*. The innkeeper left to see if he could borrow a *challah* from a neighbor.

"Rebbe," one of those present asked R' Yoshe Ber, "aren't we told that a person can fulfill the *mitzvah* of *shalosh se'udos* with Torah? Why don't you give us a morsel of Torah, and we will both study Torah and fulfill the requirement of *shalosh se'udos*."

"I am afraid," smiled R' Yoshe Ber, "that someone may disprove what I say. Then I will remain without the Torah and you without the *shalosh se'udos*."

Rosh Hashanah

◈§ Elul Is Elul

R' Israel Salanter would say: "Each person should consider the entire year like the month of *Elul* and *Elul*, of course, is *Elul*."

◈§ You Recite The Selichos on Our Behalf

R' Levi Yitzchak of Berdichev was late for *Selichos*. They waited and waited. Finally, he arrived, stood before the Ark and said, "Lord of the universe! I am a mortal, born of woman, an old man who is no longer able to arise before dawn to say all the *Selichos*. But You are eternal, You are mighty, You do not become old, You do not sleep. The *Selichos* that You recite are short. They consist of one word: *Salachti* — 'I have forgiven.' Please recite Your *Selichos* and tell us, 'I have forgiven.' "

ও§ The Best Intentions

R' Levi Yitzchak of Berdichev was looking for a *baal tekiyah* — someone to blow the *shofar* on *Rosh Hashanah*. Many people vied for the honor of blowing the *shofar* for him, and he set about interviewing the various candidates. He called each one in and asked him, "What do you think about when you blow the *shofar*?"

Each one spoke of lofty thoughts that were rooted in the *kabbalah*, and yet R' Levi Yitzchak was not satisfied.

Finally, one answered, "Rebbe, I'm not a learned man. I have four daughters who are all of marriageable age. When I blow the *shofar*, I think: 'Lord of the universe! I have done whatever You wanted, and have obeyed all Your commandments. Now, please do what I want, and help me find husbands for my daughters.' "

R' Levi Yitzchak was overjoyed, and said, "Your thoughts are true ones. You will blow the *shofar* for me this *Rosh Hashanah*."

ও§ The Proper Intention

R' Moshe Sofer, the *Chasam Sofer*, did not appreciate those who had all types of mystical intentions and meanings when they blew the *shofar*.

A *baal tekiyah* asked him, "Rebbe, please teach me what thoughts I must have when I blow the *shofar*."

"Think that you are fulfilling your duty and that you are also acting for those who are listening," said R' Moshe.

ও§ Buying on Credit

R' Yaakov, the *Maggid* of Dubno, would say, "Why is it that when we say the prayer *Avinu Malkeinu* (Our Father, Our King), with its constant repetition of those two words, we say all the verses aloud, except for the very last one: 'Our Father, Our King, take pity on us and answer us'?"

He would then give a parable. "A merchant came to a large city to buy merchandise for his store. He brought a long list of things he needed, and he ordered them in a loud voice. The supplier had his workers scurrying about, taking down the bolts of cloth, measuring the required lengths and packaging them. When everything had been packed, the merchant said very softly, 'I don't have any money right now. Please do me a favor and give me credit.' "

"We too," said the *Maggid* of Dubno, "ask Hashem for all sorts of things in a loud voice. We want health and prosperity and so much more. However, when it comes time to pay for all of these, we realize we don't have any credit. Then we whisper, 'Our Father, Our King, take pity on us and answer us, for we have no good deeds.' Give us credit."

◄§ Composing Prayers

R' Levi Yitzchak of Berdichev prepared himself for the blowing of the *shofar*. He immersed himself in the *mikveh* and put on the white cotton *kittel* that is worn by the one who blows the *shofar*. He said the chapter of *Tehillim* seven times, and the congregation said it with him. He said the verses from the *Zohar*, took the *shofar* in his hand, and waited. Everyone waited expectantly for the blessing and the blowing of the *shofar*, but in vain.

"My friends," said the Rebbe, "near the door there is a Jew who was forced to spend most of his life in the Czar's army, and who doesn't know how to pray. When he saw everyone else praying, he became very jealous. He began crying and pouring out his heart to Hashem. And this is what he said as he cried, 'Merciful Father, You know that I am not able to pray. In fact I don't know anything at all except the letters of the Hebrew alphabet. I want to recite them for You: *Alef, Beis, Gimmel.* You, in Your great mercy, fit them together into a proper prayer.'

"Now Hashem is busy fitting together the letters of that holy man, and we must wait for Him to finish."

➳ Not Even One Commandment

R' Leib, the Zayde of Shpola, rose on *Rosh Hashanah*, looked up to the heavens, and said, "Lord of the universe, why do You have complaints against Israel? I swear that had I not seen it with my own eyes, I would not have believed they could have performed even one of Your commandments, because of their bitter exile and their great oppression."

➳ Priorities (I)

R' David of Lelov once came to Lublin to spend *Rosh Hashanah* with his Rebbe, the *Chozeh*. Just before they were due to blow the *shofar*, it became apparent that R' David was not in the synagogue. Someone went back to his inn, and found him feeding a horse. The horse's owner had been so intent on praying that he had forgotten to feed the animal.

➳ Priorities (II)

R' Naftali Tzvi Yehudah Berlin, the *Netziv*, would never sit down to eat until he was assured that the chickens had been fed first, as it states: "And I will give grass in your fields to your animals, and you shall eat and be satisfied" (*Devarim* 11:15). The animals receive their grass before man can take up his meal.

One *Rosh Hashanah*, they had all come home after the long services and they could not find the key to the chicken coop. They looked and looked, to no avail. The *Netziv* decided that a non-Jew should be asked to break the lock. That meant that someone had to be sent to the other side of town to find a non-Jew who would come and perform the task.

Meanwhile it was getting later and later. No one had yet eaten. The *Netziv* was old and weak, and he, too, had not tasted a thing.

Finally a non-Jew was found, the lock was broken, and only

then did the *Netziv* and his family sit down to make *kiddush* and to eat.

⊷§ *Listening for Selichos*

R' Nachman of Breslov would say: "As soon as *Yom Kippur* is over, I place my ear to the wall to listen for the banging of the *shamash* on the doors as he calls the Jews to the *Selichos* prayers in preparation for the next *Rosh Hashanah* and *Yom Kippur*."

⊷§ *I Am the Sinner*

During the entire Ten Days of Repentance, R' Yisrael of Horodno would give passionate speeches calling the people to repent. The day before *Yom Kippur*, however, he would change his tone and would speak gently, telling the people of Hashem's goodness and His desire to forgive man. And he would tell a story:

A man had a son who suddenly became ill. The doctor came and treated the son, but nothing he did seemed to help. The boy became sicker and sicker, and was on the brink of death.

Finally, they decided that they needed the top specialist from the big city. There was a catch, however, for the man was poor, and could not afford to pay the fee of the specialist. Out of desperation, the father spread the word that a plague was striking the village, and that only by bringing the specialist could the village be saved. Of course, everyone agreed to contribute, and the specialist was brought in and saved the boy's life.

"I know that *I* am a sinner," R' Yisrael would add. "*I* am the one who needs Hashem's mercy; *I* am the one who should repent. However, the repentance of an individual does not have the same force as the repentance of a community. I therefore, like that father, filled you with concern, telling you that you are all sinners, in order for my repentance to be accepted within the community's repentance. You are, in truth, all good and will be blessed with a good year, a year of life and peace, of redemption and mercy."

ᴼᴐ *Who Can Compare?*

R' Zushia of Hanipol left the synagogue on *Rosh Hashanah* just before the blowing of the *shofar*. He saw a young boy. The child was obviously from a very poor family. He was dressed in rags and was thin as a rail.

"My child," R' Zushia asked him, "do you envy the non-Jews, who have enough to eat and drink, and who wear decent clothes?"

"No," said the child, "I am not jealous of them at all. My portion is greater than theirs, because I am a Jew and believe in the God of Israel."

R' Zushia returned to the synagogue and exclaimed, "Lord of the universe! Look from the Heavens and see how there is none like Your people Israel. A Jewish child, even when he is hungry and thirsty and dressed in rags, nevertheless, accepts all of this lovingly, as long as he is a Jew."

ᴼᴐ *A Plea to Hashem*

R' Levi Yitzchak of Berdichev would often, when a prayer moved him, stop, and begin a debate, as it were, with Hashem.

Once, during *musaf* of *Rosh Hashanah*, at the words "May Your throne be established in mercy, and may You sit on it in truth," he said:

"Lord of the universe! You want Your throne to be established in mercy and You wish to sit on it in truth, so that You will preside in a way appropriate to the King of kings; so that You will make decrees and they will be obeyed.

"I suggest that You deal with Your children in mercy and lovingkindness, and may Your decrees for us in the coming year be good ones, with salvation and consolation. If, however, You treat us with strict justice and decree evil decrees against us, Heaven forbid, Your throne will not be established before

You and You will not sit in truth. The righteous men of the generation will not permit You to sit on Your throne. You will decree, and they will annul Your decree. I therefore beg of You, O great Hashem, 'May Your throne be established in *mercy*, and may you sit on it in *truth*.' "

⋅⧖ Piku'ach Nefesh

On a *Rosh Hashanah* which fell on *Shabbos*, R' Levi Yitzchak rose and said: "Lord of the universe, today You judge each person for the coming year, and grant him life or condemn him to death. But, on this *Rosh Hashanah* You are forced by Your own Torah to write that You grant Your entire people a good life in the coming year. After all, on *Shabbos* You have decreed that one cannot write. How, then, can You fulfill 'On *Rosh Hashanah* it is written down'? There is no way You can inscribe anyone in the Book of Death, because writing is forbidden on *Shabbos*. On the other hand, You may certainly inscribe us in the Book of Life. For, when there is *piku'ach nefesh* (danger to human life), the prohibition against writing on *Shabbos* falls aside."

⋅⧖ Getting Ready for the Right Holiday

R' Simchah Zisel, the Alter of Kelm, once heard one yeshivah student ask another between *Rosh Hashanah* and *Yom Kippur*, "Have you already bought an *esrog* for *Sukkos*?"

"I'm amazed," said R' Simchah Zisel. "I see you are already preparing for *Sukkos*. Have you then finished your preparations for *Yom Kippur*?"

⋅⧖ When Will I Attain That Level?

R' Chananiah Yom Tov Lipa of Sighet, the author of *Kedushas Yom Tov*, would be besieged by countless chasidim during the *Selichos* period. Everyone wished to receive his blessing. He would spend some time with each one, and this would take time away from learning.

He would say, "I wish that I could attain the level of the average Jew. The average Jew, when *Elul* arrives, spends less time on his job and more time in learning Torah and doing good deeds. But when *Elul* arrives, I spend more time on my job and less time in learning Torah and doing good deeds."

ᴁ§ *In One Ear. . .*

R' Yisrael Salanter would gather together his congregation during *Elul* and speak to them about the importance of the time and the need to repent. Once, a man said to him, "Rebbe, you're wasting your time. What you say goes in one ear and goes out the other."

"Thank you!" said R' Yisrael. "I was afraid that what I said didn't even go in one ear. Now that I hear that it goes in one ear and out the other, I am sure that at least something will remain inside."

ᴁ§ *What to Check*

A chasid came to R' Mordechai of Denaburg, and asked permission to leave early.

"Why are you in such a hurry?" asked R' Mordechai.

"Rebbe," the chasid answered, "I will be leading the *tefillah* on *Rosh Hashanah* and I need to review the *machzor* and prepare."

"The *machzor*," said R' Mordechai, "will not change. It is more important for you to review your deeds and to prepare yourself."

Yom Kippur

◆§ Who Needs More Mercy?

R' Yekele Orenstein, author of *Yeshu'os Yaakov,* was lenient in his decisions, while his *dayan,* R' Hirtzel, was always severe.

Just before *Yom Kippur,* as they were parting and wishing each other a good year, R' Yekele said to R' Hirtzel, "I hope you realize that you need more mercy from Hashem than I do."

"Why?" asked R' Hirtzel in astonishment.

"Well, when I rule that something that should be forbidden is permitted, I am committing a sin against Hashem alone, for having caused a Jew to eat something that might be non-kosher. Sins between man and his Creator are absolved by repentance on *Yom Kippur.* But when you forbid something that should actually be permitted, you are depriving a person of that which is rightfully his, and thus your sin is one between man and his fellow man. Such sins are not atoned for by repentance alone."

◄§ Who Needs to Forgive Whom?

R' Yoshe Ber of Brisk publicly rebuked a butcher who was not acting properly. The butcher did not mend his ways.

On the day before *Yom Kippur*, R' Yoshe Ber came to the butcher and asked for his forgiveness.

"Rebbe," the man said, "why do you ask me to forgive you? On the contrary, I should ask you to forgive me, because I didn't listen to you."

"No," said R' Yoshe Ber, "since you didn't listen to me anyway, it meant that my words of rebuke were in vain. All that I managed to do was to embarrass you in public."

◄§ Quoting in the Name of the Author

R' Levi Yitzchak of Berdichev once rose just before the *Kol Nidrei* prayer and announced, "Our sages tell us that 'Whoever quotes something in the name of the one who originally said it, brings salvation to the world' (*Avos* 6:6). Therefore, I want to quote something in the name of Hashem Himself, and thereby I too can bring salvation to the world: 'And Hashem said: I have forgiven them as you asked' (*Bamidbar* 14:20)."

◄§ Who Is Forgiven?

The *Chafetz Chaim* would say, "It is not the one who pounds on his chest who is forgiven, but the one whose chest pounds within him because of the sins which he has committed."

◄§ A Sense of Priorities (I)

R' Yisrael of Salant was delayed for *Kol Nidrei* and the congregation would not start without him. They said verses of *Tehillim*, and still the Rav had not appeared. It was almost dark and the time was running out. The *shamash* then went to the

Rav's house to call him. But there was no one there. The entire community went looking for R' Yisrael.

They combed the market area and the streets. No R' Yisrael. As they were going back to the synagogue, by chance, someone glanced into the window of a house. There he was. He was sitting rocking a baby in its cradle.

"Rebbe," they said, "we've been searching for you everywhere! The whole congregation is waiting for you so that we can start *Kol Nidrei*."

"Sh!" said R' Levi Yitzchak. "The baby just fell asleep."

"But, Rebbe," they asked, "what are you doing here?"

"I was on my way to the *shul*," he explained, "when I passed and heard a baby wailing. I went in, and found the house empty; everyone had gone to the synagogue. So I sat down and rocked it until it fell asleep."

◆§ A Sense of Priorities (II)

R' Zundel of Salant was in the middle of the *Yom Kippur* prayers when he saw a goat jump over the fence and begin grazing in the neighboring field. Everyone else who saw this ignored it; after all, one does not interrupt the most solemn prayers of the year because of a goat. Not so R' Zundel. He left the *shul* and returned the goat to its owner's field.

"The Torah commands us to respect the property of others," he explained.

◆§ I Have Forgiven

R' Yisrael, the *Maggid* of Kozhnitz, was sickly during his entire life. He had to wear special fur clothes and was confined to his bed for long stretches.

On *Yom Kippur* he would force himself to get up and lead the congregation in its prayers.

Once, when he got to the words: "I have forgiven them as you requested," he interrupted his prayer, looked up to the heavens and said, "Lord of the universe: You Yourself know my weakness and You alone know Your strength. I, the weak one, have summoned up all my strength and am here praying on behalf of Your children. Is it then so hard for You, Who are the source of all strength, to utter two simple Hebrew words: *Salachti Kidvarecha*, 'I have forgiven them as you requested'?"

◆§ The Shabbos Table

R' Leib, the brother of R' Meir of Premishlan, always took great pains in observing *Shabbos*. He would always set the table with the best foods and delicacies for the *Shabbos* meals, and all his dishes and silverware would sparkle in honor of the day.

When *Yom Kippur* fell on a *Shabbos* and the fast forbade eating, he would have the table set before going to the synagogue for *Kol Nidrei*. Everything would be arranged as beautifully as on any other *Shabbos*. After he would return from his prayers, he would sit down at the table for a little while, and would say, "Lord of the universe: I want to fulfill the commandment of celebrating *Shabbos*, to eat and drink and to enjoy Your blessings. You, however, have decreed that today we are to fast. Therefore Leib will obey Your decree."

◆§ Blessings in Vain

R' Levi Yitzchak of Berdichev would say, "Why is it that when we pray on *Yom Kippur*, we conclude the blessing of the *Shemoneh Esrei* with the words: 'King Who forgives and pardons our sins'? And if, God forbid, He doesn't pardon our sins, are we not then guilty of having made a *berachah levatalah* (a blessing in vain), which is forbidden?

"Let me give you a parable. A young child sees his father holding an apple. He realizes that if he asks his father for the apple, he may get it, but then again he may not. What does the clever child do? He makes a blessing on the apple in a loud voice. His father now has one of two choices: Either he ignores the child and thus forces the child to be guilty of making a blessing in vain, or else he wants to avoid having his son commit a sin and gives the child the apple. Of course, being a father, he will take the latter course.

"When we pray to our Father and ask His forgiveness, we are not sure whether He will forgive us or not. But we make the blessing, 'King Who forgives and pardons our sins,' and being the compassionate Father that He is, Hashem will forgive us. After all, He wouldn't want us to be guilty of making a blessing in vain."

◆§ We at Least Are Telling the Truth

R' Levi Yitzchak would also say, "Our generation is not like previous generations. In previous generations nobody used to tell the truth when they prayed on *Yom Kippur*. They would confess and say: 'We have sinned, we have deceived.' But there wasn't a word of truth in what they said. They never ever sinned. Not so in our generation. When we confess and say, 'We have sinned, we have deceived,' every word we say is the whole truth. For telling the truth alone, we deserve to be pardoned."

◆§ Sound Psychology

R' Chaim of Sanz was approached for a halachic ruling on *Yom Kippur*. He was asked what should be done for one who was ravenously thirsty, and was sick as a result.

"Give him a teaspoon of water," R' Chaim ordered.

They did so, but soon came back to report that the man's thirst was still unquenched.

"You may tell him," said R' Chaim, "that he may drink as much as he wants, but he is to donate one hundred kopeks to charity for each spoonful that he drinks."

When he heard the condition, the man suddenly no longer felt thirsty.

✑ Only Twenty-two Letters

R' Yisrael Meir of Gur, the *Chidushei HaRim*, once explained why the confession prayer is arranged alphabetically: *Ashamnu*, *Bagadnu*, etc.

"If it weren't for that fact," he commented, "we would have had to recite an infinitely long prayer, because we have an infinite number of sins."

✑ Life Is Even More Important

R' Yisrael of Salant was in Vilna when a cholera epidemic swept the country. During the Ten Days of Penitence between *Rosh Hashanah* and *Yom Kippur*, R' Yisrael instructed all the Rabbis in Vilna to announce that no one was to fast that *Yom Kippur*, because the fasting might weaken the people and make them more susceptible to the disease.

Immediately after the *shacharis* service on *Yom Kippur*, the *shamash* pounded on the table and announced, "By order of the Rabbis, everyone is required to return home and eat now."

No one moved. Each looked down, not daring to look his friend in the face. Who could eat on *Yom Kippur*?

R' Yisrael tried to reason with the people, explaining to them that the commandment "to protect one's life" (*Devarim* 4:16) was more important than any other. Still no one moved.

Finally, R' Yisrael motioned to the *shamash*, who brought out wine and poured a cup for the Rabbi. In a broken voice R' Yisrael recited the required blessing and drank the wine in full public view. Everyone answered "Amen" tearfully, and one by one they slipped away to their own homes to eat.

✑ An Epidemic on Yom Kippur

When R' Elye Chaim of Lodz was the Rav of Pruzhina, an epidemic once befell the area. R' Elye Chaim immediately gathered together a group of young people to take care of the ill and to supply them with their needs. He stood at the head of the group, and whenever he found out that someone had fallen ill, he would run to the man's home and take care of him until he was out of danger. Throughout the day and night he would go from home to home.

On the night of *Yom Kippur* that year, immediately after the prayers, he ran to look after the sick. He spent the entire night tending to their needs. In the morning, he was found dozing on someone's doorstep.

◆§ At Any Time

R' Nasan Zvi of Slobodka would say, "A man is liable to sin at any time. You can see this from the fact that immediately after the concluding *ne'ilah* prayer of *Yom Kippur*, we start *ma'ariv* with *Vehu Rachum* — "He, being merciful, will forgive sin."

◆§ Preparing for Sukkos

Immediately after *Yom Kippur*, the Gaon of Vilna summoned R' David Shmuel, one of the leaders of Vilna, who was extraordinarily wealthy. R' David Shmuel came without delay.

"Let us start our work on the *Sukkah* now," said the Gaon.

David Shmuel agreed.

The Gaon took out the tractate *Sukkah*, and said, "This is an excellent start."

And the two of them spent the night learning the tractate.

◆§ Learning After Yom Kippur

R' Itzele of Volozhin would spend the night after *Yom Kippur*, until midnight, learning in his yeshivah.

"The yeshivah students are tired because of the fast," he explained, "and cannot sit down to study. I do not want the yeshivah to remain, Heaven forbid, for an hour without the study of Torah."

$\mathcal{S}$ukkos

✦ Why Not Ask Four Questions?

The Duke of Mannheim once asked R' Zvi of Berlin, "Rebbe, why do the children all ask the Four Questions on *Pesach* and not on *Sukkos*? After all, *Sukkos* certainly brings a greater change in their lives than does *Pesach*. During *Sukkos* the Jew leaves his home and spends his time in the *sukkah*."

"On *Pesach*," R' Zvi answered, "the child sees everyone sitting around the table, at ease like free men, and not like a people in exile. Seeing this, the child becomes curious and asks: 'Why is this night different?' But on *Sukkos* he sees Jews exiled from their homes, without a true roof over their heads. That doesn't surprise him at all. Jews have always lived that way, ever since we went into exile."

◆§ God's Pity

R' Uri of Strelisk would say, "The *Yamim Nora'im*, with their demand to repent and mend our ways, might very well have caused our death. Hashem therefore took pity on us and commanded us to enter the *sukkah*."

◆§ A Great Mitzvah

R' Simchah Bunim of Pshischa would say, "The *mitzvah* to sit in a *sukkah* is a very great one, because the Jew fulfills it with every single part of his body."

◆§ Comparatively Speaking

Whoever bought an *esrog* in Slonim would bring it to the *Rav*, R' Eizel Charif, to have him pass judgment on whether it was a proper *esrog*.

One year, the stock was very bad, and every *esrog* that was brought to the Rav was given the same verdict — "No, this is not a very nice *esrog*."

Finally the *esrog* dealer came to R' Eizel and said, "Rebbe, do you know what you're doing to me? I'll be left with my entire stock at this rate."

"What am I supposed to do if your *esrogim* are not very fine? I can't lie. But let me give you a piece of advice. Whenever anyone comes to you to buy an *esrog*, send him along with two to show me. This way, when he comes to me, I can tell him: 'This *esrog* is better than that one.' That way he will at least buy one of them."

◆§ See What Happens?

R' Chaim of Sanz was invited to be the Rav of a community. He refused the offer, because he did not want to enter the Rabbinate. His wife, however, was very disappointed.

As a result she began trying to persuade him to accept the offer.

Finally, just before *Sukkos*, R' Chaim told her, "If you buy me an extremely beautiful *esrog*, I'll consider it."

His wife, seeing her chance, bought the very best *esrog* that money could buy, and brought it to her husband.

Soon word got around the village that R' Chaim had an exceptional *esrog*, and on the first day of the festival everyone came to fulfill the *mitzvah* of the *lulav* and *esrog* with R' Chaim's beautiful *esrog*. By the time everyone had finished handling it, it was rather the worse for wear, and had lost its original beauty.

"Look!" said R' Chaim to his wife. "The most beautiful of *esrogim* only needs to fall into the hands of the community to lose its beauty."

✑§ *Pronouncing the Blessing over a Horse*

R' Mordechai of Mezhibozh was extremely poor. Each year he would save penny after penny to be able to buy a really beautiful *esrog*.

Once, he went to Brody just before *Sukkos*, with six rubles that he had carefully saved over the previous year. As he was on his way, he met a man who was sitting at the side of the road crying bitterly. R' Mordechai approached him and asked, "My brother, why are you crying?"

"I'm in great trouble," said the man, sighing mightily. "I'm a water carrier and earn my living with great difficulty by filling my barrel with water and bringing it to the village by horse and wagon. Just now my horse died, and I have no way to support myself. I'll have to go begging."

R' Mordechai took out his six rubles, handed them to the man, and said, "Go and buy yourself a horse." He then turned about and went home.

When he entered his home he said with great joy, "Thanks to Hashem, this year I was able to find the most beautiful of beautiful things. All the other Jews will pronounce their blessing over an *esrog*, while I will pronounce mine over a horse."

◄§ *Measure for Measure*

R' Levi Yitzchak of Berdichev would invite many simple and ordinary folk into his *sukkah*, to the consternation of some of his disciples. Once, one of his disciples asked him to explain himself.

"When I enter the World to Come," he said, "I will find all the greatest sages sitting in their *sukkah* discussing Torah. I will ask to be allowed in that *sukkah*, but they will not allow me in. After all, I am but a simple man, and who am I to be allowed into a *sukkah* with all the great sages? But I can say, 'I, too, allowed the simple into my *sukkah*.' "

◄§ *One Doesn't Recite a Blessing*

R' Leibele, the son of R' Ber, was one of the leading Jews in Vilna. He was extremely rich, and willingly spent money to fulfill the *mitzvos* in the most proper fashion.

One year the crop of *esrogim* was very poor, and the prices went up accordingly. Almost no one could afford to buy an *esrog*. As a result, there were only two *esrogim* in the entire city that year, one of them belonging to R' Leibele.

On the first day of the festival, R' Leibele rose at sunrise to be able to perform the *mitzvah*, which had cost so much, at the earliest possible instant.

His servant had risen even earlier, hoping to perform the commandment before his master was up. As he began, he heard his master approaching, and out of fear he dropped the *esrog* and ruined it so that it could no longer be used.

R' Leibele walked in and saw his servant's pale, fearful face, and the *esrog* lying on the ground. R' Leibele picked up the *esrog*, and with a smile said, "Well, if one doesn't have an *esrog*, one doesn't recite a blessing."

ৰ্৶ A Heart Condition

R' Leibele of Kelm became sick just before *Sukkos*. On the evening of *Sukkos* his wife begged him: "Listen to me and don't sit in the *sukkah*. You'll catch a cold and get sicker."

R' Leibele refused to listen, went to sit in the *sukkah*, and soon started having heart pains.

"You see," said his wife, "I was right."

"No, you are wrong," said R' Leibele. "It is true that I have heart pains after sitting in the *sukkah*, but imagine how much more my heart would hurt if I didn't sit in one."

ৰ্৶ Raising One up

Throughout *Sukkos*, it was the custom of the yeshivah students of Radin to celebrate the *Simchas Beis HaSho'evah* each night. The *Chafetz Chaim*, too, would join them.

Once, in the middle of the celebration, as all were dancing around the *Chafetz Chaim*, one of the young men got carried away and picked up the *Chafetz Chaim* and raised him high.

The *Chafetz Chaim* objected, and somewhat later he told the young man, with a smile, "It is not proper to raise a person above his own height."

ৰ্৶ A Contest of Wills

When he was young, R' Levi Yitzchak of Berdichev was known as a great Torah scholar. In time, he married the daughter of a noted wealthy man, R' Yisrael Peretz of Levartov, and was supported by his father-in-law as he learned Torah.

One *Simchas Torah*, the *gabbai* of the *shul* honored R' Levi Yitzchak with saying *Ata Hareisa*. The *shamash* of the synagogue then called him up, using all types of fancy musical flourishes. Everyone leaned forward expectantly to hear the young sage.

R' Levi Yitzchak rose, put his *tallis* over his head, and then removed it from his head. Again he put it over his head, and again he removed it. Finally, R' Levi Yitzchak called out in a loud voice, "If you are a Torah scholar and a chasid, then you go to the ark and say *Ata Hareisa*."

In the end, someone else recited the verses.

His father-in-law was angry at him, but R' Levi Yitzchak returned from the synagogue in a particularly joyous mood.

During the meal, his father-in-law asked, "Levi Yitzchak, why did you humiliate me publicly?"

"Let me explain what happened," said R' Levi Yitzchak. "When I put my *tallis* over my head to go to the ark, I saw the *yetzer hara*, the Evil Desire, standing next to me. 'Who are you?' I asked him.

" 'And who are you?' he asked me in return.

" 'I am a Torah scholar,' I said.

" 'I, too, am a Torah scholar,' he told me.

" 'And where,' I asked him, 'did you learn?'

" 'And where,' he asked me, 'did you learn?'

" 'I studied with this-and-this Torah scholar,' I told him.

" 'And I too,' he said, 'was with you, and my hand did not leave yours for a moment.'

" 'But,' I went on, 'I am a chasid.'

" 'I, too,' he said, 'am a chasid.'

" 'Where,' I asked him, 'did you learn your way in chasidus?'

" 'And where,' he asked me, 'did you learn?'

" 'I learned it all from the *Sefer Yere'im*,' I said.

' "I was with you,' he said, 'and we learned together.'

"I saw that he refused to leave me alone. I therefore took the *tallis* off my head and said, 'If you are a Torah scholar and a chasid, then you say *Ata Hareisa*.' "

◆§ Simchas Torah

R' Yoshe Ber of Brisk would say: "*Simchas Torah* means the rejoicing of the Torah. This teaches us that it is not enough for a man to rejoice in the Torah, but the Torah must also rejoice in the man."

✺ Learning from the Lulav

A man came to R' Yitzchak Elchanan Spektor to ask his advice. He was interested in uprooting himself and going to America.

"Do you earn a living?" R' Yitzchak Elchanan asked him.

"Thank G-d," replied the man, "I have enough to keep me going, but not enough to really save money."

"If that is so," said R' Yitzhak Elchanan, "I suggest you stay where you are. When we say *hoshia na* ('save us') in the *hallel* of *Sukkos*, we wave the *lulav* in all four directions as well as up and down, but when we say *hatzlichah na* ('make us successful'), we do not move the *lulav* or wave it at all."

✺ Knowing the Bride

R' Akiva Eiger was given the honor of *Chasan Torah* each *Simchas Torah*. Once, after he had received this honor, he burst into tears.

"Rebbe," the people asked, "why are you crying?"

"Woe is to me," he sighed. "For sixty years I have been the *Chasan Torah* and I still do not know the *kallah* — the Torah."

Purim

⋘ The Purim Meal

R' Yisrael Salanter would say: "A person who truly knows how to fulfill the commandments properly can accomplish more in his *Purim se'udah* (festive meal) than in *Ne'ilah* on *Yom Kippur*."

⋘ Customs Are Not to Be Discarded

R' Yaakov Berlin, the father of the *Netziv* of Volozhin, lived in Mir. He was a very wealthy man and was known for his learning and good deeds.

In Mir, the bakers began selling *hamantashen* and other special *Purim* treats from the beginning of *Adar*.

Once, as *Purim* approached, R' Yaakov discovered that none

of the traditional baked goods were available. "Why are things different this year?" he asked.

"There has been a drought," he was told, "and the price of flour has gone up. The bakers can barely afford to buy enough flour for bread."

R' Yaakov called together all the bakers, placed thirty gold coins before them, and said, "Here is money for flour. Go and bake the traditional baked goods for *Purim* as you have done every other year. One does not give up a Jewish custom."

⋖§ Obviously a Favor

When R' Shlomo Kluger was in Brody, there was a rich man who would send him a gold coin along with his *mishlo'ach manos* each year. Once, the man sent along six gold coins. R' Shlomo returned five of them.

"It appears," he said, "that there is some favor he wants from me."

And that was indeed the case. After *Purim*, the man asked R' Shlomo to endorse his wine as kosher for *Pesach*.

⋖§ Stay in Your Place

On *Purim*, R' Yosef Shaul Natanson of Lvov saw a very wealthy and learned man sitting in the *beis midrash* learning. R' Yosef Sha'ul approached the man, closed his *Gemara*, and evicted him from the *beis midrash*.

"Your place today is not in the *beis midrash* studying Torah, but in your home, in front of a plate full of money which you have to distribute to the poor," he said.

⋖§ Certain Things Don't Go Away

R' Yoshe Ber of Brisk always kept his house open for the poor, and whoever came for help was given a decent coin. This was especially true on *Purim*.

One *Purim*, the members of the community sent him money

for the festival, as was customary. The *rebbitzen* took the money, and placed it on his table. R' Yoshe Ber distributed it among the poor.

The next day, when the *rebbitzen* wanted money to buy some household needs, she saw that there was absolutely nothing left on the table.

"Yoshe Ber," she asked her husband, "where is the money from *Purim*?"

"And the poor of *Purim*," he answered, "where are they?"

◄§ Taking Care of Important Things

At the funeral of R' Moshe Isserles, the *Rama*, his *shamash* mentioned that it had been the *Rama's* custom to go to the different homes at the time of the *Purim* feast and ask for a glass of water. In the course of his visit, he would, as if speaking to himself, exclaim, "We still have to pray *ma'ariv*."

In this way, he managed to remind the townsfolk of the need to say the *ma'ariv* prayer, something which is at times forgotten in the midst of the *Purim* feast.

◄§ Poor Proof

Moshe Landau of Uman, a descendant of the *Noda BiYehudah*, became involved in the *haskalah* movement, and would often address meetings of Jews, where he would try to stress the importance of learning the language of the country.

Once, in an effort to prove his point, he noted that Mordechai, by knowing the language of the country, was able to foil the plot of Bigsan and Teresh. This, he said, proved that the Jews of that time knew other languages in addition to their own.

"That's a very poor proof," one of the chasidim present called out. "Had the Jews of the country all known its language, Bigsan and Teresh would never have dared to talk openly in front of Mordechai. This proves that Mordechai was the exception, not the rule."

❧ How Precious It Is

One *Purim*, R' Avraham Yehoshua Heshel of Apta took all the money he had been sent on that day and began to count it over and over.

"Father," his son said to him, "I thought you hate money."

"I want to distribute this money to the poor," said the Rebbe. "If it means nothing to me, then my gift will be of no significance."

❧ And Afterwards?

R' Shalom of Belz would gather the poor of his town on the day after *Purim*, on *Shushan Purim*, and would distribute charity to all.

"On *Shushan Purim*, the average person does not think of giving charity; he feels that yesterday was *Purim* and he has already fulfilled his obligation. But what then is to become of the poor?" he said.

Pesach

❧ A Guaranteed Charm

A Rabbi from a nearby village came to R' Shlomo of Radomsk before _Pesach_ with a request. Since the laws of _Pesach_ were so complicated, he said, and there were so many of them, would R' Shlomo give him a charm or amulet to prevent him from making any errors in his decisions concerning the laws?

"I have a charm that is guaranteed to prevent you from making any mistakes," said R' Shlomo.

"What is it?" said the Rabbi excitedly.

"A very simple charm," said R' Shlomo, "and it has been tested. Study the laws and restudy them. This way you can be guaranteed not to make any mistakes."

◆§ Four Cups of Milk

Just before *Pesach* a man came to R' Yoshe Ber of Brisk with a question. "Rebbe," he asked, "is it permitted to use four cups of milk instead of the customary four cups of wine for the *Pesach seder*?"

"Are you, Heaven forbid, sick?" asked the *Rav*.

"No, I'm fine, thank G-d," said the man, "but," and here his voice dropped, "wine is very expensive this year."

Calling in his wife, R' Yoshe Ber told her to give the man twenty-five rubles.

"Rebbe," the man protested, "I came to ask you a question, not to ask for a donation."

"This money," said R' Yoshe Ber, "is a loan until you can afford to repay me." After a good bit of persuasion, the man eventually took the money and left.

After he had gone, his wife asked, "Why did you give him twenty- five rubles? Even the best wine doesn't cost more than two or three rubles."

"I assume you heard his question, didn't you?" said R' Yoshe Ber to his wife. "He wanted to know if he could use four cups of milk instead of wine. If he had been able to buy what he needed for *Pesach*, he would have had fish and *meat* at his table, and then he wouldn't have been able to have milk at all. I understood that he had none of the necessities and had him take twenty-five rubles to buy whatever he lacked."

◆§ "We'd Be Eating Bread on Pesach"

The wife of R' Yehoshua of Kutna was very exacting in her observance of the *halachah*. Before *Pesach*, R' Yehoshua saw her spending much time and effort cleaning the wood chairs.

"You've done enough," said R' Yehoshua, while she was still at the task. "As far as the *Shulchan Aruch* is concerned, the chairs are perfectly kosher for *Pesach*."

"You and your *Shulchan Aruch*," said his wife. "Between the two of you we'd be eating bread on *Pesach*."

◆§ The Laws of Matzah Baking

R' Yisrael of Salanter would take personal charge of the baking of the *matzos* for *Pesach*. He supervised the kneading, the rolling out of the dough, and the baking, making sure that everything was in accordance with the *halachah*.

One year, shortly before *Pesach*, he became sick and was not able to attend to the supervision. Instead he sent his disciples. Before they left for the bakery, they asked, "Rebbe, what do we have to be most concerned about?"

"The thing that should concern you most," said R' Yisrael, "is that the woman who kneads the dough is a widow. Take special care not to get angry at her."

◆§ Like Matzah Dough

R' Yechezkel of Kuzmir would say, "The Jew is like the dough from which *matzah* is to be baked. As long as one works it and kneads it, it is fine. If it is left alone unattended, it becomes *chametz*."

◆§ The Rav Must Set the Example

R' Yitzchak Elchanan of Kovno was very lenient when ruling for the poor.

In a year of drought when very little was available to eat, he permitted all the members of his community to eat *kitniyos* (beans, peas, corn and other such produce that Ashkenazic Jews normally do not use during *Pesach*). R' Yisrael of Salanter heard of this and felt uneasy. Finally, R' Yitzchak Elchanan said to him, "Rebbe, I'd like you to know that I and my entire household and all the leaders of the Kovno community are going to eat *kitniyos* this year. I hope you do the same. I don't want the poor people to have their conscience bothering them so that they will not rejoice during the festival."

✢§ Not the Soldiers

R' Shmuel Mohilever was very involved in helping those Jews who had been drafted into military service in Russia. He arranged for a kosher kitchen to supply their needs and would invite many of them to his home for *Shabbosos* and Festivals.

Once, before *Pesach*, the community head came in to him and said, "Rebbe, we're suffering from a bad drought this year. The prices have been going up by the day and people simply cannot afford to pay the costs involved in buying their *Pesach* needs."

R' Shmuel said, "Let us assemble the Rabbinical court judges and permit the use of *kitniyos* this year."

"Rebbe," said the man, "you have taken a load off my shoulders. I was trying to see how we could feed the soldiers during *Pesach*, but now that you have permitted the use of *kitniyos* I can rest easier."

"Jewish soldiers?" said R' Shmuel in indignation. "That I will not allow. I, you, and all the members of the community will eat *kitniyos* this *Pesach*. But as far as the soldiers are concerned, it is our duty to feed them only the best, just as in any other year."

✢§ Reconciling the Rambam

R' Mendel of Lizhensk gave the traditional *Shabbos HaGadol* speech and discussed the importance of donating money to the poor for their *Pesach* needs.

"My friends," he said, "you know that when Rabbis speak on this *Shabbos* they normally attempt to reconcile apparent differences in the laws of the *Yad HaChazakah* of the *Rambam*. I too will attempt to do so.

"The *Rambam* rules that each Jew, even the poorest of the poor, must eat *matzah* on *Pesach*. In another place he states that it is forbidden to steal. What should the poor do on *Pesach*? They don't have any money to buy *matzah*, yet they are not permitted to steal to get money to buy the *matzah*.

"And now I will solve this apparent contradiction. There is indeed one solution: Let the rich donate money to the poor, and in this way the two laws in the *Rambam* will be reconciled."

৵ Halfway There

After having given his *Shabbos HaGadol* speech, R' Naftali of Ropshitz appeared very tired.

"Naftali," his wife asked, "why are you so tired?"

"I gave a very difficult speech today," he answered. "There are many poor in the city, and their number grows day by day. I gave a long speech trying to persuade the rich to help them."

"And were you successful?" she asked.

"My speech was half successful," he answered. "The poor have accepted what I said and have indicated their willingness to accept the money. There is still grave doubt, though, whether the rich are willing to give."

৵ Who Needs Policemen?

On the day before *Pesach*, after noon, R' Levi Yitzchak of Berdichev took his *shamash* with him for a walk. On the way, they met a well-known smuggler. "Do you have any cloth that was smuggled across the border?" R' Levi Yitzchak asked him.

"Of course," was the answer.

"How many yards do you have?" said R' Levi Yitzchak.

"As much as you want," answered the smuggler.

They continued walking until they met a Jew.

"Do you happen to have any bread?" asked R' Levi Yitzchak.

"Bread?" the man said in shock. "Of course not! No Jew would have bread in his possession by this hour!"

They approached another Jew, and again they asked if he had any bread.

"Bread, Rebbe? Do you think I've converted?"

R' Levi Yitzchak looked up to the heavens and exclaimed, "Lord of the universe! Look down and see how Your people are scrupulous in their observance of Your laws. The Czar has his soldiers and policemen, his courts and his prisons. Yet all kinds of things are smuggled in and they are all freely available in the marketplace. All You said is: 'Leavened bread shall not be seen' (*Shemos* 13:7), and without any policeman or soldier to stand guard, You will not find a Jew who has bread in his possession."

◆§ A Jew up to Your Pockets

When R' Eizel Charif was the Rav of Slonim, there was a very rich man in the town who was a miser. He never gave any money for charity and turned away any poor man that came to his door.

On the day before *Pesach*, R' Eizel went out to the market and saw the miser standing by the fire where he had burned all his bread. He was busy emptying out his pockets into the fire, in case there were any crumbs left in the linings.

"You're wasting your time," R' Eisel told him. "There is no reason for you to empty your pockets."

"Why?" said the miser.

"Because," said R' Eisel, "the law states that the only *chametz* we have to get rid of is that which belongs to a Jew, and you're only a Jew *up to* your pockets."

◆§ Eating Matzah on Pesach

R' Zundel of Salant, the mentor of R' Yisrael of Salant, would spend day and night learning Torah. In the process, he became so engrossed that he often forgot to eat or drink.

When he once fainted, a doctor was summoned. After examining him, the doctor announced that the one tooth remaining in R' Zundel's mouth had become infected and had to be extracted. No sooner said than done and the tooth was pulled.

When R' Zundel came to and realized that his tooth was no

longer there, he sighed and said, "Woe is to me! How will I be able to fulfill the *mitzvah* of eating *matzah* on *Pesach* from now on?"

◆§ *"Our Table Is Wobbly"*

R' Akiva Eiger took pains in observing the commandment of *hachnasas orchim*, inviting guests. Each *Shabbos* and festival he would have a number of them.

Once, on the night of *Pesach* eve, during the *seder*, as they were all discussing the Exodus, one of the guests accidentally spilled his cup of wine. The snow-white tablecloth was ruined.

As soon as R' Akiva saw what had happened, he tilted the table so that his own cup of wine spilled as well. "It appears," he said, "that our table is wobbly."

◆§ *The Proper Attitude to Decision-Making*

A woman once came to R' Yechiel Michel of Novarodok, the author of the *Aruch HaShulchan*, shortly before the *Pesach seder* was due to begin, with a complicated question concerning *chametz*.

R' Yechiel Michel went into his study and leafed through this volume and that, striving to find a way to permit the woman to use her food.

R' Yechiel Michel's grandson finally entered and said, "Grandfather, we're all waiting to begin. If you can't find a way to permit the food, why don't you tell the woman that it's forbidden?"

"What are you saying, my son?" R' Yechiel Michel exclaimed. "How can I sit at the table with my whole family and enjoy the *seder* when the poor woman will be in distress and her whole festival will have been ruined?"

Again he began searching through the sources. After some time he came out of his study, went over to the woman, and told her, "It is permitted." Only then did he sit down to conduct the *seder*.

◆§ Why Hard-Boiled Eggs?

A gentile once asked R' Meir of Lublin, "Rabbi, why do the Jews eat hard-boiled eggs on *Pesach*?"

"Israel is like an egg," said R' Meir. "The more an egg is cooked, the harder it gets. The more the Jews are persecuted, the more stubborn they become."

◆§ I Am Embarrassed

Once, when R' Yisrael of Ruzhin was conducting his *seder* and he got to *LeShanah HaBa'ah BiYerushalayim*, "Next year in Yerushalayim," he stopped and exclaimed, "Lord of the universe! Each year I repeat *LeShanah HaBa'ah BiYerushalayim*, praying that next year we will be in Yerushalayim, and yet we are still in exile. I am really embarrassed in front of our non-Jewish maid."

◆§ Next Year in Jerusalem

R' Pinchas Cohen of Pressburg always desired to go up to *Eretz Yisrael*. Each year, at the *Pesach seder*, he would exclaim with all his might, "*LeShanah HaBa'ah BiYerushalayim*."

When he finally was able to do so, he moved to Yerushalayim, where he lived in the greatest of poverty, but also in the greatest of happiness. The first *Pesach seder* he spent in Yerushalayim, he again repeated with all his might, "*LeShanah HaBa'ah BiYerushalayim*."

"Father," his son asked him, "isn't that a prayer in vain? You are already living in Yerushalayim."

"My prayer," said R' Pinchas, "is that next year, as well, I will be in Yerushalayim, and that I will not, Heaven forbid, be forced to leave it for any reason."

➳ A Proper Host

A number of tourists came to R' Yosef Chaim Sonnenfeld of Jerusalem, a few days before *Pesach*, and asked if they could spend the first days of the holiday with him.

"By all means," he said joyfully.

The tourists took out the then princely sum of five pounds sterling, and gave it to the *Rav*, telling him, "This is for your expenses."

The guests attended R' Yosef Chaim's *seder* and the meals thereafter, enjoying all that was served.

On the second day, when it was still *Yom Tov* for the tourists but already *Chol HaMoed* for R' Yosef Chaim, he entered their room and placed the five-pound note on the table. His guests protested vehemently, but R' Yosef Chaim told them, "Do you think that I would take money for offering hospitality to guests?"

"Why then, Rebbe," asked one of them, "didn't you say so at the outset? Why did you take the money then?"

"I wanted you to feel perfectly comfortable at my table, said R' Yosef Chaim, "like a man who eats what is his."

➳ Concern for Others

A number of students of the *Chafetz Chaim* came to rejoice with him during *Pesach* and to hear Torah from him. They ate and drank and rejoiced, and the *Chafetz Chaim* rejoiced with them. The students were carried away with the joy of the festival, and began to dance.

"My sons," said the *Chafetz Chaim*, "please be careful not to dirty the floor. The poor woman who scrubbed it spent a great deal of time in getting it clean."

➳ When to Count Sefirah

R' Asher of Stolin would say:

"Since the counting of the *sefirah* indicates our loving

anticipation of the receiving of the Torah, a person should count the *sefirah* each day, in fact each minute and every single day of the year."

~§ Obviously a Visitor

During *sefirah*, R' Yechezkel Banet of Neitra saw one of the local residents who had just taken a haircut. He went over to the man and said, "*Shalom Aleichem.*"

"Rebbe," the man exclaimed in amazement, "I live here, and I haven't been away."

"I thought that you must be a visitor," said R' Yechezkel, "for in our community the custom is not to take a haircut during *sefirah*."

✑ Offering a Sample

R' Yaakov, the *Maggid* of Dubno, was once invited to Vilna for *Shavuos*, and spent the festival with R' Eliyahu, the Gaon of Vilna. On the first night they both stayed up, as is the custom, and studied Torah throughout the night. While R' Eliyahu spent the time on the *Tikkun Shavuos*, which consists of extracts from all the books of the Bible and Talmud, R' Yaakov studied the *masechta* (tractate) which he was learning at the time.

"Why don't you say the *Tikkun Shavuos* as is customary?" asked R' Eliyahu.

"I'll tell you a story," said R' Yaakov:

A man married off his daughter to a Torah scholar and, as agreed in the wedding contract, supported his son-in-law for a number of years while the young man continued learning. After the time that had been set aside for the children's support was over, the man called in his son-in-law and said to him, "My son, until now I supported you. Now the time has come when you must support your family on your own."

"But what should I do?" said the son-in-law.

"Go out into the marketplace and see what everyone else does, and follow their lead," his father-in-law advised him.

The young man went into the marketplace and saw that there were many stores, each with its merchandise displayed outside. He rented a store, bought a few pieces of material, and hung them outside his store. When the customers came into the store, they saw the store was empty, and left.

The young man returned to his father-in-law and complained, "I did everything you suggested, and I haven't even a penny to show for it." And he told his father-in-law the whole story.

"Fool," said the father-in-law angrily, "What you saw hanging outside the other stores was simply a sample of what they had inside the store. People see the samples outside and then come in to buy the merchandise inside. However, if your store is empty, what is the use of samples outside?"

"This applies to me, too. *Tikkun Shavuos* is only a sample of the Torah," said R' Yaakov. "A chapter of each book, a *Mishnah* here and there, a sample of the *Talmud*, and so on. You, who know the whole Torah, can show these as your samples. I, however, who do not know the Torah or the *Talmud*, would be showing samples without possessing the wares."

⊷§ An Excellent Speech

R' Chaim of Sanz would always give a Torah discourse before reciting *kiddush* on *Shavuos*.

One *Shavuos*, after the *tefillah*, he asked his *shamash* to assemble some of the richest of his chasidim to hear the *kiddush*.

The men came and found a table laden with all types of delicacies. R' Chaim entered, greeted everyone warmly, and then sat down. The chasidim all waited patiently for the Rebbe to recite the *kiddush*.

Finally, R' Chaim said, "When I was younger, I would give a long and complicated Torah discourse. Now that I am old, I will be brief."

Everyone looked up in anticipation.

"I need a thousand thalers for charity," said R' Chaim, "and this particular cause cannot tolerate any delay. I will not recite the *kiddush* until you have arranged to donate that amount, each according to his ability, and I want the amount that you pledge now, to be brought in tonight." With that, he rose and left the room.

Soon enough the pledges were made, and the Rebbe returned and recited the *kiddush* prayer.

"That *Shavuos*," R' Chaim later recalled, "I gave an excellent speech."

◄§ The Season of the Giving of Our Torah

R' Yitzchak Meir of Gur, the *Chidushei HaRim*, would say, "Why is *Shavuos* known as 'the season of the giving of our Torah' and not as 'the season of the receiving of our Torah'? Because the *giving* of the Torah took place only once, at Sinai, whereas the *receiving* of the Torah takes place every single day."

The Three Weeks

⊷§ Why We Still Mourn

A freethinker once asked R' Yoshe Ber of Brisk, "Rebbe, why do we need the three weeks of mourning over the destruction of the Temple? Couldn't we do without it?"

"I will tell you a story," said R' Yoshe Ber. "Once there was a fire in a town and many people lost all their possessions. Some went sifting through the ashes to see what they might yet salvage, while others left everything as it was. Almost inevitably, whoever went through the ashes rebuilt his house soon after the fire, while the others generally never rebuilt their homes.

"As long as we mourn for Yerushalayim and the Temple that was destroyed, we can be sure that it will be rebuilt one day."

✒ Concern for the Future

A woman came to R' Yoshe Ber of Brisk just before the fast of *Tishah B'Av*, and poured out her troubles. "Rebbe," she said, "I am an honest woman and keep all the commandments and customs. Every year I make my husband noodles on the day before the fast, but this year, while I was kneading the dough, I somehow forgot myself and made farfel. What can I do now?"

"That is a serious question," said R' Yoshe Ber gravely.

He took down a thick volume and began leafing through it. He tugged at his beard and appeared deep in thought.

After some time, he looked up and said, "The farfel may be eaten, but you must take care from now on to make noodles for the last meal before the fast."

When the woman had left, those who were there asked him, "Rebbe, what was that all about? Why did you make such a big to-do over something that was unimportant?"

"From her question I could see that the woman was unlearned," said R' Yoshe Ber. "I felt that I must show that I treated her question seriously. If I would have dismissed her out-of-hand, she would never come and ask me another question, even when such a question might relate to a really important and serious law."

✒ We'll Have to Wait Another Year

After the concluding meal before the beginning of the fast of *Tishah B'Av*, R' Levi Yitzchak of Berdichev stood before the window for a long time, staring out.

It was getting dark, and everyone was rushing to the synagogue to say the *kinos* — the lamentations — but without the Rebbe, no one would dare begin.

Finally the *shamash* came and told R' Levi Yitzchak, "Rebbe, the congregation is waiting for you."

"Yes," said R' Levi Yitzchak, "the *Mashiach* has not yet come. We will have to say *kinos* this year too."

⊸§ Rather than Lie

R' Levi Yitzchak of Berdichev saw a young man eating in public on *Tishah B'Av*. "My son, you have no doubt forgotten that today is *Tishah B'Av*," said the Rebbe.

"No, Rebbe," the young man replied, "I know that today is *Tishah B'Av*."

"Well then, you probably don't know that one is not permitted to eat or drink today."

"No, Rebbe," said the young man. "I know that one may not eat or drink today."

"Well then, you are obviously sickly and must eat today."

"No, Rebbe," said the young man, "I am perfectly fit."

R' Levi Yitzchak looked up to the heavens and exclaimed, "Lord of the universe! Look down and see how holy a people You have! A Jew would rather admit to having transgressed a commandment than be guilty of telling a lie."

⊸§ Self-Evident Fast Days

R' Avraham Heshel, the Rebbe of Apta, was not fond of the fast days.

He would say, "If I could, I would have abolished all the fast days except two: *Tishah B'Av* and *Yom Kippur*. As far as *Tishah B'Av* is concerned, when the Temple was destroyed, how is it even *possible* to eat? And on *Yom Kippur*, when each person is judged for the entire year by Hashem, who *wants* to eat?"

⊸§ Do We Honestly Believe?

R' Mordechai of Lechovich would say, "If we really truly believed each day that the *Mashiach* will come today, we would not save the *Kinos* booklets from one year until the next."

~§ On the Other Hand . . .

R' Avraham Kamai, the son of R' Elye Baruch of Mir, entered a bookstore on the day before *Tishah B'Av*, to buy a *Kinos*. He haggled about the price before finally buying the booklet.

"Rebbe," the bookseller said in astonishment, "since when have you started bargaining? I know that you have bought some of the most expensive books without questioning the price, yet here you have been so insistent on getting the lowest possible price."

"I will use the other books for all time, even when the *Mashiach* comes," said R' Avraham. "On the other hand, the *Kinos* I buy today will not be needed next year, because by then the *Mashiach* will have come."

This volume is part of
THE ARTSCROLL SERIES®
an ongoing project of
translations, commentaries and expositions
on Scripture, Mishnah, Talmud, liturgy, ·
history, the classic Rabbinic writings,
biographies, and thought.

For a brochure of current publications
visit your local Hebrew bookseller
or contact the publisher:

Mesorah Publications, ltd

4401 Second Avenue
Brooklyn, New York 11232
(718) 921-9000